Perspectives on Teaching Language and Content

Perspectives on Teaching Language and Content

Stacey Katz Bourns
Northeastern University

Cheryl Krueger
University of Virginia

Nicole Mills
Harvard University

Yale UNIVERSITY PRESS
New Haven and London

Published with assistance from the
Mary Cady Tew Memorial Fund.

Copyright © 2020 by Stacey Katz Bourns,
Cheryl Krueger, and Nicole Mills.
All rights reserved.
This book may not be reproduced, in whole or in
part, including illustrations, in any form (beyond that
copying permitted by Sections 107 and 108 of the
U.S. Copyright Law and except by reviewers for
the public press), without written permission
from the publishers.

Yale University Press books may be purchased in
quantity for educational, business, or promotional use.
For information, please email sales.press@yale.edu
(U.S. office) or sales@yaleup.co.uk (U.K. office).

Set in Joanna and Nobel types by Tseng Information Systems, Inc.,
Durham, North Carolina.
Printed in the United States of America.

Library of Congress Control Number: 2019954077
ISBN 978-0-300-22329-3 (paperback : alk. paper)

A catalogue record for this book is available from the
British Library.

This paper meets the requirements of ANSI/NISO
Z39.48-1992 (Permanence of Paper).

10 9 8 7 6 5 4 3 2 1

To Jeff, John, and Jamie

Contents

Acknowledgments   ix

Chapter 1 • Context   1

Chapter 2 • Frameworks   9

Chapter 3 • Beliefs   38

Chapter 4 • Interaction   61

Chapter 5 • Grammar   90

Chapter 6 • Vocabulary   121

Chapter 7 • Texts   143

Chapter 8 • Writing   177

Chapter 9 • Culture   207

Chapter 10 • Synthesis   223

Chapter 11 • Profession   245

Appendix A • World-Readiness Standards for Learning Languages   263

Appendix B • "Requiem," by Karen Brennan   265

Appendix C • Excerpts from *Exercises in Style*, by Raymond Queneau   268

Appendix D • Professional Organizations and Journals   270

Bibliography   273

Index   297

Acknowledgments

COLLECTIVE

We thank Jim Katz and Charlotte Kassab for our peaceful and productive writing retreats at the Nautilus at Ocean Park; H. Jay Siskin and Vanessa Wei for their feedback on earlier versions of two of our chapters; Sandra Katz for her editorial help; and Karen Brennan for her permission to use "Requiem." We appreciate the generous financial support that we received from Northeastern University, the University of Virginia, and Harvard University's Department of Romance Languages and Literatures' Potter Publishing Fund. In addition, we are grateful to our editors at Yale University Press for their support and guidance: Sarah Miller, Ash Lago, and Ann-Marie Imbornoni. We owe a great deal to our copy editor, Juliana Froggatt, for her enthusiasm and her insightful corrections, suggestions, and comments, and to our indexer, Dave Luljak, for his careful work. We thank our no longer anonymous reviewers—Lara Lomicka Anderson and Charlotte Melin (final readers) and Theresa Catalano and Eva Kartchava (proposal readers)—whose thoughtful feedback helped improve the final manuscript. Finally, we are grateful to the many colleagues and experts cited throughout these chapters. We could not have written this book without their wisdom and perspectives.

STACEY KATZ BOURNS

I acknowledge my late mentors, Knud Lambrecht and Grant Wiggins, whose influence on me is immeasurable. I am also grateful to my first teaching methods professor, the late Peter Hagiwara. I thank my many wonderful colleagues (too numerous to list) from the American Association of University Supervisors, Coordinators, and Directors of Language Programs; Northeastern University; Harvard University; the University of

Utah; Montclair State University; and the University of Texas at Austin. I have benefited greatly from conversations about topics related to this book with members of Northeastern's World Languages Center Curriculum Committee, as well as with Ericka Knudson, Glenn Levine, Jane Hacking, Johanna Watzinger-Tharp, and Carl Blyth. Finally, I am grateful to my family—especially to Jeff, Sarah, Missy, Andy, Charlie, Max, and my parents, Sandra and Bill Katz.

CHERYL KRUEGER

I thank my colleagues in French at the University of Virginia. I am grateful to be in a department that allows me to create new courses and try new techniques. I also acknowledge Karen James, our language program director, for her wisdom and generosity; Connie Knop, who taught the methods course when I was a new graduate student and who has never stopped motivating and supporting her former students; Robert Davis, Elise Leahy, Sarah Nelson, Loren Ringer, Tim Scheie, Madeline Spring, Nancy Virtue, and Dolly Weber, who have shared countless teaching materials and who are always ready to discuss ideas related to teaching and the profession; all the undergraduate students who have inspired me to experiment with teaching strategies; and all the graduate students whose teaching and research have inspired me. I am deeply grateful for the ongoing support of my family: my husband, John Urbach; my parents, Patricia and Richard Krueger; and my sisters, Heidi Erickson and Karen Pollard.

NICOLE MILLS

I thank Carol Herron Lustig, for her patient guidance and enthusiasm, and the late Frank Pajares, who was an inspiring scholar, teacher, and mentor. I also acknowledge my graduate students and TAs—current, former, and future—who inspire me with their creativity, knowledge, and innovation in our collaborations. In particular, I acknowledge the following instructors, who have allowed us to reproduce some of their pedagogical materials: Matthew Barfield, John D'Amico, Caroline Gates, Cécile Guédon, Samuel Harvet, Fanny Macé, Grégoire Menu, and Christina Svendsen. I am also grateful to my undergraduate students, who are always willing to try something new. Finally, I thank Jamie and my parents, who have always supported me and encouraged me to do what I love.

Perspectives on Teaching Language and Content

1 · Context

NOT A "ONE SIZE FITS ALL" MODEL

Experienced language instructors usually have a vivid memory of the first day that they stepped into the classroom to teach—that overwhelming combination of excitement, enthusiasm, high expectations . . . and trepidation. Many look back on their entire first semester as the most challenging teaching performance in their career. Everything was so new, and even with the excellent preparation and mentorship that they might have received, they were humbled by their lack of control over the material and/or methodology. At the same time, they usually also recall how satisfied, and even amazed, they were by how much their students had learned by the end of that first semester. They knew that there was still room for them to grow as instructors, but they were eager for new opportunities and experiences. Language faculty tend to continue to embrace opportunities for professional development at all stages of their careers; it is for this reason that some of the most dynamic teaching and learning on university campuses often take place in language departments.

This book is designed with two intrinsically related audiences in mind. Just like the students who come to our classes with diverse backgrounds, needs, and expectations, teachers in language departments possess expertise and training in various areas, as well as different levels of pedagogical experience. On the one hand, this book is intended for new language instructors who have not yet explored the fields of second language acquisition or applied linguistics. It contains insights into the trajectory of language teaching in the United States, focusing on the present and including new theories and frameworks as well as concrete models and examples. On the other hand, we also want to engage experienced language, literature, and cultural studies faculty who would like to stay in touch with ideas and innovations in the increasingly coactive worlds of language, culture, literature, and pedagogy. Today's TA is tomorrow's professor, and every language program director was once a first-time teacher. By addressing readers at various stages of their careers, we recognize the "whole" teacher who adapts to new professional challenges by building on knowledge and experience.

Though we do not promote one "best" method, approach, or perspective, this book is built on the premise that language and meaningful content are deeply connected and mutually reinforcing. We are aware of the differing environments in which our readers may teach and the fact that extensive curricular reforms are not always an option, due to institutional constraints. The book therefore brings together multiple perspectives and insights with the understanding that there is more than one effective way to fuse the teaching of language and content within various types of courses and academic programs. Approaches to language teaching today recognize the influence of larger social and educational currents, including attitudes about language study and the humanities, as well as the impact of technology on learning across the curriculum. Students come to the language classroom with different educational backgrounds, experiences, learning styles, and motivations. An individual's learning goals may not always correspond to programmatic aims. Do students simply want to fulfill a language requirement? Are they studying a language to prepare for research or to pursue a particular career? Have they enrolled for personal reasons (for example, a familial connection to the language or the desire to live in a country where the language is spoken)? Are they pairing language study with work in another field, such as linguistics or anthropology? Or might students be taking language classes just because of intrinsic interest? As Kramsch explains, some "collect languages like others collect butterflies" (2009, 4). One thing is certain: students in marketing who are learning Chinese in order to navigate basic, day-to-day situations during a business trip to Beijing have different goals from those of comparative literature graduate students who want to learn Russian so that they can read Pushkin in the original language. Nursing students studying Spanish to interact with patients have specific needs and goals, as do sports management majors who aspire to work as interpreters for Japanese baseball players.

Students are sometimes drawn to a particular language for indefinable reasons and are then surprised to realize that when speaking that language, they become slightly different versions of themselves. As Taylor explains, "the inextricable link between language and identity has long been acknowledged by psychologists, sociologists, anthropologists and philosophers alike" (2013, 26). Subjects in Kramsch's (2009) study report that they began to feel they were a different person when speaking another language. They experienced "such subjective aspects as: heightened perceptions and emotions, awareness of [their] body, feelings of loss or enhanced power, together with imagined identities, projected selves, idealizations or stereotypes of the other" (5). Instructors therefore have the chance not only to teach students to speak another language and learn about another culture but also to transform their lives in meaningful ways. We can lead students to develop into what Kramsch calls "multilingual subjects" instead of simply "language learners." Learning another language can help students better understand themselves and their place in the world; it can also facilitate their acquiring empathy, a quality that many see as much needed in today's world and a compelling reason why the humanities matter.

Of course, not everyone recognizes the value of learning another language. The study of the humanities in general has waned considerably in recent years (see Looney and Lusin 2018 for statistics), as many students (and perhaps even more important, their parents) believe that one should take courses in college that will directly lead to lucrative career options. Learning to speak another language may be seen in some cases as instrumental to that goal, but the study of literature, philosophy, history, or the arts may be viewed as a privilege that is difficult to afford or justify, especially considering the skyrocketing costs of higher education. Even Lawrence Summers, once the president of Harvard University, publicly disparaged the learning of other languages: "English's emergence as the global language, along with the rapid progress in machine translation and the fragmentation of languages spoken around the world, make it less clear that the substantial investment necessary to speak a foreign tongue is universally worthwhile" ("What You [Really] Need to Know," *New York Times*, January 20, 2012). Others have asserted that there are no intellectual or educational arguments for English speakers to learn a "foreign" language and that use of a common international language (English) in a global economy would obviate the need for multilingualism among Anglophones. Clearly, the question of cultural sensitivity has little impact on this unidimensional view of how language operates. Yet even putting aside mutual respect and general etiquette, it seems odd that proponents of global business ventures do not always grasp the social advantage of multilingualism. If colleagues speak your language and you do not speak theirs, from the outset they know more about you than you do about them. In addition, knowing the language of others allows you to gain access to their world in important and meaningful ways. The following quotation, attributed to Nelson Mandela, captures the emotional connection that learning another language can facilitate: "If you talk to a man in a language he understands, that goes to his head. If you talk to him in his language, that goes to his heart." Today more than ever, it falls upon educators to articulate, in the classroom and beyond, the value of language learning.

GUIDING PRINCIPLES

Every program determines its pedagogical priorities based on specific goals and available resources. There are, however, some generally acknowledged guiding principles upon which effective second language (L2) pedagogy in the twenty-first century are based (these may be reordered, reworded, fine-tuned, and adapted to specific program goals and institutional missions):

- Because input is vital to language acquisition, students work with *authentic language* from various linguistic registers, used in multiple contexts, to acquire target grammar and vocabulary.
- Students interact with *texts*, broadly defined to include everything from literature to movies to music to maps to artwork to photos to graffiti (and everything in between).
- The development of students' *critical thinking* skills and the integration of intellectually stimulating content are components of classes at all levels of instruction.
- Classroom and homework oral and written activities and *tasks* are scaffolded, containing specific, guided, step-by-step instructions and support.
- Courses are developed around *themes* that intersect with and reinforce other disciplines (art, history, science, etc.).

- Classes contain a thorough integration of and emphasis on *target cultures*, along with critical comparisons to students' own lives and beliefs.
- Learning environments are designed to foster *motivation* through the integration of engaging and student-centered pedagogical initiatives.
- Students have ample opportunities for *interaction* and collaboration, not only with peers but also with target language communities.
- An *expansion of classroom boundaries* provides variable contexts and experiential learning opportunities.
- Language learning fosters self-expression, *self-awareness*, and confidence within and beyond the language learning classroom.

These guiding principles are couched in the larger framework of blended language and content in which the study of language, literature, and culture provides students with the chance to become not only fluent and proficient second language users but also thoughtful and culturally well-informed global citizens. In the chapters that follow, we provide models that demonstrate how language and content can be intertwined within thematic lessons at various levels of instruction.

ROAD MAP

This is not a "methods book" per se, in that it does not espouse one particular approach or method. The main goal is to encourage readers to become knowledgeable, reflective, critical, and creative practitioners. At the same time, it provides insights into frameworks and initiatives that modern research currently advocates. Most important, it focuses on supporting and cultivating the intellectual and pedagogical growth of the teacher. It presents models that connect theory and practice, and it also offers mechanisms for reflection that nourish lifelong, effective teaching practices.

Certain chapters may be more beneficial for readers with particular backgrounds. For example, experienced teachers may already know a great deal about the evolution of teaching methods, covered in Chapter 2. At the same time, the later sections of Chapter 2, which treat the current state of the field, are relevant for all audiences. Graduate students may find Chapter 11 especially helpful as they begin to develop their professional profile. However, seasoned instructors may also be interested in some of the resources that are provided therein, since professional development is an ongoing process. Chapters do not need to be read in any particular order, and they can also be used on their own.

We hope that readers will regard our proposals in the field of language pedagogy as at least partially a result of what we have learned and adapted from previous approaches (see Chapter 2). We also make the case that many of the teachers' beliefs about language teaching presented in Chapter 3 are based on their own past experiences as students, as well as teachers, in the language classroom. Our trajectories may unintentionally bias us. At the same time, language department faculty members are known for their commitment to innovation. Blending their insights into the effectiveness of techniques and initiatives from the past with current, research-based frameworks, they embrace and enhance curricular and pedagogical changes that align with the needs of their students, departments, and institutions.

As this book demonstrates, modern language teaching refutes the separation of the teaching of "language" versus content (which can be very broadly defined). For logistical purposes, however, we have divided the book into chapters dealing with recognizable topics and skills. For example, we include chapters dedicated specifically to vocabulary and grammar pedagogy (Chapters 5 and 6). Our goal is to provide easily referenced guiding principles and models that can be integrated into meaningful lessons. In other chapters, which appear to focus more broadly on content (Chapters 7 and 9) or tasks (Chapters 4 and 8), we show not only how these elements are intertwined with the teaching of language but also that they are all connected to one another in important ways. In Chapter 10, we bring together topics and themes from all the earlier chapters to provide, using a backward design approach, a model for a pedagogical unit. Finally, in Chapter 11, we encourage readers to look beyond the classroom and to consider their professional identity and options for professional development.

We have kept many of the recommendations in this book flexible so they can be adapted to various settings. We also understand that not everyone who teaches languages is an applied linguist or an expert in foreign language education. The corps of language instructors in universities is a strikingly heterogenous group, bringing together a wide range of insights and talents to the task at hand. This diversity should be considered an asset. At the same time, even the non-specialist language teacher needs to remain cognizant of developments in applied linguistics. This book intends to give readers the tools that they need to be successful not only in teaching but also in engaging with pedagogical scholarship moving forward, even if colleagues' interests lie elsewhere or if a heavy teaching load prevents them from conducting their own research. The field needs excellent practitioners as well as strong scholars.

Regarding the perspectives of the three authors, although we have all conducted research in applied linguistics, our training is different, including respective expertise in theoretical linguistics, literary and cultural studies, and education. In addition, even though we have all completed doctorates whose titles contain the word "French," we have had a great deal of experience educating and mentoring teaching assistants and collaborating with colleagues in other languages, including "less commonly taught languages" such as Arabic, Chinese, Hebrew, Japanese, Persian, Russian, and Turkish. We understand the challenges that instructors teaching these languages may face. In particular, we realize that some languages simply take a lot longer for an anglophone student to learn, either because they do not contain many English cognates, because they have different writing systems, or because their grammatical structures are complicated and vastly different from what one finds in English.

Although applied linguistics researchers tend to use the term "foreign languages" to refer to languages taught in a context where they are not spoken outside the classroom and "second languages" for languages that are, we use both terms somewhat interchangeably throughout the book. We include references to numerous other languages but have provided many examples in English, French, or Spanish (the latter two glossed), since these are the languages and corresponding cultures about which we are most knowledgeable. We feel that readers are better suited than we are to adapt our materials and recommendations to align with their own areas of expertise.

In the chapters ahead, for the purpose of illustration, we have included texts that reflect what we believe to be some of the most compelling issues that might be explored in various ways within language and culture classes today. They deal with the changes in perspective that humans experience, personally and collectively, moving through time and space. For example, we explore the notions of identity, self and others, nostalgia, idealization, disillusionment, home, and exile. Both learning and teaching another language can be transformative, ongoing processes that lead us, students and instructors alike, to understand who we once were and imagine who we can become. Each chapter includes pauses ("Reflections") that allow readers to think, discuss, and brainstorm before moving on to a new topic. "Perspectives" sections present real-life teaching or learning challenges for which there is no single "right" answer. Readers are encouraged to analyze and solve problems, taking into account the multiple points of view represented. The "Perspectives" vignettes offer a composite of situations and commentary that the authors, and most likely our readers, have encountered many times. There are no direct citations, and details and contexts have been changed.

This book focuses on both the big and the small pictures. It discusses the overarching issues and frameworks that are prominent in today's research, and it provides insights into managing the day-to-day practices of language teaching, lesson planning, and curriculum development. It offers practical support and guidance to help teachers and their students acquire specific skills and knowledge, and it acknowledges the larger context of pursuing a teaching career. We hope that readers will reflect upon the following questions as they move through the chapters that follow: How can teaching a beginning course inform the future teaching of an advanced course? How can the materials and approaches that worked well in one institutional setting be adapted to a new position at another university? How can applied linguistics/pedagogy specialists and literature/cultural studies scholars communicate and work together, becoming stronger as a result of their collaborations? We hope to provide opportunities for all teachers to consider questions about research, teaching, and the profession as a whole. Whether the reader's career leads to or includes teaching elementary or more advanced courses, or (as is the case for most teachers) a combination of levels, we hope that the book will serve as a helpful and informative resource and that its emphasis on reflective teaching will foster confidence and creativity.

2 • Frameworks

METHODS AND APPROACHES

The guiding principles generally recognized today as promoting effective second language pedagogy have evolved from a dynamic, responsive history of methods and approaches. Richards (2018) differentiates between methods and approaches in the following way: "When an instructional design is quite explicit at the level of theory of language and learning, but can be applied in many different ways at the level of objectives, teacher and learner roles and activities, it is usually referred to as an approach. . . . Teachers adopting an approach have considerable flexibility in how they apply the principles to their own contexts. When an instructional design includes a specific level of application in terms of objectives, teacher and learner roles and classroom activities, it is referred to as a method." Some researchers use the two words interchangeably or refer to approaches within a given method. Others use the terms "model" or "framework."

We often hear that we are now in a "post-methods era." This notion may be considered promising, since pedagogical flexibility allows for adjusting curricula and lesson planning to suit the goals and contexts of particular programs, students, and classes. At the same time, the lack of an overarching pedagogical framework may tempt new (as well as experienced) teachers to fall back on familiar initiatives unrelated to empirically based findings about second language acquisition (SLA). Fostering a connection between theories and practice has always been one of the biggest challenges in second language education, and it persists today. Theorists and practitioners do not always communicate well with each other, ironically even in the field of language pedagogy.

Language instruction has never existed in a vacuum; it has always aligned with its historical context. This chapter describes a number of pivotal moments and changes in perspective regarding language pedagogy over the years and explores the motivations for change. Shifts in pedagogical approaches offer insights into the needs of each era. For example, although students who studied languages using the grammar translation method (described below) did not focus on learning to speak or write the target language, they were able to read and translate quite well (and much better than students studying language within the more orally focused approaches that followed). When speaking became a primary goal of language study, translation did not serve the needs of language learners eager to hone pronunciation and oral proficiency skills. Professional certificates in translation and courses in translation theory or translation for research purposes still thrive today, but communication-focused approaches have replaced translation methods in the L2 classroom.

The fact that certain methods and approaches that were once advocated do not address the needs of today's learners and curricula reminds us that adapting to new goals and perspectives is an ongoing, dynamic process. If successful language learning is contingent on social and cultural contexts, as well as individual learner variables, then finding the most effective approaches for the here and now may be a more realistic goal than seeking an essential, "right" method. As long as pedagogical goals and contexts change, approaches will evolve along with them.

Effective course design combines empirical research in SLA with practical curricular initiatives and realistic expectations for learners who will have limited exposure to the target language. Students who do not have access to a prolonged immersion experience should not be expected to excel in every aspect of language learning after one year, two years, or even three years of study. The question is how to provide students with the best language learning experience possible, one that will lead them to achieve their personal goals, along with the carefully constructed and articulated outcomes of the particular academic context in which they are studying.

Below, we chronologically explore the most influential teaching methods used in American language programs over the past century. For each, we outline its tenets, goals, and activity types, and we evaluate its advantages and shortcomings.

> **Reflection**
>
> 1. Why should we study new approaches for teaching language when traditional methods may have worked well for us personally?
> 2. Why is it important to understand the tenets of the methods and approaches of the past when we are teaching in the present?

HISTORICAL METHODS AND APPROACHES

Grammar Translation

Dating back to the mid-nineteenth century, grammar translation (GT) was once the dominant method for teaching modern languages in North America, Europe, and beyond. Versions of GT are still sometimes used in specific contexts, often for courses that focus on language as a research tool. The goal of GT is for students to learn the mechanics and vocabulary of a language via the translation of texts, traditionally works of literature, philosophy, and history. Students study long lists of vocabulary words and detailed grammatical explanations at home, and class time is then usually devoted to translations, relying on the teacher's corrective feedback. Students do not communicate in the target language in class, although occasionally they may translate sentences from English into the target language as a pedagogical activity. There is little emphasis on speaking.

GT activities usually consist of a passage for students to translate line by line, followed (or preceded) by fill-in-the-blank activities in which they manipulate the grammar points in question (conjugate verbs, supply the appropriate articles, etc.). Students develop keen metalinguistic awareness of grammar, and they acquire a large lexicon. Although the academic texts used in GT may not necessarily address issues in popular culture today or include vocabulary that is relevant to students' everyday lives, they are often intellectually stimulating and historically important. Students in GT classrooms have the opportunity to study the original versions of philosophical passages and great works of literature, and they engage with thoughts and ideas that are central to the human condition.

> **Reflection**
>
> Search online for "Life of Brian romanes eunt domus," and watch this scene from the film *Monty Python's Life of Brian*. Make a list of elements from the GT method that you find embedded in the scene.
>
> 1. Do you think many language learners can relate to this scene? Why or why not?
> 2. Why do you think that GT is still used in certain classrooms across the globe where the goal is to teach students to speak the language, not to translate literary texts?

The Direct Method

The direct method (DM) arose in reaction to GT. The overriding criticism of GT was "Students can't speak!" Of course, speaking had never been the point of GT. It is, however, a vital component of the DM. DM classes are therefore intended to be immersive, so the target language is the only language permitted in the classroom. For example, an instructor might spend five minutes trying to act out the word for "bored" instead of simply providing the translation. In addition, the focus is on vocabulary that is used in everyday conversations, not literary prose. There is a great deal of back-and-forth between teachers and students; the teacher models usage, asks questions, and cues responses in the target language. DM programs tend to prefer native speaker instructors, since they are considered better models of "authentic" pronunciation and accurate language use.

The DM persists today in Berlitz-type programs and has specific goals for a particular audience, which includes learners who do not necessarily seek fluency but would like to master everyday, practical language so that they can communicate with native speakers when traveling, as well as those who are out of practice and want to refresh their skills. The DM is more effective (especially at the beginning levels) when used to teach a language that has a large number of cognates with the student's first language.

Reflection

1. Search online for "Alec Baldwin French Class Saturday Night Live" and watch the sketch, keeping in mind the DM's goals. What elements of the DM do you see in practice here? Why is the last segment particularly revealing?
2. Does this method prepare students to communicate with native speakers? Why or why not?
3. What general differences do you see between the goals of GT and the DM, as reflected in the *Saturday Night Live* and *Life of Brian* scenes that you have watched?
4. Which method appeals to you more? Why? Do you think that certain types of learners would prefer one approach over the other? Explain.

Audiolingualism

Like the DM, the audiolingual method (ALM) emerged as a response to GT. ALM was used extensively in American language courses beginning in the 1950s and persisting well into the 1980s. It is based on the tenets of behaviorism, with the underlying theoretical assumption being that learning a language is equivalent to habit formation; in other words, practice makes perfect, like learning to play the piano with the correct fingering or to hit a baseball using a proper batting stance. Language learners are thus encouraged to imitate what they hear and to use only the phrases and paradigms that they have studied. Mistakes are unacceptable, so students are discouraged from creating novel utterances or taking linguistic risks. They are therefore often limited to reproducing sentences from the conversations that they have been required to memorize, even though a lot of those sentences are not particularly relevant to their lives or even something that they would ever think to say on their own. "My name is Jean Hughes, and I'm an engineer," a former ALM prodigy spouts out mischievously in French when he meets Québécois tourists in Maine, even though his name is Lou and he is a doctor. It has been more than thirty years since he has studied French, but remnants of the dialogues he once memorized have remained with him. He actually finds some of them useful, although sometimes his stock phrases are not effective for accomplishing his communicative goals.

ALM's main aim is for students to produce grammatically correct utterances. Instructors therefore regularly correct students' errors (or cue for self or peer correction) and conduct carefully sequenced, often quick-paced, drills (described in Chapter 5). ALM tends to be a better fit for energetic, outgoing, charismatic teachers who enjoy the performative nature of teaching. The Rassias method, created by the Dartmouth professor John Rassias in the late 1960s, is a larger-than-life version of ALM that, as he explains in a video of himself teaching English in China, is "a dramatic interpretation of language infused with an avalanche of energy" (https://vimeo.com/40409810). As is apparent in the video (if it is still available; otherwise, just search for "Rassias approach"), Rassias is an impressively animated instructor who incorporates a series of movements, including hand signals and snaps, that elicit the behaviors and responses (both oral and physical) that he seeks from his students. Although some instructors are able to emulate Rassias, others are not as comfortable using the method and may not be able to pull it off with such aplomb. Just as students have different learning styles that work best for them, instructors also have their own preferred teaching personas.

Critics of ALM assert that envisioning language learning as a series of drills and memorized conversations limits students' ability to converse naturally. At the same time, there are some elements of ALM that may still be useful, such as learning lexical "bundles" or "chunks" (Lewis 1993, 1997); we discuss this topic in Chapter 6.

Reflection

1. Search online for "Qué hora es Mexican soap opera part 1."
2. What aspects of this video suggest that the creators may have once been students in ALM classrooms?
3. The native speaker of Spanish realizes after trying to communicate to the rest of the cast that they do not actually speak Spanish: "¡Ustedes no hablan español!" (You don't speak Spanish!). Then he modifies his Spanish to include the phrase that they all understand (¿Qué hora es?), for which they are all grateful. Is there a deeper significance to his speech act here?

Continued . . .

> 4. If you have had any experience with ALM, can you recite some of the phrases that you memorized from the dialogues that you studied?
> 5. Of the three methods that we have seen so far (GT, the DM, and ALM), which do you think would be the most appealing to students? Why? How about to teachers? Which aligns most with your own learning style?

The Natural Approach

The natural approach framework (Krashen and Terrell 1983) set the stage for communicative language teaching (discussed below). The underlying premise is that second languages are acquired in the same way as first languages. The natural approach and the DM share many features. For example, classes are taught entirely in the target language, and the focus is on communication (similar to that which one would experience when learning one's first language). There is not a lot of emphasis on grammatical form in the natural approach, however. Like a parent talking to a child, the teacher provides students with comprehensible input—that is, exposure to the target language at a level they can grasp without knowing every word or structure. Typical classroom interventions include the teacher telling stories, showing images, and using mime and gestures to present new vocabulary. Lessons move from the students' comprehension of input to their participation in role plays and other oral activities.

The main difference between the DM and the natural approach is that students are not required to produce as much output in the natural approach; the reasoning is that they will speak when they are ready, as is the case for children acquiring their first language. Another difference is that the natural approach classroom atmosphere should be very relaxed, and teachers should not correct students when they make errors. A staple of the natural approach classroom is the integration of techniques from the Total Physical Response (TPR) approach, developed by James Asher in the 1960s. TPR advocates having students respond physically to instructions repeatedly given by the instructor in the target language (such as asking the students to sit down or open their books), so that the commands become automatically entrenched in the learner's memory.

The theoretical basis for the natural approach is Krashen's (1981, 1982, 1985) "monitor" model, which rests on five hypotheses:

- Acquisition-learning hypothesis: Krashen makes a sharp distinction between learning and acquiring another language, insisting that languages should be acquired through input and not learned through studying and mastering rules.
- Monitor hypothesis: The monitor, which is related to learning (and not acquiring) a language, represents the part of the learner's mind that is intent on memorizing rules, scrutinizing errors, and producing "correct" language. Krashen does not see the monitor as useful for language acquisition.
- Natural order hypothesis: Learners acquire forms in a particular order (for example, certain verb tense endings before others), in second as in first language acquisition.
- Input hypothesis: Krashen explains that languages are acquired through the assimilation of comprehensible input. He proposes an "input + 1" (or "i + 1") construct, recommending that second language learners receive exposure to input that is slightly beyond what they already know.
- Affective filter hypothesis: Learners who are feeling anxious are less successful; negative emotions create a metaphorical filter that blocks the learner's ability to comprehend input. Therefore, classes should be more relaxed and teachers should not correct every error.

Reflection

1. The natural approach relies on the theory that SLA is similar to the acquisition of one's first language. What are the major differences in the settings in which first and second languages are acquired? Do you believe that the classroom can adequately mirror the environment in which a first language is learned?
2. Have you ever experienced a "monitor" in your brain when you are speaking your second language? When has it snapped into service? How about in your first language? Do you monitor your grammar? If so, in which situations?
3. Some argue that errors may become "fossilized" (unable to be

Continued . . .

> fixed) if they are not corrected early enough. Have you ever heard speakers whose grammar, vocabulary, or pronunciation seemed fossilized to you? Which area do you think is most likely to fossilize? Have you experienced this phenomenon in your own language learning?

Communicative Language Teaching

Communicative language teaching (CLT) overlapped somewhat with the natural approach and ALM; it began to pick up steam in the late 1970s and early 1980s and then established itself as the predominant approach in the US in the late 1980s and early 1990s. In fact, we hesitated as to whether it would make more sense to discuss CLT here or in the "Today's Context" below, since it is still widely used. Many applied linguists insist that we are now in a post-CLT era. The reality, however, is that CLT is not dead yet. In addition, many researchers agree that certain elements of CLT should be retained as we move into the next era of language pedagogy.

Like the natural approach, CLT came into existence in reaction to the rigidity of ALM. It is intentionally categorized as an "approach" and not a "method," because it is flexible in its interpretations and implementations. Like the natural approach, CLT is dependent on students' receiving copious target-language input, based on real-life situations and everyday vocabulary and consisting mostly of spoken language. The main difference between CLT and the natural approach is that CLT includes an emphasis on output and, in most of its iterations, at least some explicit attention to grammatical form. The basic premise is that students develop practical language skills through interacting with their peers to complete various types of tasks using authentic materials. CLT interventions might include completing charts, interviewing partners, participating in information gap activities (where students need to exchange information to complete a task, such as filling in a table), or engaging in mingling activities where classmates go around the room asking one another questions and then reporting on their collected data to the class. We present some model CLT grammar activities in Chapters 5.

The CLT classroom focuses on students' being able to express their own experiences, thoughts, and opinions. For instructors trained in ALM, the transition to this more communicative and student-centered approach can be challenging, since it means allowing some errors to go uncorrected, as well as stepping back and giving students more ownership of their learning. The teacher's role is more that of a facilitator, as students participate in various types of group activities.

CLT aims to develop students' "communicative competence," a term coined by Hymes (1967) whose definition has evolved and expanded over the years. Canale and Swain (1980) broke down the concept into three components: grammatical competence (knowledge of grammar, vocabulary, pronunciation, spelling, etc.), sociolinguistic competence (the ability to use language appropriately in various discourse settings), and strategic competence (the ability to circumlocute when needed). In 1983, Canale added the notion of discourse competence (the ability to express language within various types of texts, both written and oral) to the definition. The idea of communicative competence continues to evolve even today. For example, Celce-Murcia (2007) has updated it to also include linguistic, formulaic, and interactional competence.

CLT and its focus on communicative competence overlapped with the creation of the American Council for the Teaching of Foreign Languages (ACTFL) proficiency guidelines, which were first rolled out in 1986. ACTFL is the largest organization of language teachers in the US, and it has had a strong influence on curricular innovation, particularly at the secondary level. ACTFL defines proficiency as "the ability to use language in real world situations in a spontaneous interaction and non-rehearsed context and in a manner acceptable and appropriate to native speakers of the language. Proficiency demonstrates what a language user is able to do regardless of where, when or how the language was acquired. The demonstration is independent of how the language was learned; the context may or may not be familiar; the evaluation of proficiency is not limited to the content of a particular curriculum that has been taught and learned" (2015, 4). ACTFL divides proficiency into four skills: speaking, writing, reading, and listening. Its Oral Proficiency Interview (OPI) is a well-known instrument to assess an individual's ability to speak a particular language, based on specific descriptions of what it means to have achieved the status of a novice, intermediate, advanced, superior, or distinguished speaker (with further sub-rankings from low through mid to high in all but the superior and distinguished levels). In 2012, ACTFL published proficiency guidelines for all four skills (not only speaking), which identify levels similar to those of the

OPI. CLT classes have striven to help students develop these four skills and thus acquire linguistic proficiency.

A criticism of CLT is that it lacks sufficient intellectual rigor. It seems incongruous that students who might be studying molecular biology or philosophy must respond to banal questions about vegetables or hair color in their language classes. In addition, since there is little focus on grammar (which is usually expected to be acquired implicitly), CLT students tend to make a significant number of errors. When they enroll in upper-level classes, their instructors often disparage their writing proficiency. These criticisms have led to current initiatives that seek to integrate more academic content in language classes of all levels.

> **Reflection**
>
> 1. Did you learn or have you taught using CLT? Based on your experiences or the framework outlined above, what do you think are the advantages and disadvantages of this approach?
> 2. One criticism of CLT is that it overemphasizes the *self*. How might we focus more on the *other*?
> 3. Find a textbook that claims to be communicative. Do you see any activities that appear to fit better into earlier frameworks?

TODAY'S CONTEXT

Methods and approaches for teaching languages have followed a somewhat pendulous path. Language pedagogy has always been linked to societal values, perceptions, and demands, and pedagogical changes reflect these external influences. Grammar translation guided students to understand philosophical, historical, and literary texts in order to become well-educated citizens. The direct method addressed perceived deficiencies in grammar translation, in particular, learners' limited ability to produce the target language orally. The audiolingual method, with its militarized format (drills!), emerged as a response to Sputnik and the national obsession with keeping up with the Russians and strengthening national defense. The shift to the natural approach and communicative language teaching highlighted the focus on the well-being of the individual, aligning with the self-expression goal of the "me" generation.

What does it mean to teach languages in the twenty-first century? New and experienced instructors alike find opportunities and resources as well as challenges and obstacles that were unimaginable in the past. Consider, for example, the nuts and bolts of class planning and classroom management. Teachers must adapt and readapt to a plethora of technological tools developed at an increasingly rapid pace, but often with a brief shelf life. Twenty-first-century students have grown up in a digital world where their phones and tablets allow them to remain connected to others at all times, but technological skills do not automatically translate into successful learning strategies. The lure of texting and social media can lead to classroom distractions. Teachers must therefore find innovative ways to keep students engaged. As Kramsch explains, students "no longer want to be passive recipients of grammar and vocabulary; they now demand to be given agency and autonomy in order to manipulate knowledge and work collaboratively with others" (2013, xii). Many of the techniques and activities that were once mainstays of the second language classroom may no longer be viable for students accustomed to in-person and virtual interactions.

On the curricular level, teachers are encouraged to frame lessons and courses within culturally stimulating contexts and to guide students to interact with the world in meaningful ways. More and more university mission statements call for their students to become "global citizens." What this term actually means is open to debate (see Olds 2012). In any case, the concept appears to be here to stay for a while, at least in some form. It is therefore vital to frame the learning of other languages (and cultures) as not only an intellectually important endeavor but also a vital component of leadership in today's globalized world. Van Houten, Couet, and Fulkerson cite the Department of Defense's white paper that states, "To maintain a position of global leadership, the United States must broaden and deepen its language, regional, and cultural capabilities" (2011, 9). They explain that "in a 21st century global marketplace, serious competitors must have language and cultural skills to work collaboratively with people from a variety of linguistic and cultural backgrounds at home and around the world" (Van Houten, Couet, and Fulkerson 42). Therefore, if fewer students are eager to study languages for intrinsic reasons, departments must adjust and focus on making the instrumental goals clear and persuasive. Programs need to stress reasons why remaining monolingual is a poor choice in today's world. The following section offers insights into these and other twenty-first-century challenges.

Technology and the Myth of Quick and Easy Language Acquisition

One of the most important pedagogical initiatives that overlapped with the advent of CLT was the integration of technological resources into the second language classroom. In CLT's early years, instructors were encouraged to present "visuals" via transparencies projected onto a screen. Transparencies could contain anything from illustrations of new vocabulary to short grammar presentations to instructions for group activities to photos or drawings for students to discuss. Today's students (and even some of today's instructors) would be amazed that the only way to show a clip from a movie back in the day was to wheel a stand containing a TV and VCR into the classroom.

Technology can be a double-edged sword, however. All over the web, and even showing up on screens uninvited, advertisements and testimonials claim that individuals have learned a language in a strikingly short time. Popular myths abound. Consider the "language teachers hate him" ads that frequently pop up. You can learn a language in thirty days! Another online app promises that you can learn a language for free, with minimal effort, just through completing grammar and vocabulary exercises on your phone. This app asserts that it is "science based"; however, in reality, no linguists were involved in its development. The science behind it is the science of gaming and motivation. These are certainly important components of an online program, but integrating the expertise of applied linguists, who have insights into how language is actually acquired, is vital.

Commercial app and site users often end up disappointed. DeWaard (2013, 66–69) exposes major flaws of the Rosetta Stone program, many of which are relevant for other technology-based programs as well: misleading claims, shaky theoretical foundations, nonstandard (and again misleading) proficiency scales, lack of cultural authenticity, limitations of a nonhuman system, and some technical issues (which may have been addressed by now). At the time of this book's publication, there is no empirical evidence that any of the commercial online apps or programs that currently exist can, *on their own*, ensure that learners will acquire documentable proficiency in the target language. Even if they may be well intentioned, these apps can be deceptive. Because they are so technologically advanced, they may appear to be pedagogically sophisticated as well (which may not be the case). Many commercial apps offer practice and support, much like flashcards and workbooks of old. They may be helpful in certain ways, such as for memorizing vocabulary or practicing verb conjugations. However, they often fail when it comes to putting everything together. As Lord explains, "until [Rosetta Stone] and other stand-alone programs are able to effectively promote proficiency as measured not just by lexical and grammatical assessments, but through true communicative competence, they will never come close to replacing classroom-based instructor-led learning" (2015, 403–4). Commercial apps should be appreciated as practice tools; they are not approaches or methods or curricula or replacements for language classes. The good news, however, is that applied linguists have been getting on board and are now contributing to the production of noncommercial computer-assisted language learning tools that show great promise. These initiatives (some of which are discussed in Chapter 4) align with research in the field of language learning (and not only gaming); thus, they help students develop not only language skills but also cultural insights.

Reflection

One language learning app developer has conceded that he has always seen his product as an accompaniment to language classes, not a replacement for them (although this statement contradicts the advertisements for the program that one finds on the internet).

1. Do you see a role for language apps as an ancillary to courses? How might they be effective?
2. Choose one "language learning" app and analyze its strengths and weaknesses.
3. Can you think of reasons why many researchers in the field of computer-assisted language learning (CALL) believe that hybrid language classes are superior to classes that are taught completely online (see Rubio and Thoms 2012)?

"Humanics" and Language Learning

Whereas some technology-based programs claim that they can help students master another language in a remarkably short time, others boldly proclaim that their technological innovation makes it unnecessary to learn another language in the first place. For example, portable interpretation devices are now available; the technology, however, is not perfect yet. Like online translation software, these devices can produce comprehensible yet error-filled and distracting results. The software is constantly evolving, though, and it is likely that the quality of translation will improve as well, especially if computational linguists become more engaged in the endeavor.

In his 2017 book *Robot-Proof*, Joseph Aoun, the president of Northeastern University, discusses the fact that robots are replacing human beings in many spheres: "The impetus for the book was a realization that robotics and artificial intelligence are advancing more rapidly than anyone predicted. Even scientists appear to be caught off-guard by the sudden and unprecedented capabilities of their creations. These technological advances have vast implications, especially for the future of work. Some studies predict that half of all U.S. jobs will be at risk within the next 20 years" (Nicodemo 2017). In response, Aoun proposes the framework of "humanics," which he believes will enable humans to distinguish themselves from robots: "We need a new model of learning that enables learners to understand the highly technological world around them and that simultaneously allows them to transcend it by nurturing the mental and intellectual qualities that are unique to humans—namely, their capacity for creativity and mental flexibility. We can call this model *humanics*. . . . Humanics is a discipline that teaches mastery of content as well as the development of particular skills" (Aoun 2017, 53). The goal is to "cultivate the best of what it means to be human. . . . Society is changing, the world is changing, and I believe higher ed has the responsibility and opportunity to make every learner robot-proof" (Nicodemo 2017).

Aoun proposes the following human literacy skills as vital to humanics: creativity, entrepreneurship, systems thinking, empathy, cultural agility, and teamwork. One could argue that the language classroom is the perfect environment for students to hone their cultural agility and empathy, among the other skills mentioned. For those whose goals are purely pragmatic, however, cultural agility can be beneficial for becoming not only global citizens but also global (business) partners. Aoun explains that "cultural agility involves more than just knowing how to behave in a video conference or at a foreign restaurant. It requires a deep enough immersion in a culture so that we can fit seamlessly into multicultural teams or get results from people who have dramatically different lives from our own"

(2017, 70–71). Below, we discuss two frameworks that merge culture, content, and language learning within L2 curricula.

ACTFL World-Readiness Standards

The ACTFL Standards, also known as the "Five Cs" (Communication, Cultures, Connections, Comparisons, and Communities), were developed in 1996. They were "refreshed" in 2015 and are now called "World-Readiness Standards for Language Learning." Appendix A provides a chart containing the refreshed standards.

As is clear from the chart, the Standards reflect the impetus to connect language learning, cultural understanding, and the advancement of global citizenship. Many secondary school programs in particular use the ACTFL Standards as the cornerstone for curriculum development and assessment, although universities have not adopted them with the same consistency.

The revised framework also includes the 2012 Performance Descriptors, which cover three "modes" of communication: interpersonal, interpretive, and presentational. Unlike the four skills (speaking, listening, reading, and writing), which reflect proficiency levels, the performance descriptors assess "language performance that is the result of explicit instruction in an instructional setting" (ACTFL 2015a, 3). In other words, the modes provide guidelines for teachers to evaluate students' work. Each mode requires the use of more than one skill, sometimes several at the same time. For example, to interpret a text, students need not only to read it but also to write about it or to discuss it orally with peers (speaking and listening). The Performance Descriptors reflect the fact that language skills do not exist within a vacuum; they are inherently linked to one another.

The 2007 MLA Report

With the exception of GT classes, beginning-level classes have traditionally emphasized everyday, real-life communication, unambiguous and literal meaning, and concrete situations. In contrast, upper-level courses have addressed critical thinking, ambiguous and metaphorical meaning, and open-ended ideas (Swaffar, Arens, and Byrnes 1991). Fifth-semester "bridge" courses have been charged with the nearly impossible task of crossing this language-content divide in one semester. This rift has often led to instructor (and student) frustration at all levels. Beginning-level instructors often feel unsatisfied by banal discussions about students' favorite weekend activities. Faculty teaching upper-level courses report that students do not have the linguistic preparation to focus exclusively on context in their classes, and advanced students miss having the opportunity to continue to build their language skills. In an analysis of four upper-level content courses, Rodgers (2015) found that students had limited opportunities to engage in extended discourse and to enhance their language proficiency, due to the instructors' emphasis on content and teacher-centered lectures with only incidental focus on form. The only linguistic feedback that students received was through the correction of errors in their writing assignments.

The MLA's "Foreign Languages and Higher Education: New Structures for a Changed World" (2007) aimed to address the shortcomings of this artificial philosophical and pedagogical division with a call for "replacing the two-tiered language-literature structure with a broader and more coherent curriculum in which language, literature, and culture are taught as a continuous whole." The report envisioned curricular attention to both form and content at all levels of instruction, with engagement of critical thinking and critical language awareness across the curriculum. Its recommendations suggested that students at all levels should "1) consider alternative ways of seeing, feeling, and understanding; 2) reflect on the world and themselves through the lens of another language and culture; 3) analyze differences in meanings, mentalities, and worldviews; and 4) engage in interpretation and translation, historical and political consciousness, social sensibility, and aesthetic perception in the course of acquiring functional language abilities" (3).

The report has inspired curricular reform that seeks to foster the acquisition of two kinds of competence: *translingual* and *transcultural*. It explains that "the idea of translingual and transcultural competence ... places value on the ability to *operate between languages* [emphasis ours]. Students are educated to function as informed and capable interlocutors with educated native speakers in the target language. They are also trained to reflect on the world and themselves through the lens of another language and culture" (MLA 2007, 3–4). In addition, the report argues that "at one end, language is considered to be principally instrumental, a skill to use for communicating thought and information. At the opposite end, language is understood as an essential element of a human being's thought processes, perceptions, and self-expressions; and as such it is considered to be at the core of translingual and transcultural competence. While we use language to communicate our needs to others, language simultaneously reveals us to others and to ourselves. Language is a complex multifunctional phenomenon that links an individual to other individuals, to communities, and to national cultures" (2).

Kramsch, a member of the committee that composed the MLA report, clarifies that it "understands language as much more than just the acquisition of forms in the lower division taught by graduate students or lecturers, to be filled with meaning in the upper division courses taught by literature professors. It is, from beginning to end, about the traffic in meaning through reflection, translation, and an awareness of the power of language in discourse" (2010, 19). In her earlier research, Kramsch (1997) argues that the glorification of native speakers is misguided. She believes that the goal of the second language classroom should not be to try to make students indistinguishable from native speakers but to help them develop a sense of their own multilingual selves and thrive in that capacity. The MLA report, clearly influenced by Kramsch's work, thus argues for setting a goal that transcends communicative competence to advocate for a focus on the learner's personal relationship with, and interactions within, the target language and culture.

Criticism of the MLA report has focused on the fact that it does not specifically outline how to achieve its goals, both at the broad, curricular level and in everyday lesson plans. As Lomicka and Lord explain, "Reactions to the MLA 2007 report generally concur that the report clearly identifies several issues facing language departments but does not provide useful solutions or implementation strategies for a different kind of language instruction" (2018, 117). In response, applied linguists have proposed and continue to hone curricular models and pedagogical approaches that align with the report and seek to accomplish its goals. We discuss these initiatives below.

Reflection

1. The Five Cs/Standards are more often linked to the K–12 environment than to the college level. How do needs differ at the two levels? Are they always different?
2. How do the MLA report and the ACTFL Standards differ? Are they complementary? Contradictory?

Continued ...

3. How does Aoun's notion of "cultural agility" align with the Standards and the MLA report?

SPIRALING LANGUAGE AND CONTENT: CURRICULAR MODELS

How do we merge form and content effectively at the lower levels of instruction? How do we avoid overpersonalization and a focus on self-referential topics when students have a limited command of form? How do we develop students' "translingual and transcultural competence" while reviewing the necessary vocabulary and grammar to develop linguistic proficiency? How do beginning-level students engage in critical language and culture awareness when they have a limited proficiency? The curricular models presented here propose some solutions to these challenges. We should point out that the merging of language and content is not a new initiative; the first three frameworks we discuss (Content-Based Instruction, Languages for Specific Purposes, and Foreign Languages across the Curriculum) have been implemented in programs for quite some time. The last two ([multi]literacies/genre-based pedagogy and social pedagogies) are newer frameworks.

Content-Based Instruction

A Content-Based Instruction (CBI) focuses on "the learning of language through the study of a content area" (Rodgers 2006, 373). Content areas can include anything from chemistry to mathematics to history. Immersion programs are a common example of CBI. Content-based or immersion approaches provide students with meaningful, comprehensible input from which they may gain tangible skills to interpret written and spoken language. Research suggests, however, that the emphasis on content in immersion instruction may sometimes be at the expense of language instruction. In her well-known large-scale study of French immersion students in 1985, Swain found that there were discrepancies in students' mastery of grammatical structures despite their strong achievements in comprehension, interpretation, and subject-matter content knowledge. She suggested that these results were likely due to an imbalance in the opportunities for students to produce language *output*, despite the many occasions to process input. Although teachers and students regularly discussed content in the target language, these interactions did not include interventions that focused on metalinguistic exploration of grammar, likely owing to the instructors' belief that language acquisition would occur naturally within the meaningful context. Based on these and similar findings, Pica (2002) describes the fallacy of the "two for one" promise of language acquisition in a content-based classroom that does not contain carefully designed interventions that call attention to form.

Recent studies, however, have provided suggestions for balancing *form* and *meaning* or *content* and *language* in the foreign language classroom. For example, Gibbons (2002) recommends that teachers design lessons that emphasize both knowledge construction and language development by envisioning an hourglass image. Within this template, meaning and content are found at the top wide part of the hourglass. At this stage of the lesson, the context is established, and students explore meaningful and comprehensible content. For example, if the students watch a clip from a documentary (see Chapter 7), they can be asked to take notes and collaboratively complete a table that responds to the who/what/where/when/why of the clip's content. Students can explore the *meaning* of the documentary in both small- and large-group discussions.

In the next stage, as the hourglass tapers, the instructor would highlight language details. Examples include the analysis of tense and aspect, stylistic features, and discourse markers in targeted text(s). For instance, teachers could distribute one sentence from the documentary to each student and then ask all the students to work together to reconstruct the narration by placing the sentences in order, paying particular attention to verb tenses, which would be highlighted in boldface. Students could then discuss their choices and, with the instructor's guidance, engage in collaborative discussions of how various past tenses are used within discourse. This type of activity provides a focus on both content and grammatical form; in addition, it allows the teacher to offer targeted error-correction feedback to students. Likewise, instructors can modify their responses to student contributions in ways that encourage more student output (e.g., Can you elaborate with an example? That's an interesting point—could you expand on your thoughts? Why? Is there an alternative way of looking at this situation?).

The bottom wide part of the hourglass then includes activities that allow students to apply their understanding of the linguistic features within the established context. For example, students could reimagine and renarrate the same scene from the perspective of one of the historical figures in the documentary using the targeted past-tense structures. Within an hourglass framework, the language-focused activities are organically linked to the content. Cummins (1998) sums up a similar pedagogical approach with the following easy-to-remember stages: (1) focus on message, (2) focus on language (in context), and (3) focus on language use (in context).

Some researchers also distinguish between "content-obligatory" and "content-compatible" language in a content-rich environment (Snow, Met, and Genesee 1989). Content-obligatory language is academic-style language, whereas content-compatible language is everyday language that is used for negotiation, social encounters, and interaction. The University of Minnesota's Center for Advanced Research on Language Acquisition (CARLA) provides a model formula to help articulate language goals in content-rich environments: "Students will use X (language structure) to do Y (functions) with Z (words/word groups)" (https://carla.umn.edu/cobaltt/modules/curriculum/formula.html).

CARLA also provides model objectives created by Tara Williams Fortune, the director of its Immersion Research and Professional Development Program, in the context of a lesson on the geography of Spain. A sample content-obligatory language objective for this lesson is "Students are able to identify geographic features using *hay* (there is/are) and terms like *el río* (river), *el desierto* (desert), *el bosque* (forest), and *la costa* (coast)." A complementary content-compatible language objective is "Students are able to use what/where questions, such as *Dónde están los pirineos?* (Where are the Pyrenees?) to ask about geographic locations in Spain with the verb *estar* (to be) and question words such as *dónde, qué* (where, what), etc." Some researchers suggest that it may be more effective to place emphasis on transferable, content-compatible language in certain classroom contexts so that students can acquire everyday language that can be applied to a variety of situations outside the academic context. Fortune and Tedick (2008), for example, propose a lesson plan template that reminds instructors to call attention to the language and content features of a text, including

- content and cultural concepts;
- text genre;
- discourse and linguistic features;

- content-obligatory language structures, expressions, and vocabulary; and
- content-compatible language structures, expressions, and vocabulary.

Regardless of one's lesson-planning approach, developing specific and detailed course objectives can help fuse language and content instruction in important ways.

> **Reflection**
>
> Reflect on one of your recent lesson plans. How could you reconfigure the lesson to emphasize both language and content? How could you incorporate attention to content and cultural concepts, text genre, discourse and linguistic features, content-obligatory language structures, and/or content-compatible language structures?

Languages for Specific Purposes

Languages for Specific Purposes (LSP) curricula provide students with training to use language within a professional context. Examples of such courses include Spanish for Social Justice, German for Engineering, and Chinese for Business. Because LSP courses aim to link language study to other professional disciplines, they can be a true representation of the Connections goal of the World-Readiness Standards for Learning Languages, which is to "connect with other disciplines and acquire information and diverse perspectives in order to use the language to function in academic and career-related situations" (ACTFL 2015b, 2). Following such calls to action in the profession, LSP curricular models have gained popularity over the past twenty years. The competitive global job market has raised awareness that future employers may highly value the language competence that students gain in LSP courses. Furthermore, the mission of LSP courses to integrate language, cultural understanding, and professional content in practical ways has responded to the needs of different populations of students (Grosse and Voght 2012).

Foreign Languages across the Curriculum

Foreign Languages across the Curriculum (FLAC) courses have also emerged in departments across the country, with support from large foundations such as the National Endowment for the Humanities and the Fund for the Improvement of Postsecondary Education. The goal is to provide students with opportunities to use their foreign language skills to study content in other academic courses outside or in conjunction with language/literature/culture departments. In this format, an academic discipline such as art history or psychology could be taught in conjunction with the target language. Many researchers claim that engagement with academic materials in multiple languages can provide meaningful opportunities for students to develop their language skills (Klee and Barnes-Karol 2006).

FLAC courses can take on a variety of formats. Sample models include

- content courses taught primarily or partially in the target language;
- content courses in English with modules in the target language;
- courses co-taught by both content and language pedagogy specialists; and
- lecture courses taught in English with discussion sections in other languages.

In the discussion section model for FLAC courses, content-based texts in the target language can provide an alternative perspective that may subvert the viewpoint of a parallel reading presented in English. This approach allows students to engage in thoughtful dialogue regarding how the targeted content might be framed or articulated differently. Klee and Barnes-Karol (2006) suggest preparing study guides that include prereading tasks, comprehension questions, and vocabulary support activities. These study guides can prepare students for discussion sections by activating their prior knowledge of the content. In-class activities facilitated by a language instructor, such as small-group discussions, debates, and roundtables, can help students link the course material presented in English to the content presented in the target language.

Literacy, Multiliteracies, and Genre-Based Models

Kern's influential work on literacy serves as the impetus for curricular models based on the integration of texts in the L2 classroom. In their advocacy of a "multiliteracies" approach (a term coined by the New London Group [1996]; see Chapter 7), Allen and Paesani (2010) cite Kern (2003, 43), explaining that this type of instruction offers "a way to narrow the long-standing pedagogical gap that has traditionally divided what we do at the early levels of language teaching and what we do at the advanced levels. That is, it offers up a way to reconcile the teaching of 'communication' with the teaching of textual analysis" (121). They also cite Kern's (2000, 16) definition of "literacy" as "the use of socially-, historically-, and culturally-situated practices of creating and interpreting meaning through texts. It entails at least a tacit awareness of the relationships between textual conventions and their contexts of use and, ideally, the ability to reflect critically on these relationships.... It draws on a wide range of cognitive abilities, on knowledge of written and spoken language, on knowledge of genres, and on cultural knowledge" (Allen and Paesani 2010, 121). (For more on genre, see Chapter 7.) Paesani, Allen, and Dupuy present a detailed description of the tenets of the multiliteracies framework, including its four crucial "pedagogical acts": "situated practice, overt instruction, critical framing, and transformed practice" (2016, 37).

Georgetown University's German program is known for its genre-based model, which is designed to develop students' multiple literacies. Specifically, it aims to "dismantle the Language/Literature division" and to "focus on the integration of intellectually stimulating content/texts from the beginning class onward." A description of the initiative likewise appears on the department's website: "The curriculum project, which we have called 'Developing Multiple Literacies,' reflects a literacy orientation that recognizes that foreign language instruction of adult learners, as contrasted with second language instruction, is fundamentally about engaging these already literate learners in imagined textual worlds which provide the occasion for thought-full language acquisition. The curriculum draws its content and its socially situated language use for the acquisition of advanced competencies in listening, speaking, reading, and writing from a wide range of oral and written genres. These are sequenced in a principled way across the curricular levels, thereby contributing to program articulation" (https://german.georgetown.edu/page/1242716500101.html). By focusing on texts that contain different genres as well as various linguistic registers, the Georgetown model attempts to connect classes from the lowest to the highest levels offered in the department.

Social Pedagogies

New opportunities in the area of experiential learning, broadly defined to include study abroad, service learning, internships, and project-based learning, have expanded the environments in which students interact with the target language and develop linguistic and cultural expertise. This trend reflects interest in interaction-based initiatives that align with the framework of social pedagogies. Charitos and Van Deusen-Scholl describe this framework as follows:

> Drawing insights from the work of Randy Bass and Heidi Elmendorf (2010, 2011), social pedagogies are design approaches that seek to provide students with the tools and the opportunities needed to engage and interact with authentic audiences (i.e., anyone other than the formal classroom instructor) in iterative cycles of engagement. As students move through a cycle of discovery, exploration, and engagement with a set of disciplinary concepts, they begin to establish a personal relation to knowledge in the context of audience and community. Social pedagogies thus allow students to position themselves as actors who experience how "acts of communication and representation connect authentic tasks to learning processes, learning processes to adaptive practices, practices to learning environments and intellectual communities, and how the constellation of these elements help [them] integrate their learning by connecting to larger contexts for knowledge and action" (Bass and Elmendorf, 2011). (2017, 20)

The kind of engagement residing at the core of a social pedagogies orientation differs significantly from what one finds in other approaches, as it is related not only to students' linguistic and cultural growth but also to their personal transformations and potential impact on the world around them (see Clifford and Reisinger's [2019] rationale and guidelines for service learning models and community-based language learning [CBLL]). Experiential learning is based in large part on the connections that students establish with others. It therefore links in important ways with the MLA report's notion of "operat[ing] between languages."

Dubreil and Thorne explain that

> the framework of social pedagogies aligns in striking ways with the critical pedagogies framework (i.e., Freire, 1970) applied to Second Lan-

guage Acquisition (SLA) by Norton and Toohey (2004) in that it envisions language as "not simply a means of expression or communication" but rather as "a practice that constructs, and is constructed by, the ways language learners understand themselves, their social surroundings, their histories, and their possibilities for the future" (Norton and Toohey, 2004, 1), a characterization akin to what Kramsch (2006) identifies as symbolic competence. Seen from this perspective, L2 teaching and learning is positioned as an agent for personal as well as societal transformation. (2017, 3)

A social pedagogies orientation is also compatible with the notion of an "ecological" or "complexity" language pedagogy, defined by Levine and Phipps as an approach that "sees all aspects of language—its use, [its] structures, and the ways these change and, of course, its development in individuals and groups—as complex, dynamic systems.... With regard to language pedagogy, a complexity approach means viewing the entire system in which learners learn a new language, which includes the curriculum and all its components, as a social ecosystem" (2010, 10). Within the same chapter, Levine and Phipps propose "Five New Cs," not to replace but to add to the established ACTFL Five Cs. Their Five Cs are Context, Complexity, Capacity, Compassion, and Conflict (8–13). In sum, they support the conviction that true transformations, both within the student and within society, rely on the exploration of contextualized interactions.

A social pedagogies approach also allows us to consider, in particular, the goals of study-abroad initiatives and their integration into programs. Although virtual connections with the target culture today are much more sophisticated than ever before, the actual physical experience of living abroad (i.e., the engagement of all one's senses, as well as the challenges of adapting to a foreign environment) cannot truly be duplicated. Levine (2014) makes the argument, however, that programs do not currently prepare students adequately for their experience abroad. He states that "we need to rethink what we teach students (and how) from the beginning of introductory classes, focusing more on the learner as a developing 'multilingual subject' than an effective 'talking head' who can process and generate accurate utterances based on (primarily) quotidian themes and topics" (78). In his ethnographic study, which he structured while he was leading a semester study-abroad program in Germany, Levine concluded that most students tend to engage abroad in the same ways that they have participated in the L2 classroom. In particular, they are able to use the target language to accomplish everyday tasks and to complete coursework. On the other hand, their interactions with target communities tend to be superficial and instrumental, consisting mostly of transactions and small talk. Levine links this result to the tenets of CLT, thus leading to a call for curricular innovation (93). He states that "moving away from the talking-heads model means seeking ways to design curriculum and then teach by way of communication in which the learners have a personal stake" (94). Even if students do not have the opportunity to study abroad, we should still cultivate their multilingual identities and lead them to become thoughtful global citizens. Through interactions with classmates, with global partners (by using technology), or with texts of various types, students can transcend the talking heads model and participate in a deeper and more meaningful multilingual experience.

> **Reflection**
>
> 1. Compare the curricular models outlined above, citing their differences and overlap. Which one seems to correspond most to the language classes you have either taken or taught?
> 2. Do any of the models correspond in certain ways to earlier approaches/methods? How? How are they different?
> 3. What elements from each framework would you prioritize in your own language classroom? Why?
> 4. Which of the models mentioned above seem the most promising for your current academic context? Why?

MOVING FORWARD

Specialists in SLA underscore the importance of backing up curricular reform with empirical studies that provide evidence of language acquisition. VanPatten's work on input processing (presented in detail in Chapter 5), for example, was groundbreaking and has led to innovation in the way that grammar is presented in the L2 classroom. VanPatten is outspoken in his view that he and his SLA colleagues are researchers, not scholars, and that their work is based on science. In a 2015 white paper in *Hispania*, he laments the "perpetuation of myths about language" and the "perception about language acquisition and language teaching" that one finds in many language programs throughout the country:

> As a field of empirical research, second language acquisition does not have answers to all questions. But there is a wealth of accumulated evidence that points to what we might call fundamental facts about language acquisition. Among these facts are the necessity of communicative input for the development of an underlying mental representation, that communicative ability cannot be practiced but develops from acts of communication, that there are severe constraints on the role of explicit teaching and learning in development, that the acquisition of "grammar" does not precede communication but emerges along with it, that variation in learner output is expected, among a number of others. It is precisely these facts that elude most language departments in the twenty first century. (8–9)

VanPatten's remarks point to a somewhat recent divide found between the language "scientists" and the more humanistic scholars in the field. The two groups seem to be heading in different directions in terms of how they believe languages should be taught and for what purposes.

A discourse-based model might serve as a middle ground for effectively merging text-focused and communicative orientations. Celce-Murcia and Olshtain state that "using a language entails the ability to both interpret and produce discourse in context in spoken and written communicative interaction, which is why we assign such a central role to discourse in our discussion of frameworks that should inform language teaching" (2000, 4). Likewise, Kern proposes that integrating texts into the L2 classroom provides students with insights into authentic discourse, prompts for meaningful communication, and an understanding of the underlying linguistic code: "Texts—whether written, oral, visual, or audiovisual—offer more than something to talk about (that is, content for the sake of practicing language). They offer students the chance to position themselves in relation to distinct viewpoints and distinct cultures. They give students the chance to make connections between grammar, discourse, and meaning, between language and content, between language and culture, and between another culture and their own—in short, making them aware of the webs, rather than strands, of meaning in human communication" (2008, 380). In other words, texts can represent an enhancement of, and not necessarily an alternative to, CLT.

There is significant overlap among the curricular frameworks presented in this chapter, and they are not mutually exclusive. For example, Blyth (2018) describes a project in which students engage with a poem using a multiliteracies approach and, in so doing, make important discoveries about their multilingual selves (more of a social pedagogies construct). Twenty-first-century language teaching therefore reflects a diversity of approaches that are employed, often in unexpectedly blended ways, to suit the particular contexts in which they are found.

3 • Beliefs

INSTITUTIONAL IDENTITY, CONTEXT, AND GOALS

Beliefs, motivation, and identity are traits often attributed to individuals, but they also characterize the ethos of departments and institutions and are closely linked to their expressed missions. It is therefore crucial to design curricular and pedagogical initiatives so that they align with the goals of multiple stakeholders. As we discussed in Chapter 2, although foreign language study traditionally aimed to prepare students to read and analyze literature in the target language, today's student learning outcomes vary considerably from one context to another. For example, the Massachusetts Institute of Technology, whose mission is "to advance knowledge and educate students in science, technology, and other areas of scholarship" (http://web.mit.edu/facts/mission.html), may approach language and culture instruction differently from Amherst College, whose mission is "expanding the realm of knowledge through scholarly research and artistic creation" (https://www.amherst.edu/amherst-story/facts/mission/node/7854). An institution's location also can play an important role in curricular development, sometimes inspiring departments to offer courses to meet the needs of the community and its local businesses, programs, and agencies. Bernhardt (2002) has characterized the intersections of people and institutions that inform a program's goals as networks of culture. She explains that "language departments are cultures; they consist of subcultures, and they are cultures within cultures" (248).

Various frameworks advocated in twenty-first-century language teaching, in tandem with institutional identity, often influence the curricular model that a department implements. For example, the University of Massachusetts Lowell's World Languages and Cultures Department was inspired by "the university's mission to prepare our students to be 'Work Ready, Life Ready, World Ready'" (https://www.uml.edu/catalog/undergraduate/fahss/departments/languages-cultures/). The Pillars of Excellence, established by the university for its 2020 Strategic Plan, encourage goals such as "transformational education" and "global engagement and inclusive community" (https://www.uml.edu/2020/Pillars-of-Excellence.aspx). To align with the university's mission, the department chose to use the ACTFL's World-Readiness Standards as a curricular framework when redesigning its curriculum in 2015. The department's new curriculum emphasizes community engagement, service learning, interdisciplinary collaborations, and an increasing number of internship and study-abroad opportunities.

At Stanford University, a Committee on Undergraduate Education recommended the development of a Language Center to oversee more than forty language programs in order to strengthen and standardize foreign language instruction. The Language Center was established in 1995, with the mission of creating language performance benchmarks, organizing professional development for instructors, and conducting research on language teaching and learning. While the Language Center coordinates the administration of lower- and intermediate-level foreign language courses, however, the upper-level courses in foreign languages, literatures, and cultures are housed in the Division of Literatures, Cultures, and Languages; thus, one finds separate oversight for lower- and upper-division courses.

The German Studies Department at Emory University developed a different curricular and structural framework. Similar to the Georgetown program established in the early 2000s (see Chapter 2), this department believed that the great "language-literature divide," which focuses on "language" at the lower levels of instruction and "content" at the upper levels, was counterproductive to the language learning experience. To integrate form and content at all levels, the department developed a genre-based four-year curriculum in 2007. This departmental curriculum emphasizes the genres of narration, explanation, and argumentation at the lower, intermediate, and upper levels, respectively.

In this chapter, we invite instructors to think critically about both their department's identity and mission and their own socialization into the world of teaching. We also discuss the strength of instructor beliefs and their long-lasting influence on pedagogical practices. The final portion of the chapter addresses students' beliefs, goals, and motivation and offers strategies to engage students with meaningful, useful, and purposeful learning experiences.

Reflection

What are the identity, goals, and values of your institution and department? Go through the list of questions below. If you are unsure of some of the answers, interview the language program director(s) and other faculty in your department to gain more information.

Analysis of Institutional Context

Community
1. Are particular languages prominent in the community surrounding your institution? Does the community influence the institutional attitude toward foreign language study? If so, how?
2. Does the institution offer courses to meet the needs of the community and its local businesses, programs, and agencies?
3. Does your institution have a relationship with feeder schools? How might this connection have an impact on the curriculum?

Institution
1. What is the institution's mission? What is the relationship between the mission of the institution and the mission of the department?
2. What are the relationships between the foreign language department and other departments within the institution? Are there interdisciplinary or joint programs?
3. What is the relationship between the department and the general education requirements?

Department Goals
1. Has the department established a common curricular framework for beginning through advanced courses (e.g., proficiency-

Continued . . .

oriented curriculum, Standards-based curriculum, genre-based curriculum, or literacy-based curriculum)?
2. Do the department's targeted goals emphasize linguistic proficiency and the four skills of reading, writing, listening, and speaking? The ACTFL Standards? Translingual and transcultural competence? Students' understanding of literature and culture? A combination?
3. Do the department's goals differ significantly in lower- versus upper-level courses?
4. How does your program integrate content in lower-level courses and language in upper-level courses? Is there articulation from beginning- through advanced-level courses?
5. Has the department outlined particular goals and learning outcomes for students? For example, is there an exit assessment for language requirement students, majors, and minors (i.e, a proficiency exam, or a portfolio)?
6. Does the department offer students the opportunity to participate in study-abroad, exchange, internship, and work-study programs? How do these programs align with course offerings and departmental goals?
7. Are there various tracks within your department with different goals (e.g., linguistics, literature, history, culture)?

Teaching
1. Are there particular teaching approaches or methods advocated within your department? Do they vary by level? By language? By instructor?

Students
1. What is the profile of the students at your institution? What are their areas of interest and specialization?
2. Do students in beginning, intermediate, and advanced courses have different profiles? How might their diversity influence departmental goals or instruction?
3. What common career and professional interests do students have? Do they differ by course level?

Source: Adapted from ADFL 2001.

TEACHER BELIEFS AND PRACTICES

Freeman and Johnson explain that "teachers are not empty vessels waiting to be filled with theoretical and pedagogical skills; they are individuals who enter teacher education programs with prior experiences, personal values, and beliefs that inform their knowledge about teaching and shape what they do in their classrooms" (1998, 401). New teachers' beliefs are therefore influenced by their own experiences as students or their projected self-images as teachers. Lortie characterizes these images and beliefs as coming from the "apprenticeship of observation" (1975, 62), or the vivid memories of over thirteen thousand hours spent in classrooms as students. Teachers often embark on their first day of teaching with strong preconceived ideas about language learning, often stemming from their own first language learning experiences. They may rationalize, "Hey, it worked for me! And I'm fluent. Certainly it will work for my students." They may be forgetting that they happened to be particularly adept at learning languages or comfortable adapting to various learning strategies and that most of the students in that same class did not thrive in the same way that they did.

New teachers' previously established beliefs, which may be based on outdated conceptions of foreign language instruction, can persist for their entire professional careers, influencing their pedagogical decision-making, their willingness to implement innovative pedagogical interventions, and their choice of classroom activities and assessment strategies. Even when enrolled in teacher education programs and presented with theory-based practices and research that contradict their outdated beliefs, teachers often remain resistant to change. The strength of their beliefs is undeniable. Therefore, if they do not identify and challenge their deep-rooted beliefs and make thoughtful attempts to explore innovative teaching practices, teachers, often unknowingly, may unintentionally rely on ineffective strategies.

Teachers who intend to teach in line with current research and theory in SLA sometimes do not follow through for logistical reasons. For example, a new instructor may read several articles about the importance of merging language and content, and she may believe in and advocate for this approach. However, when she attempts to merge language and content in her own classroom, she may not yet have acquired the experience or the requisite pedagogical content knowledge (the ability to organize content in ways that are pedagogically appropriate) to do so successfully. Interactions with the students or classroom management issues might also influence her ability to put her beliefs into practice, and she may revert to familiar practices. As instructors gain more experience, receive constructive feedback from trusted supervisors and colleagues, and regularly reflect on their instruction, they will feel more at ease implementing new pedagogical strategies and navigating the moment-to-moment pressures of the classroom environment.

In addition to their language learning experience and training, teachers bring to the classroom their unique backgrounds and personalities. Instructors who have big or engaging personalities, a lot of confidence in themselves, and a warm and enthusiastic rapport with their students are often praised as being excellent language teachers. But is their teaching effective? Here is the testimony of one of those teachers:

Perspectives

I was a twenty-two-year-old, first-year TA at a large public university in the mid-1980s. I had never taught before, and my Italian wasn't all that great. I was also a failed actress. I loved the spotlight, and I realized on the first day that I stepped in front of that class that I was meant to be a teacher. I arranged my students' desks in a semicircle (as I had been told to do), and the area between my students and my desk felt like my stage. I genuinely loved my students—every single one of them. I wanted so badly for them to like me, and I was willing to do whatever it took to ensure their success (which included being very generous with my time outside of class).

But my pedagogy. Oh, my pedagogy. I was trained in ALM, although we had had only a week's worth of preparation before we were thrown into the classroom to teach (alone and unsupervised). I did the drills from my textbook that I was supposed to do, and my students memorized the textbook conversations. I hate to admit it, but I also used some grammar translation. I'll also confess that I used a lot of English in class, especially when I wasn't being observed. I explained grammar to my students in great detail whenever they asked, and I was so proud of my detailed clarifications and charts. I have always loved grammar! My students ate it all up, since they wanted to know all the rules. The weird thing was that they still made a lot of

Continued . . .

mistakes even after they had seemed to understand how the grammar worked.

My evaluations were always nearly perfect, and students flocked to my classes, begging me to increase my cap so they could switch into my section. My supervisors raved about my classes after visiting them, mostly because my students were so engaged and I was so energetic and encouraging. But was I truly a good teacher? To be honest, I'm not so sure. My students' exam grades were not among the highest of all the students taking first-semester Italian (we group-graded all the exams to ensure consistency and fairness). And did my students become proficient in Italian? I'm not sure about that either. Did they enjoy coming to my class, and did they like me? Absolutely. But did that make me a good teacher? I don't know . . . Define "good teacher."

1. In your opinion, what is a "good" teacher? Is there a difference between a "good" and an "effective" teacher? Reflect on your experiences as a student.
2. Are student evaluations a reliable measure of effective teaching? What factors may influence students' perceptions of effective teaching? Personality? Likability? Gender? Rigor or lack thereof?

It is helpful to remember that personality and "sense of self" play an important role in who one becomes as a teacher. Gender, cultural identity, and academic background as well as beliefs and values all inform one's teaching persona. Ghanem states that "foreign languages differ from any other subject in that the subject that is taught is also the medium of instruction, which can often complicate the construction of teacher identities. . . . These identities, in turn, are often intertwined with issues of proficiency and a sense of legitimacy of being a [foreign language] instructor" (2015, 170).

Shulman (2000) identifies three domains of knowledge necessary for effective teaching: general pedagogical knowledge, content knowledge, and pedagogical content knowledge. In foreign language instruction, linguistic proficiency and knowledge of the target culture are key components of content knowledge and may influence beliefs and practices (Chacón 2005). For example, in a study of the self-efficacy, or perceived competence, of native versus nonnative teaching assistants, Mills and Allen (2007) found that nonnative speakers often believed themselves to be less competent foreign language instructors than native speakers, despite supportive feedback from the language program director that indicated otherwise. In an evaluation of English as a Second Language (ESL) instructors working in Korea, Defeng Li (1998) found that nonnative English instructors who believed that they had limited communicative ability often chose not to use advocated CLT approaches. Because of a self-perceived lack of proficiency, they felt more at ease implementing grammar-focused teaching practices. Hu's (2002) research reveals that many English teachers in China have learned English through teacher-centered, rote learning approaches and revert to these practices when faced with very large class sizes, heavy teaching loads, and examination-oriented external assessment. These studies (and others) suggest that new instructors can often perceive themselves to be unqualified to teach for one reason or another.

Despite the strength of these beliefs and their influence on classroom practices, nonnative teachers can have powerful advantages in the foreign language classroom. They often possess strong metalinguistic awareness, an excellent understanding of grammatical rules and concepts, and knowledge of effective language learning strategies, since they have learned the target language themselves (Medgyes 1996). Most important, they can be a source of motivation for their students, since they serve as role models.

Reflection

1. Are you a native or nonnative speaker of the language that you teach? What advantages do you have in the foreign language classroom? Which skills would you like to develop?
2. In terms of the three domains of knowledge deemed essential for effective instructors (general pedagogical knowledge, content knowledge, and pedagogical content knowledge), where are your strengths and weaknesses? Do you ever feel as if you have not received adequate preparation?

Some teachers have complex linguistic and cultural backgrounds and thus cannot be labeled simply "native" or "nonnative" speakers. For example, a teacher born in Brazil could have then spent her childhood in

Japan and attended high school and university in the United States. These experiences would have influenced her linguistic proficiency, as well as exposed her to a diverse repertoire of cultural and pedagogical practices. Her beliefs about teaching and learning today would be based on how she processed, labeled, and perceived these educational experiences.

Preconceived beliefs about language teaching are amenable to change only if instructors are open to problematizing their current practices and reflecting critically on their own teaching (Barcelos and Kalaja 2003). Teachers can take courses in foreign language pedagogy and participate in pedagogical workshops, observe teacher models, teach collaboratively, and request feedback on their teaching from respected and knowledgeable supervisors (Borg 2003; Vélez-Rendón 2010). With concerted effort and mentorship, new instructors will be able to apply their knowledge of SLA theory directly to their practice.

Teacher socialization is defined as "a complex, communicative process by which individuals selectively acquire the values, attitudes, norms, knowledge, skills, identity positions, and behaviors of the teaching profession and of the particular school or educational culture in which they seek to work" (Staton 2008, para. 1). Teachers' professional identities may be influenced by a variety of contextual factors, including their institution's demographics, practices, policies, and resources. Although this complex process occurs at the institutional, departmental, and disciplinary levels, Golde (2005) suggests that the department and discipline often have the most profound influence on an instructor's socialization. Faculty within a department establish disciplinary values and norms, which graduate students observe and internalize. In short, the beliefs and practices of a department often influence the beliefs and practices of its teachers—for better and for worse.

Graduate students receive a variety of messages—sometimes conflicting—about foreign language teaching from a number of sources, including department chairs, language coordinators, professors, and the popular media. These messages may not always align with the theory and research studied in language pedagogy courses. For example, following a teacher observation session, a new instructor told her teaching supervisor, "Wait, I'm confused. I was told by my advisor that the best way to learn a language was to memorize and recite the lines of a Shakespeare play!" Navigating these mixed messages is challenging; the key is to evaluate them critically alongside current SLA research and theories. As Ling and Mackenzie have stated, "Without [critical reflection], teachers are disempowered and dependent on outside forces to control their work" (2001, 96).

Action research is a process in which teachers become teacher-researchers, developing their own research questions and critically examining their own teaching practices. In a study on the influence of an action research course on teachers' beliefs and practices, one instructor described the challenges that she faced when implementing new pedagogical approaches in a traditional teaching environment: "Other colleagues . . . [support] me in my work, as long as I don't ask [them] to change what/how [they teach]. That is sometimes frustrating because I feel like new doors have been opened to me and want us all to take advantage of it, but I am 'treading patiently and carefully' . . . , hoping to change [their minds] about certain things" (Mills 2013, 99). This instructor believes that the knowledge gained from the foreign language pedagogy course has positively influenced her classroom practices. In return, she feels a sense of responsibility and determination within her teaching context to "tread patiently and carefully" to cultivate curricular innovation.

> **Reflection**
>
> 1. How do you think your department's identity and mission have influenced your socialization into the world of teaching and/or academia?
> 2. Are there challenges within your teaching context that you may need to overcome? Can you imagine ways in which you can innovate in your own courses while "treading patiently and carefully"?

STUDENTS' BELIEFS, GOALS, AND MOTIVATION

Questioning one's long-held beliefs about language teaching and aligning one's pedagogical practices with current SLA frameworks can provide the opportunity to create innovative lessons that engage and motivate students. Researchers have long been interested in student motivation because of its key influence on effort, persistence, and, ultimately, success in learning a language (Ushioda 2009). Although the definition and conceptualization of language motivation have evolved over the years, all the research in this domain attempts to answer this fundamental question: Why do foreign language students behave the way they do? To understand students' motivation to learn a language, it is important to look at individuals and determine why they are learning a foreign language, when, and with whom. Rather than labeling students as "abstract depersonalized learners," Ryan and Dörnyei have called for an intertwined "person-in-context" perspective (2013, 91), emphasizing that language learners cannot be isolated from their context and background.

For example, a heritage language learner, defined by the Center for Applied Linguistics as "a person studying a language who has some proficiency in or a cultural connection to that language through family, community, or country of origin" (http://www.cal.org/heritage/research/faqs.html#2), may have unique motivations for studying the target language. Van Deusen-Scholl (2003) asserts that heritage learners often wish to gain literacy skills, acquire academic language proficiency, and fine-tune their understanding of grammar. Others suggest that heritage students' motivation to learn (or even relearn) the language may be linked to a desire to reconnect with their family's cultural heritage and to communicate better with their parents and extended family (Kondo-Brown 2003). Jin Sook Lee (2005), however, discusses the complex nature of heritage learner backgrounds and motivations and highlights the challenges that teachers face when they use static "heritage learner" labels. For example, there may be a Pakistani student who is learning Arabic so that he can read the Koran, a student from Germany who believes himself to be a heritage speaker of Hindi because he lived in India for several years and closely identifies with the Hindi community, or a student raised in a Korean-speaking household in the US who does not believe that she is a heritage learner because she does not think that she is as linguistically proficient as her peers. Heritage learners, like all language students, can also find their beliefs starting to shift as they develop their linguistic proficiency, gain life experience in the target culture, or reassess their ethnic, religious, or cultural identity. In addition, they may face particular challenges, due to expectations from their teachers and classmates that they have had more exposure to the language than is actually the case (some "heritage" speakers may have picked up a few words here and there from their grandparents, but that is the extent of their linguistic background). Heritage learners are a diverse group. As such, it is important that teachers remain attentive to their evolving needs, motivations, and beliefs. As Ushioda states, "Within the context of institutionalized learning, the common experience would seem to be motivational flux rather than stability" (1996, 240).

Mismatches in the beliefs of students versus teachers about what constitutes "good" language learning and teaching can have a negative impact on student satisfaction and long-term motivation. Alan Brown (2009), for instance, found that students and teachers of Spanish had significantly different perceptions about the importance of target language use, error correction, and the teaching of culture in the foreign language classroom. Of course, just because students value certain approaches does not mean that teachers should entirely adapt their practices to match student expectations. Instructors need to clarify their goals and explain to students the reasons behind their pedagogical decisions. Midsemester teacher evaluations are often a great way for teachers to receive student feedback, and even experienced instructors are often surprised, for example, to read evaluations that express students' frustrations that the teacher did not explain grammar points in English in class. Paying careful attention to what students value and expect and why they feel that way may allow teachers to motivate them effectively.

THE PSYCHOLOGY OF LANGUAGE LEARNING

Studies of motivation and the psychology of language learning have traditionally attempted to understand the reasons for human behavior. Self-determination theory, for example, is grounded in the notion that student motivation is centered on a sense of autonomy. This theory groups motivation into two main types: intrinsic and extrinsic. Intrinsic motivation to engage in an activity is a result of an associated personal interest, enjoyment, or satisfaction from that activity, while extrinsic motivation views an activity as a means to an end, such as a reward, praise, the easing of parental pressure, a grade, or the fulfillment of a foreign language requirement (Schunk, Meece, and Pintrich 2014). Busse (2013), for example, conducted a longitudinal study that explored the motivational changes of first-year German students. She found that students' intrinsic motivation was closely linked to their engagement during classroom tasks. From this study, Busse concluded that intellectual challenge was of key importance for the intrinsic motivation of beginning language learners.

Expectancy value theory similarly suggests that students are more motivated when they perceive an activity or academic subject as worthwhile. The challenge is that not all students appreciate the same learning experiences. Students' perception of the academic subject as interesting, enjoyable, and important to their future professional and academic goals contributes to its perceived value. Teachers and program directors are not always aware of what students hope to take from their classes. For example, in a study of students' and instructors' perceived values of language- and content-oriented goals, Mills and Moulton (2017) found areas of alignment and misalignment. Students and instructors placed the same values on interpersonal communication; presentational communication in speaking; presentational communication in writing; and learning about cultural perspectives, symbols, and products. However, whereas the students placed the most value on language-oriented goals, instructors placed the most value on *both* language- and content-oriented goals. In addition, advanced students and instructors teaching advanced courses valued different goals than their counterparts in introductory courses.

What should happen when there is a mismatch between student and teacher beliefs and values? Schunk, Meece, and Pintrich (2014) suggest that teachers should explain the importance and utility of assigned work and engage in transparent discussions about expectations and goals. Students may then see more clearly how the content and teaching approaches enhance the language learning process and how the skills that they will thus gain are critical to their professional and personal goals in today's world. Open discussions between teachers and students about the rationale for learning about culture, for example, could create solidarity, validate perspectives, and allow students to gain a better understanding of the motivation for teachers' instructional practices. Critical reflection on one's own teaching practices is also important. If a syllabus highlights communication-oriented goals and the instructor attempts to teach those skills by assigning fill-in-the-blank grammar worksheets and rote, decontextualized exercises from a textbook, students may not be able to understand how these activities will allow them to communicate effectively in the target language. Thoughtful attention to aligning classroom goals and practices is crucial. Horwitz's "Beliefs about Language Learning Inventory" (1988, 285–90) and the "Perceived Value Survey of Language and Content Goals" used in Mills and Moulton's (2017, 724) study are helpful tools to learn more about how teacher beliefs correspond to those of their students. The findings from these surveys (or their adapted forms) could be a catalyst for productive classroom discussions about rationales for studying foreign languages and cultures. These discussions will help students understand that their input is respected, even if not always implemented, because not all students have the same preferences or goals.

IDENTITY AND MOTIVATION IN LANGUAGE LEARNING

Students do not enter their first language class as tabulae rasae. They come from various cultural, ethnic, and linguistic backgrounds; possess different attitudes, beliefs, and perceptions; and have varied ages, aptitudes, and academic experiences. For some students, the class could be a first exposure to a new language and culture. Others may be influenced by previous language courses or cultural experiences. All these factors can influence students' ability to set language learning goals, prepare and plan for learning, select and use language learning strategies, and manage their time effectively to reach their goals.

Pavlenko and Norton (2007) assert that learning a new language can alter one's identity, no matter how many languages one already knows. Our use of language can shape who we are and show where we come from. With such an inseparable relationship between language and identity, learning a new language can open up new worlds to students—with the foreign language providing them with the power to express themselves differently in social contexts, elaborate on and explain who they are to others in alternative ways, establish their positions and roles in a new society, understand a new culture better through inquiry and dialogue, and help others understand their own culture. Through the language learning experience, students can shift their identities and create what Kramsch (1993, 233–47) calls a "third place" that lies somewhere between their own linguistic and cultural identity and that of the target culture and language. In this new, hybrid space, as Vivian Cook states, the learner is "not becoming an imitation native speaker, but a person who can stand between the two languages, using both when appropriate [and stand] . . . between two cultures . . . seeing both in a new light" (1992, 583–84). This in-between place can constantly be reformed and renegotiated throughout the language learning process.

> **Reflection**
>
> 1. As a proficient speaker of more than one language, do you feel that you experience a "third place" between your own linguistic and cultural identity and that of the target culture and language? Describe this experience with examples. How might you help your students recognize this third place?
> 2. Do you think that you have a different personality when you are speaking your second (or third) language? Why do you think that is the case? Has this personality evolved as you have become more proficient in the language?

ENVISIONING GOALS

Research in motivational psychology suggests that it is easier for students to sustain motivation when they are able to articulate what they would like to do with their foreign language skills in the future. Dörnyei's (2005, 105–9) "L2 Motivational System" includes three components: (1) the ideal self, (2) the ought-to L2 self, (3) and the L2 learning experience. He claims that the system's most important component is the learner's ability to articulate her ideal self, because there is a powerful motivation to reduce the gap between the current self and the imagined ideal self. The ought-to self reflects the expectations of others, such as family and society, and the learner's perception of who she needs to be to meet these expectations and avoid any negative consequences associated with failure to achieve these goals. The L2 learning experience then encompasses the language learning environment and how the teacher, curriculum, and fellow students may influence students' perceived competence and language learning success. According to this system, it is particularly motivating if students can describe a desired future L2 self that is in harmony with their own expectations as well as those of their family and social environment.

It is difficult to motivate language requirement students to continue their language studies if they feel pressure to pursue other academic fields or if they are unable to see how language learning aligns with their personal and professional goals. If students are unable to make the connection between language learning and their ideal selves on their own, they may need direction and guidance from teachers. When the instructor creates meaningful activities and assignments, critically frames these assignments with rationales, and discusses the greater importance and value of course goals and coursework, students may be able to envision in a new light their future ideal selves—which include foreign language, culture, and literature at the center.

Research suggests that it is helpful for students to visualize themselves as eventual proficient speakers of the target language. Dörnyei, Henry, and Muir (2016) suggest that vision may be one of the most reliable predictors of motivation and commitment to language learning. Vision involves an element of fantasy, including sensory, visual, and imagery representations. For example, the vision of becoming a Foreign Service officer in Senegal goes beyond passing the Foreign Service Officer Test; learners can also imagine and thus transport themselves into the rich, sensory experience of traveling and promoting peace abroad. Through Skype, online discussion forums, and social networking platforms, students can interact with alumni who are using their language skills in meaningful ways, both domestically and abroad. Pamphlets, classroom activities, and community engagement that involve students in discussions about the professional avenues available for proficient speakers can help them visualize the role of the foreign language in their future. In short, as Dörnyei and Kubanyiova state, "where there is a vision, there is a way" (2014, 11).

Emerging technologies such as virtual reality (VR) offer valuable opportunities for foreign language learners to immerse themselves in a foreign language and culture by using multiple sensory modalities (visual, auditory, tactile, etc.). These immersions can be so vivid that students feel as if they have been transported into other cultures to witness and experience them. In a VR narrative project developed for a beginning French course, four people who live in the same Parisian neighborhood were asked to document their lives with 360-degree cameras over the course of two months (Mills and Gant 2018; Mills, Dede, and Dressen 2019). Their VR vignettes allowed students to see and experience not only the architecture and cultural landmarks but also some unexplored or unexpected practices and sights of the foreign city. The narratives immersed students in the diversity of life in the neighborhood as they walked in the Parisians' shoes, engaging in discussions with friends at a local café or visiting the local market on a Saturday morning. In classroom surveys, one student in the course stated that the VR experience allows participants to "truly feel like you are living and breathing with the other people in the scene," and another stated that he "was temporarily immersed in a language without fear of embarrassment" and "finally able to see firsthand how [those from the target culture] truly interact."

VR is therefore a tool that can help students imagine and envision the proficient speaker whom they would like to become. Ryan and Irie state, however, that "it is not enough to simply have a clear vision of who or what one wants to become; an individual needs to simulate in detail how to become that person" (2014, 115). This notion is the premise of an experiential curricular framework called global simulation. In experiential learning environments, students engage in imaginative and creative thinking, self-directed collaborative work, and authentic and meaningful language use (Nunan 1999, 7). Global simulation allows language learners to establish a vision of a future self, to transport themselves into an imagined cultural environment, and to "experience" life in this context—students take on the roles of self-developed characters and engage with other participants in the simulation as creators and inventors of this imagined yet culturally grounded world (Magnin 1997). A common example of a global simulation for a foreign language course is the collective story line created by "neighbors" living in a virtual building. In other examples of global simulation frameworks, language learners could develop a start-up company or assume the roles of hospital staff for a simulation of medical training. In these highly participatory and semistructured environments, students learn about culture experientially and use language in meaningful ways to interact socially or professionally with friends, peers, and co-workers. Levine states that global simulation "validates [students'] sense of self in the process of cultural exploration and importantly allows students' cultural and linguistic learning to proceed primarily experientially in ways that approximate life" (2004, 27).

Mills (2012) outlines a global simulation format for an intermediate Persian course. Students (or characters) develop a collective story in Shiraz, a city that is widely known as the leading center of arts and letters in Iran. Course themes include Shiraz and its housing, cuisine, neighborhoods, history, arts, and contemporary life, and each theme is paired with targeted linguistic functions, grammatical structures, and vocabulary (see Table 3.1). A premed student enrolled in the class could choose to play the role of a medical resident doing a fellowship at the Shiraz University of Medical

Sciences. Alternatively, a student with a professional interest in creative writing could envision and play a writer such as the son of Shahriyar Mandanipour, a famous contemporary Iranian author. Through carefully organized tasks and activities, students could organize weekend excursions to the ruins of Persepolis with their neighbors in which they would explore the region's transportation, food, and activities. Through memoirs and social networking interactions, the students could participate in simulated dinners, site visits, and discussions of Shiraz before and after the Iranian Revolution. Oral exams could include informed discussions about Shirazian arts, history, or contemporary life while targeting important linguistic functions, grammatical structures, and vocabulary reviewed in the course.

> **Reflection**
>
> 1. Which approaches could you use in the classroom to help your students articulate the vision of whom they would like to become as L2 users?
> 2. Global simulation is one form of experiential learning. Can you brainstorm other ideas for experiential learning inside or outside the foreign language classroom? How can you connect students with communities or organizations (local or abroad) as a means to enrich their understanding of language and culture?

ADOPTING A MOTIVATIONAL TEACHING PRACTICE

Paired with a vision, a sense of purpose and ownership can play an important role in students' motivation. For example, advanced students of Italian can learn about commedia dell'arte, the masked, improvised theater practiced in Italy beginning in the sixteenth century, by listening to lectures and later answering essay questions in an exam on the topic. Or, in a different approach, they could learn about commedia dell'arte by breaking into small groups to examine various masks and costumes, match them to the archetypes presented in the text, and provide justification in Italian with both visual descriptors and textual examples. In place of an exam, the students could instead write a modern commedia dell'arte sketch and perform it at the local campus theater for members of the Italian Cultural Society.

Table 3.1. Sample Global Simulation Course

Cultural Themes	Linguistic Functions	Grammatical Structures
Analysis of stereotypes of Iran and Iranians Theme: Personal identities	Describe people (physical characteristics, personality traits, etc.)	Nouns: plural vs. singular Present tense Adjectives Comparative and superlative
Housing in Shiraz Theme: Daily life	Talk about where they live Make suggestions Describe settings	Compound verbs Direct object markers
Cuisine in Shiraz Theme: Daily life	Order food at a restaurant Express what foods one likes and dislikes	Negation Question formation Subjunctive
Sites/activities in Shiraz Atigh Jame' Mosque Qur'an Gate Eram Garden Theme: Contemporary life (leisure activities)	Extend, accept, and refuse invitations	Imperative
Neighborhoods and transportation in Shiraz Abivardi, Farhang Shahr, Ghasrodasht, etc. Theme: Geography (travel)	Ask for directions Talk about public transportation Give advice	Prepositions Adverbs
Kish-o-Mat, Iranian movie filmed in Shiraz Theme: Synthesis	Express opinions about film Discuss representation of Shiraz in film	Review/recycle previously reviewed grammar points

Continued . . .

Continued . . .

Table 3.1. Sample Global Simulation Course

Cultural Themes	Linguistic Functions	Grammatical Structures
History of Shiraz Pre-Islamic age, Islamic period, Iranian Revolution Theme: History	Narrate events in the past tense	Active vs. passive voice Past tenses
Arts in Shiraz Gardens, mosaic work, poetry, carpet weaving Theme: Art and aesthetics	Describe and analyze arts and crafts Express hypothetical situations	Hypothetical sentence structures Future tense
Shiraz today Media and the electronic curtain, sanctions, politics, US-Iranian relations, etc. Theme: Contemporary life	Express emotions State opinions Express hypothetical situations	Subjunctive vs. indicative Conditional tense Review: hypothetical sentence structure

They could create the concept, draft and edit the script in Italian, craft the masks and theatrical set for the performance with the help of a local theater group, and practice the sketch for correct delivery and pronunciation so as to ensure that their archetypes come to life. Which learning scenario seems more compelling? In the second scenario, the students feel a sense of purpose and excitement because they are not only reaching a goal and showing evidence of their understanding of both language and content but also experiencing personal ownership and satisfaction. This experience is what Muir and Dörnyei (2013, 363–63) describe as a directed motivational current. Within this framework, students experience powerful motivational drives that allow them to feel as if they are on a path toward their goals. For a directed motivational current to occur, students typically need to have a guided, step-by-step structure with goals and subgoals (often established by the teacher), to receive positive support and feedback from teachers and peers, and to know that they are making progress along the way.

Dörnyei, Henry, and Muir explain that "the deep feeling of pleasure experienced within a directed motivational current is not a giddy, temporary sensation of happiness as experienced through everyday 'fun' activities, but rather stems from a complete feeling of connectedness with an individual's core understanding of who they really are" (2016, 115). This profound engagement typically happens only when the work feels meaningful, useful, and purposeful. For example, a teacher could engage students in a "fun" activity that asks them what they would prepare for an imaginary picnic (with the goal of practicing indefinite articles). Without a meaningful purpose, however, this type of lesson is not likely to foster motivation in students for the long term. On the other hand, preparing students to use the same food vocabulary to work as Spanish-speaking volunteers at a local *comedor de indigentes* (soup kitchen) can allow them to see how their skills can be applied to the real world. Teachers can establish a variety of frameworks to foster these motivational currents—for example, an essential question (e.g., What does it mean to be German?) or concept (e.g., beauty, nationalism, identity) that drives the curriculum and provides a thematic focus for the course. Other ideas might include setting up an intriguing problem or mystery that students investigate collaboratively throughout the semester. Visits to cultural sites, engagement with community organizations, and discussions with native speakers (through Skype or other means) can also help energize students as well as provide opportunities for them to apply their skills to meaningful contexts.

Project-based learning is a useful format for encouraging directed motivational currents. In project-based learning, students are asked to engage in a series of language- and content-oriented tasks with the ultimate goal of creating a tangible final product—encouraging both a process and a product orientation. Student ownership and accountability are encouraged, as well as the integration of various modes of communication (interpretive, interpersonal, and presentational) to accomplish tasks. In addition to providing motivation, project work can engage students in productive collaborative work, inspire critical and creative thinking, and enhance students' self-efficacy, or perceived competence in language learning tasks.

> **Reflection**
>
> 1. Can you think of moments when, as a foreign language student, you were critically engaged in experiences that felt meaningful and purposeful?
> 2. This chapter describes how a "fun" lesson may not foster motivation in students in the long term. Can you provide a lesson variation on the "imaginary picnic" that would engage learners on a purposeful level? Can you also provide meaningful variations of the following activities: (a) describe your home; (b) describe your morning routine; (c) describe your plans for the weekend?
> 3. Can you think of an appropriate final project within the project-based learning framework for the course that you are currently teaching?

A beginning language course titled "Identity through Visual Media" has a project-based learning format (Mills 2014). Course themes include the exploration of various facets of identity: family, social, academic and professional, and culinary. Throughout the term, students explore grammar and cultural content through interactive, interpersonal tasks; interpret visual media in the target language; and present their perspectives. They write blog entries in the target language, engage in roundtables with native speakers, and participate in oral exams centered on questions of identity. As a culminating final project for the course, the students are put in groups to create short "mash-up" films that combine voice-over and dialogue with footage from media sources in the target language. Each group explores a different facet of identity (e.g., family identity or academic identity) and engages in a variety of steps and subtasks. The project concludes with a screening in a large movie auditorium, followed by a group discussion of the films (in the target language) and then a vote for prizes (e.g., best actor, best film), which are awarded in a ceremony where the winners are required to give brief (yet emotional!) speeches in the target language. Students experience a powerful motivational drive and sense of ownership when they screen their films and accept awards for their accomplishments in front of an enthusiastic audience.

Whether their project is a film, theater performance, exhibit, concert, poetry reading, or business proposal, when students are able to observe their progress and see how their knowledge can have meaningful real-world applications, they feel a sense of profound motivation and establish their trajectory toward their ideal L2 selves.

4 • Interaction

THE SOCIAL TURN IN SECOND LANGUAGE ACQUISITION

Do we acquire languages socially or cognitively? SLA scholars initially viewed language learning as an entirely cognitive process. Language instruction emphasized the memorization of rules, and research focused on how people learn a language as opposed to how they use it in various contexts. By the late twentieth century, however, researchers were debating the validity of this paradigm. In an influential article, Firth and Wagner (1997) questioned the importance placed on cognition in SLA and challenged the idea that language learning occurs solely inside the learner's head. Their work called for an awareness of language use as dynamic, contextual, and interactional. They emphasized the idea, grounded in sociocultural theory, that languages are ultimately acquired not just for but also *through* social interaction. Block (2003) described this shift as "the social turn in second language acquisition." At this turn, SLA scholars began to view language learning as both a cognitive and a social process.

In this chapter, we define "communication" and emphasize the importance of meaningful interactions in language learning. With this definition in mind, we discuss how teachers can enhance students' interactional competence through the use of authentic discourse, comprehensible and meaningful input, collaboration and feedback, community building, and language play. The chapter's final section offers practical examples for encouraging student interaction with tasks, texts, debate, and online media.

> **Reflection**
>
> How do you foster authentic interactions in the classes that you teach? Provide examples.

COMMUNICATION AND INTERACTION

What does it mean to be able to communicate? In general, many researchers would say that competent communicators know *what to say, how to say it, and when to say it*. In his discussion of language acquisition and classroom practice, VanPatten (2017, 3–6) highlights key terms to help instructors better understand the substance of communication: meaning, expression, interpretation, context, negotiation, and purpose. The following paragraphs provide paraphrased descriptions of each.

Meaning: Communication entails intentionally creating a message that contains meaning. Imagine that you order lunch and happily respond "That's fine" when the server informs you that the chef needs to replace your onion rings with french fries. In contrast, another client who is not so easily appeased could respond with the same words—"that's fine"—to convey frustration or disappointment.

Expression: Communication incorporates the expression of meaning (verbal and nonverbal). Gestures, use of space, tone, and intonation can all influence expression. For example, the phrase "uh huh" could be interpreted as an expression of sarcasm, happiness, or anger, depending on intonation or an accompanying nodding head or eye roll.

Interpretation: "Communication" implies that others understand the message. For example, if you explain your opinion to a colleague and he does not understand you, the message was not communicated (or not communicated effectively).

Context: Communication is closely connected to the setting and its participants. "I do" has a performative meaning when declared to your spouse at your wedding ceremony. The words have a different meaning when they are said in response to the question "Do you like jazz?" in a friendly conversation.

Negotiation: Communication sometimes requires negotiation when there is ambiguity or a misunderstanding. Clarification ("What do you mean by 'one of a kind'?"), rephrasing ("He is one of a kind: he is unique"), and confirmation ("By 'one of a kind,' do you mean that he is unique?") are all common ways to negotiate meaning.

Purpose: Communication requires a purpose—for example, social, informational, or transactional.

Celce-Murcia (2007, 48–49) included the notion of interactional competence as a component of communicative competence (see Chapter 2). Interactional competence is the ability to participate in and manage conversations in meaningful, appropriate, and relevant ways. Speakers do not simply know what to say, but they know *how to say it and when to say it*. They can open and close conversations, change topics, interrupt, collaborate, complain, apologize, and express feelings—with what sociolinguists call speech acts. Speakers can also interact using appropriate body language, turn-taking skills, and eye contact. Real conversations typically incorporate small talk ("I can't believe it's snowing again . . ."), expressive reactions ("No way!"), and comments that move the conversation forward ("anyway," "on another note"). Effective communicators are also mindful of their environment and cultural cues.

Many language instructors prioritize preparing students to communicate in a wide range of situations. The challenge, however, is to create a classroom environment where students have ample opportunities to participate in authentic conversations. In her study on discourse, Hall (1995) was one of the first researchers to highlight how interactions that take place in class may not prepare language students for real-world conversations. She describes a typical classroom discourse pattern as what has come to be known as the IRE model: (1) teacher initiates, (2) student responds, and (3) teacher evaluates. In Hall's well-known example from the 1990s, a Spanish teacher plays a Gloria Estefan song and then asks the students, "Is this music?" After confirming that the song is indeed music, the teacher asks the students a chain of questions (translated here from Spanish to English):

Do You Like the Music?

TEACHER (T): It's music, no?
JULIO: No.
T: It's music. It's music. It's music. Do you like it? Do you like it?

JULIO:	I don't like it.
T:	I don't like it.
JULIO:	I don't like it.
T:	I don't like the music. Do you like the music? I don't like the music. Do you like the music?
STUDENTS:	I do, yes. Yeah.
RAFAEL:	Aw, man, where you goin'? [in English]
T:	Yes, I like the music. Do you like the music?
ANDREA:	Yes.

Source: Hall 1995, 58.

If we return to the key words that define communication, does it seem as if the students understood and interpreted the purpose of the conversation in this exchange? Would this conversation take place in a real-world context? Does the exchange include negotiation of meaning? Are the students encouraged to change topics, interrupt, follow up, react expressively, or move the conversation forward? The answer to all these questions is no. Hall discusses how exposure to this sort of unnatural exchange in the classroom might promote communicative incompetence as opposed to communicative competence. VanPatten (2017) describes these types of interactions as language practice, not communication. He warns language teachers that "just because mouths are moving does not mean a classroom event is communicative" (14). Moreover, if there is a gap between how students communicate in the language classroom and how language is used outside the classroom, students will not necessarily become competent communicators who are able to connect with people in the real world (Levine 2014).

> **Reflection**
>
> Find an activity in your textbook that encourages students to engage in language practice as opposed to communication. Brainstorm how you would redesign the activity to include purpose, context, negotiation of meaning, and opportunities for verbal and nonverbal expression.

DEVELOPING INTERACTIONAL COMPETENCE

Students' interactional competence can be developed by instruction that includes authentic discourse, comprehensible and meaningful input, collaboration and feedback, and language play within a supportive learning environment.

Authentic Discourse

Although most language instructors would like their students to participate in real-world conversations, teaching materials do not always prepare students for authentic encounters. For example, Slade (1997) found that narratives, anecdotes, and recounts were all prevalent in workplace talk but virtually absent from language teaching materials. Based on this finding, she highlighted the importance of teaching storytelling strategies so that students could gain the skills necessary to participate in everyday conversations. Jones (2002) recommends "the reminiscence story" for teaching students how to narrate. In this split approach, students begin telling a story and then stop at crucial points, inviting fellow students to comment, interject, or hypothesize in culturally relevant ways.

In response to the IRE trend in classroom discussions, Todhunter (2007) recommends that teachers incorporate instructional conversations (described in Box 4.1) in their courses. While structured and controlled speaking tasks develop accuracy, spontaneous and unscripted instructional conversations offer students opportunities to participate in authentic dialogue.

Box 4.1. Characteristics of Instructional Conversations

Teacher's role

Teacher asks students follow-up questions.
Teacher comments on students' contributions in a meaningful way.
Teacher asks open-ended questions that offer opportunity for divergent responses.
Teacher minimizes questions with predictable answers.
Teacher encourages some incidental and unplanned chat.
Teacher allows conversation to unfold in an unpredictable way.

Continued . . .

Teacher shares control with the students in the conversation (initiation, topic development, etc.).

Students' role

Students ask questions of both other students and the teacher.
Students interject reactions and express opinions.
Students comment on other students' responses.
Students have some control over topic selection.

Classroom discourse

Spontaneous
Topically coherent
Unscripted
Natural
Meaningful and relevant

Source: Adapted from Todhunter 2007.

The exchange below transforms Hall's (1995) class discussion in a beginning-level Spanish course into an instructional conversation (translated). Note how the interactions differ from those in Hall's "Do you like the music?" example:

T:	[*after playing song*] Do you know Gloria Estefan? Have you ever heard her music?
JULIO:	I know Gloria Estefan.
RAFAEL:	You do? I don't know Gloria Estefan.
ANDREA:	Oh yeah! I know her. I like her music.
JULIO:	Really? My parents like her music!!
T:	They probably do. [*smiles*] She was very popular in the 1990s. How would you describe her music? Is it pop, jazz, . . . ?
ANDREA:	It's pop music. I love [*with emphasis*] pop music!
JULIO:	Yes [*nods head*], she sings Latin American pop music.
RAFAEL:	Oh really? [*raises eyebrows*] Where is she from?
ANDREA:	I think that she's from Cuba.
T:	That's right! She is from Cuba and has promoted Cuban American culture all over the world. In fact, in 2015

she received the Presidential Medal of Freedom for her commitment to Cuban American culture. Let's take a look at some popular Cuban Americans and discuss their influence on American culture. . . . [*refers to images in a PowerPoint presentation*]

In contrast to the IRE exchange, this conversation has a coherent topic (Cuban American music and culture), which unfolds naturally with comments that build on one another. The teacher shares control of the conversation with the students and comments on their contributions in meaningful ways. Moreover, students react to both teacher and classmate comments.

There are various ways to guide students toward meaningful communication. Handouts with lists of useful expressions give students the tools to interrupt, listen actively, check understanding, and clarify information. Instructors can also establish a topic and tell students that they need to ask one another questions and keep the conversation going for a certain period of time. Although students may initially sit in an uncomfortable silence for a few minutes, the conversation will undoubtedly take off as they participate in a lively discussion that goes in many different (yet natural) directions. By offering strategies and establishing a learning environment where students are empowered to react, interject, and express opinions, teachers give them the opportunity to experience the back-and-forth nature of real-world conversations.

In addition to promoting meaningful communication among students in the classroom, it is important to develop activities where students learn how to interact appropriately with people from the target culture(s). To do so, students need to have a general understanding of pragmatics: how (cultural) context contributes to meaning, how language can be used to perform actions, and how language can express ideas that are different from the speaker's intended meaning. To guide students in the development of pragmatic and interactional competence, applied linguists are developing online resources. The Center for Applied Second Language Studies (University of Oregon) and the Assessment and Evaluation Language Resource Center (Georgetown), for example, have created an Intercultural, Pragmatic, and Interactional Competence (IPIC) Measure (https://casls.uoregon.edu/classroom-resources/intercultural-simulation/). This tool engages students in digital simulations that resemble real-life interactions and include multiple-turn sequences, diverse pathways for conversations, and verbal and nonverbal responses (what we do not say is often just as important as what we do). Understanding how language and interactions change as a result of power dynamics, for example, is a key element of communicative proficiency. The experiential and interactive features of the IPIC Measure allow students to simulate communication in varied contexts and reflect on the ways in which they (and their interlocutors) express and interpret meaning.

Other online resources include the Columbia corpus of conversations in Spanish. To help students and instructors contextualize this collection, the interactions are organized by relationship among participants, topic of conversation, and profession, among other categories. Each conversation is accompanied by a transcription, a description, and sample classroom activities. Important features of the accompanying activities include comparing the language to the visual context established in the video (e.g., location, expressions, gestures). The format and content of such online tools can inspire teachers to develop classroom tasks that promote interactional and pragmatic awareness.

Reflection

1. Label the features of an instructional conversation (listed in Box 4.1) in the transformed student-teacher exchange above.
2. How does this exchange differ from Hall's (1995) "Do you like the music?" sample IRE discussion?
3. The IRE discussion format is standard in many traditional classrooms. How could you change the classroom dynamic to encourage your students to participate in instructional conversations in culturally appropriate ways (for example, to react, interject, question)?
4. The Center for Advanced Research on Language Acquisition has an online resource about speech acts (http://carla.umn.edu/speechacts/descriptions.html). This website includes research findings, teaching tips, and sample exercises. Review the teaching tips and exercises, and take notes on the approaches that you could integrate in your own class.

Comprehensible and Meaningful Input

Research has long advocated that language instructors provide meaningful, engaging, and comprehensible input to develop students' language proficiency. Krashen's (1985) input hypothesis suggests that to acquire a new language, learners need exposure to comprehensible input that is understandable but that integrates some new structures that are a bit beyond their language level (see Chapter 2). According to VanPatten (2017, 57–67), both the quality and the quantity of the input are important: the input needs to be presented in comprehensible and meaningful ways, and the learners need to have ample opportunities to interact with it. In short, instructors should not just "provide" input by talking *at* the students but instead create a communicative context by talking *with* them. Language learning experiences that make meaning clear lead to improved retention. In contrast, language that is unclear or incomprehensible can frustrate learners. Hall (1995) advises instructors to speak naturally while exposing students to comprehensible language. Below are a number of strategies that language instructors can use to make input comprehensible in a communicative learning environment:

Box 4.2. How Can Teachers Provide Comprehensible Input?

- Establish meaningful context
- Use gestures
- Incorporate short utterances
- Repeat
- Speak clearly
- Articulate
- Emphasize meaning with pitch and tone of voice
- Include visuals
- Use students as resources
- Ask yes/no questions
- Ask either/or questions ("Is it realistic or unrealistic?")
- Check comprehension
- Integrate tag questions ("This is realistic, right?")
- Provide examples for clarification
- Speak at a slower (but not unnatural) rate of speech
- Use known vocabulary and structures
- Frequently integrate contextualized new words and expressions
- Paraphrase
- Use simple sentence structures

Collaboration and Feedback

Language learners can become more "interactionally" competent if they receive feedback and assistance from a more capable speaker. Such facilitation can have a long-lasting influence on a student's ability to become an autonomous and competent communicator. Heron (1999) describes a simple overarching structure of facilitation for the classroom. In the first stage, the instructor guides learning in a collaborative and communicative fashion. In the second stage, the instructor allows students to participate in some self-directed communicative tasks. In the third stage, when the students are ready, the instructor provides them with more independence and allows them to engage, without support, in communicative tasks, often in pairs or groups. Facilitation is the equivalent of holding on tightly to one end of a rope and slowly giving learners (at the other end) more and more slack as they build and develop their communicative skills. This notion of facilitation is called scaffolding: "a collaborative process through which a teacher or more proficient learner provides support or guidance to assist a less proficient learner" (Rassaie 2014, 420).

Lev Vygotsky, a prominent developmental psychologist, describes how learning occurs when students move through the "zone of proximal development" (1978, 84–91). With appropriate guidance and encouragement, a more proficient speaker can gradually help the language learner master communicative tasks and move out of this zone and toward higher levels of proficiency. Today there are numerous online programs that allow students to converse with native speakers who are trained to communicate with language learners (for example, TalkAbroad). To complement group work in class, these online exchanges offer students opportunities to participate in semiauthentic conversations while receiving personalized feedback.

Perspectives

I decided to spend a week in Lisbon because I wanted to improve my Portuguese. I signed up for an intensive program in a language school, which consisted of four hours a day of class in a small-group setting. In my class, I was the only American. There were eight more students, from three countries other than the United States. Portuguese was our lingua franca, although I sometimes wondered if any

Continued ...

of my classmates spoke English. I was placed into the B2 [upper intermediate] level, which seemed a bit high for me, since it had been a long time since I had studied Portuguese. The class was very communicative, which meant that we did a lot of group work. That part of the class was, quite honestly, awful. I loved my classmates, but listening to them speak Portuguese was not helpful for me to learn. Even though I had an accent, I could pronounce Portuguese correctly enough to be understood by native speakers. Most of my classmates, however, had a much harder time. I spent a lot of time during our group work helping them with their pronunciation, for which they were grateful. One day, the teacher had some native Portuguese speakers come to class, and we interacted with them in small groups. That was the only time I felt that I had actually made progress speaking Portuguese.

1. How might the teacher have improved the group work so that it would be more beneficial for this student (and perhaps for others as well)?
2. Do you think that the speaker may have gotten more out of this experience than she realizes?
3. Was this an authentic setting for interacting in Portuguese? Why or why not?
4. Is the input that students receive from other learners necessarily bad? Can feedback from peers be beneficial to students? If so, how?

Receiving constructive and supportive feedback about one's performance from credible sources, including teachers and proficient speakers, can reinforce one's communicative ability and confidence. Belnap et al. (2015) found that students enrolled in a study-abroad program in Jordan believed that encouraging words from language teachers most strongly contributed to the development of their Arabic proficiency while abroad. Encouragement, as well as constructive teacher feedback, can allow students to attribute their language learning successes (and failures) to internal factors such as effort, preparation, and language learning strategies. Pajares states that "the teacher's challenge is to ensure that their students' internal standards are rigorous without being debilitating, realistic without being self-limiting, fluid without being wishy washy, and consistent without being static" (2002, 121). Finding this balance in student feedback can be tricky indeed. However, providing students with balanced feedback, coupled with ample opportunities for guided practice that progressively moves them through the zone of proximal development, can facilitate their interactional competence as well as nurture their motivation.

To encourage active participation in class discussions, instructors need to think carefully about how often and when to correct student errors. Glisan and Donato (2017, 146–47) offer a checklist to help language teachers navigate the use of corrective feedback:

- Does the error interfere with the learner's intended meaning?
- Is the error the linguistic target of the lesson?
- Is the error one that is being made frequently by many learners in the class?
- Would the learner benefit from receiving corrective feedback?
- Would the feedback enable the learner to perform with assistance in his/her zone of proximal development?
- Is the learner ready?
- Is the individual learner open to receiving corrective feedback (or does the learner tend to demonstrate anxiety when confronted with corrective feedback)?
- Does the learner appear to want corrective feedback assistance from the teacher?

If the answer to these questions is yes, then provide corrective feedback. If the goal is to promote an interactive discussion and the message is understood (despite the error), then corrective feedback may not be necessary. Teachers use a variety of corrective feedback strategies in the classroom. Box 4.3 has a list of commonly used approaches:

Box 4.3. Corrective Feedback Strategies

1. *Explicit correction*
   Teacher corrects student's error directly ("You should say . . .").
2. *Recast*
   Teacher corrects the error in a response to the student (S: "I have twenty years." T: "Yes, you are twenty years old").
3. *Clarification request*
   Teacher asks for clarification ("Pardon?").

Continued . . .

4. *Metalinguistic feedback*
   Teacher gives feedback about linguistic structures (grammatical hints) ("When discussing age in English, do you use the verb 'to have' or 'to be'?").
5. *Elicitation*
   Teacher repeats the words leading up to the error (S: "I don't have some brothers." T: "I don't have . . .").
6. *Repetition*
   Teacher repeats the student's mistake using a pitch accent for emphasis ("I don't have *some* brothers?").

Source: Adapted from Lyster and Ranta 1997.

Reflection

1. From Lyster and Ranta's (1997) list, which corrective feedback strategies would you label as "explicit"? Which strategies would you label as "implicit"?
2. When would you choose to use an explicit strategy? Why?
3. When would you choose to use an implicit strategy? Why?
4. If you would like students to take risks and actively participate in your classroom community, why is the choice of error correction strategies important?

Community

Although there are many variations of leadership, three styles are discussed frequently in professional and academic contexts: autocratic, democratic, and laissez-faire. In an educational context, the autocratic instructor transmits knowledge to students in a teacher-centered fashion, with limited to no opportunities for student collaboration. Democratic teachers possess a more student-centered teaching style, inviting students to share their opinions and views to build consensus. In contrast, a laissez-faire instructor displays minimal leadership behavior. In a chapter on creating a motivating classroom community, Dörnyei (2007) describes a classic study from more than seventy years ago that compares group leadership styles in a summer camp for American children (Lewin, Lippett, and White 1939). Findings revealed that children in the laissez-faire community were disorganized, stressed, and frustrated, and they completed minimal work. Students in the autocratic community were more productive than their counterparts in the laissez-faire group, but they immediately stopped working when the leader left the room. In contrast, the students' interpersonal interactions in the democratic group were described as friendly, and the learning environment was described as cohesive, collaborative, and community oriented. The quality of the children's work in the democratic group was also judged superior to the work of those in the other two leadership-type groups.

What do these findings mean for foreign language instruction? Leadership can have an important influence on group dynamics. Foreign language students who are part of a supportive, democratic community are more willing to take risks, collaborate, and communicate. The construct "willingness to communicate," unsurprisingly, refers to students' eagerness to communicate. Research has shown that individuals who are more willing to communicate will achieve higher levels of language proficiency and fluency (MacIntyre et al. 2003). Dörnyei and Murphey (2003) outline a repertoire of techniques that can help language instructors create a collaborative classroom community. Recommendations include (1) encouraging students to learn about one another (for example, through icebreakers or informal chitchat), (2) creating proximity (for example, organizing the classroom in a semicircle, to stimulate spontaneous interactions), (3) fostering a sense of group spirit (for example, with a group goal or mission), (4) encouraging extracurricular activities (for example, visits to community organizations and museums), (5) promoting intergroup competition (for example, with debates), and (6) interjecting humor (for example, with funny anecdotes or shared jokes).

Language Play

Language play, according to Guy Cook (1997), occurs when language learners interact creatively with language structures, rhythms, and vocabulary. Children regularly take part in language play in their L1 (first language). Rhymes, games, riddles, jokes, and witty banter are all common examples. Research suggests, however, that language play is also beneficial to adult language learners (Bell 2005). Through creative, fun, and memorable use of the L2, students can learn new vocabulary and practice speaking in different voices (Bushnell 2008). To play with a language, the speaker needs to have a strong understanding of its conventions, so language play is often a marker of advanced language proficiency (Belz and Reinhardt 2004). Nevertheless, students can engage in language play from the very beginning levels of language learning.

For example, in an intermediate-level French course, to simulate life in Paris, students created characters who lived together virtually, in the same Parisian building. They developed profiles for their characters and interacted in a social network community from these characters' perspectives. On several occasions, two characters participated in online exchanges: the young and hip millennial Zoé and the complicated and ornery atheist André. After a lesson on SMS language, Zoé posted a message on André's wall in which she creatively played with texting language:

> Bjr Andre! Cav? Jj'aBIT pres de toi. Est-ce que tu m'e'D trouver mon cle stp? J'tapLDkej'pE ! Rstp ! [Hello André! How are you? I live near you. Can you help me find my key please? I will call you as soon as I can! Respond please!]
>
> Source: Mills 2011, 354.

In response to Zoé's text-riddled message, the student playing André adopted the voice of his disgruntled character and responded: "I don't speak your language, mademoiselle . . . and I don't appreciate this very impolite disruption!" (translated; 354). In this fictional world, students are free to use language in novel ways, to interact with different types of people, and to speak from perspectives that are very different from their own. Through being encouraged to play with language, they gain the practice and confidence to use it in inventive ways.

INTERACTION THROUGH TASKS

The traditional teacher question–student answer format in many language classrooms does not necessarily involve students in authentic communication (as defined by VanPatten [2017, 3–6]). Without careful attention to organization and structure, group work may also not be communicative. Task-based activities, which encourage communication through group problem solving and joint decision making, became popular to address these issues within the CLT classroom. According to James Lee (2000, 32), a well-designed language learning task has the following features:

- an objective attainable only by interaction among participants
- a mechanism for structuring and sequencing interaction
- a focus on meaning exchange
- an endeavor that requires learners to comprehend, manipulate, and/or produce the target language as they perform some set of work plans

The completion of lists, charts, and tables by students who have information that their partners need is a common feature of task-based instruction. The following recommendations can be helpful when creating task-based lessons (adapted from Lee 2000, 34–36):

1. Determine the outcome.
2. Break down the task into subtasks.
3. Create and sequence the subtasks.
4. Move from simpler to more-complicated tasks.
5. Provide guidance and support (grammar reference, helpful prompts, useful expressions, etc.).

Below is an example of an information-gap task for a beginning-level ESL course. As you review the task, pay close attention to how its design facilitates communication by including purpose, negotiation, context, interpretation, expression, and meaning.

Activity 4.1. Information-Gap Task

You are in charge of organizing an end-of-the-semester dinner for your study-abroad program—*lucky you!* You want to organize the dinner for twenty people for a Friday evening.

Step 1. Review the criteria that you have received from your instructor to help you organize:

- The price should be reasonable.
- The food and ambiance should be appropriate for this large festive group.
- The dinner will be on a Friday evening, and you will need a reservation.
- The group has twenty people.

Step 2. Your friend has gathered information about some local restaurants from Yelp, and you have gathered information about the same restaurants from Google. You have some information that your friend needs, and your friend has some information that you need. Talk to each other to get the missing information and complete the chart below. Sample questions: *When is the restaurant open? Are reservations accepted?*

Step 3. After gathering all the information, talk about the various possibilities and make an informed decision about which location would be the best for this event, based on the established criteria. Sample expressions: *I think that the perfect restaurant is . . . because . . . ; I disagree/agree with you because . . .*

Student A: Google

James House Tavern
Hours: Tuesday–Saturday, 11am–1am
Price: $$
Cuisine: Upscale American fare
Ambiance: _____

Reservations: Accepted
Average rating: 4.0 stars

Maze Restaurant & Bar
Price: $
Hours: Monday–Friday, 5pm–1am
Cuisine: _____

Ambiance: Living room–type setting
Reservations: Accepted for ten or more people
Average rating: 4.6 stars

Harlow
Price: $$$

Continued . . .

Student B: Yelp

James House Tavern
Hours: Tuesday–Saturday, 11am–1am
Price: _____

Cuisine: Upscale American fare
Ambiance: Chic gathering spot
Reservations: Accepted
Average rating: 4.3 stars

Maze Restaurant & Bar
Price: $
Hours: _____

Cuisine: Unfussy American fare and creative cocktails
Ambiance: Living room–type setting
Reservations: Accepted for ten or more people
Average rating: 4.2 stars

Harlow
Price: $$$

Continued . . .

Continued . . . Hours: _____ Cuisine: Creative New American fare Ambiance: Rustic-chic subterranean restaurant Reservations: For weekdays only Average rating: 4.5 stars	Continued . . . Hours: Thursday–Sunday, 5–11pm Cuisine: _____ Ambiance: Rustic-chic subterranean restaurant Reservations: For weekdays only Average rating: 4.1 stars

As a variation on this task, students could also complete a chart listing their dietary restrictions and food preferences. Working in groups, they could then read, sort, and discuss the preferences and collectively decide which restaurant would be the most appropriate. Each group could then present its choice and supporting arguments to the class. After listening to each argument and asking relevant follow-up questions, the class would vote on the ideal restaurant. To motivate students further and connect them to the community, the instructor could even follow up on this decision by making a group dinner reservation and inviting the students.

Reflection

1. With a partner, complete the dinner organization task. What type of language did you use with your partner while completing the task? How did you interact? How did you negotiate meaning? Did you need to listen to your partner in order to complete the task? What are some phrases or expressions that students might need to complete this task?
2. Did the task include the key characteristics of communication (purpose, negotiation, context, interpretation, expression, and meaning)? Elaborate with specific examples.
3. What additional steps could you add to this task to focus students' attention on the cultural content?

INTERACTION THROUGH TEXTS

As advocated in the multiliteracies framework, texts play an important role in communication. Through the analysis of oral texts, students can gain a nuanced understanding of different spoken genres, such as debates, arguments, or friendly conversations. For example, learners can analyze the roles of turn taking and small talk in workplace chitchat or the linguistic (and culturally appropriate) strategies a businessperson might use to move a conversation forward in a professional meeting. Texts can also be used as springboards for meaningful discussions about culture. Working with art (as text) in particular can promote imaginative discussion and critical dialogue. Calvino (1988, 83) highlights two types of imaginative processes: "the one that starts with the word and arrives at the visual image, and the one that starts with the visual image and arrives at this verbal expression" (cited by Parra and DiFabio 2015, 11). In an intermediate-level unit on expressionist art, the activities oscillate between *starting with the word* and *starting with the image*:

Activity 4.2. Text-Based Interaction
Day 1: Expressionism at the Brücke Museum

Step 1. Preparatory discussion
Which modern art museums do you like? Why? What do you know about the Tate Museum in London, the Museum of Modern Art in New York, and the Institute of Contemporary Art in Boston? Are there museums that display modern art where you live?

Step 2. Description of the architecture of the Brücke Museum in Berlin
In pairs, students receive a photo of the Brücke Museum in Berlin. They are asked to describe the architecture and imagine what type of artwork is found inside the museum. Sample expressions: *The museum is . . . , therefore the artwork is . . . ; I think that the artwork . . .* Useful vocabulary: *interior, exterior, abstract, innovative, concrete, traditional, provocative, simple.*

A large-group instructional conversation follows the pair discussions.

Step 3. Interactive visit of artwork at the Brücke Museum in Berlin
The class is divided into groups, each of which receives an image of a different expressionist painting from the museum (works by Bleyl, Heckel,

Kirchner, and Schmidt-Rottluff) and a brief list of relevant vocabulary. The groups respond to the following prompts:

Describe the composition, the lines, and the characters in the painting.
Interpret the scene: In your opinion, who are the people? What are they doing?
What is the relationship between the characters and the objects?
Is the scene emotional? Exaggerated? Distorted? Does the painting evoke emotions or memories? Explain.

Step 4. Identification of paintings
The teacher displays all the paintings on a screen. Each group of students describes its assigned painting to the class, pausing at key moments to encourage their peers' reactions. The other students listen carefully to guess which of the displayed paintings they are describing.

Step 5. Instructional conversation: What are the elements of expressionist art?
Discussion topic: Based on the painting descriptions, what are the elements of expressionist art?

The teacher compiles a list of student ideas on the board and then adds relevant cultural and historical information, highlighting key features of the expressionist movement.

Source: Inspired by a lesson prepared by Samuel Harvet in spring 2012.

Activity 4.3. Text-Based Interaction
Day 2: Visit to the University Museum

Step 1. Visit to the expressionist gallery
Students visit the expressionist gallery at the university museum on campus. In groups of two or three, they walk through the gallery and peruse the works of expressionist art (virtual tours online are also possible). The instructor presents the groups with helpful talking points for their discussions of the works of art (Step 2).

1. What is it? Is it a painting? Photo? Sculpture? Is it figurative or abstract?
   Example: *It is a black-and-white photo.*
2. What can you see? Describe what you see (characters, colors, structure, etc.).

Sample expressions: *In the foreground, I can see* . . . ; *In the background, I observe* . . .
3. How do you interpret the work? What is the significance of the work?
Sample expressions: *I think that* . . . ; *I believe that* . . . ; *I doubt that* . . .
4. What expressionist elements are present in the work? Does this work move you? Why or why not?

Step 2. *What makes art beautiful?*
Small-group discussion: In your opinion, what makes art beautiful? Do you agree or disagree with the following statements? Reference the works of art in this gallery to support your opinion.

- For art to be beautiful, it must meet certain criteria.
- Beauty is born from the emotion that the artwork elicits.
- Beauty is a question of personal taste. It varies according to the person, the time period, the context, etc.

Sample expressions: *I agree because* . . . ; *I disagree because* . . .

After the small-group discussion, the teacher leads an instructional conversation in the gallery.

Source: Inspired by a lesson prepared by Fanny Macé in spring 2012.

Activity 4.4. Text-Based Interaction
Day 3: Skype Discussion with a German Expressionist Artist

Step 1. For homework, students receive images of the artist's paintings. They prepare questions and comments about her artwork and about modern art in Germany today.

Step 2. As a preparatory task in class (before the Skype discussion), students share their prepared comments with a partner. During this discussion, they are encouraged to integrate the following conversational expressions:

Okay, I understand.
That's interesting.
Can you expand on that?
Can you explain?
Do you have an example?
Do you mean . . . ?
. . . , is that right?

Step 3. Students participate in a group Skype session with a modern artist (native German speaker) in German. When the session begins, each student is encouraged to participate and ask the artist follow-up questions and request clarification.

Step 4. The lesson concludes with an instructional conversation in which the teacher and the students summarize what they have learned about expressionism, modern art, and notions of "beauty."

> **Reflection**
> 1. Which authentic texts are incorporated in the unit? How do students use these texts (artwork) as springboards for discussion with other students, the teacher, and the artist?
> 2. How is the lesson scaffolded to support intermediate language learners?

INTERACTION THROUGH DEBATE

Speakers at a superior level of proficiency can support and defend opinions, move from sentence-level to cohesive paragraph-level speech, and use idiomatic expressions and appropriate registers. To guide students toward more advanced levels of proficiency, debate is thus a useful strategy. Brown and Bown (2017) offer a number of helpful approaches to integrating debate in the language/culture classroom. One recommendation is to provide students with a debate topic and give them time to write down their opinions independently. Each student then takes a position on a taped line with endpoints "agree" and "disagree" on the floor of the classroom. Based on this positioning, the instructor places students with similar viewpoints on the same team. After small-group discussion of relevant arguments, there is a "tag-team debate" (71). In this format, each team is given a certain amount of time (for example, ten minutes) to argue its point. The first team member has several minutes to start the debate, then needs to tag the next team member, who takes the floor and continues the argument, and so on. The debate could also include a "paraphrase passport" task (72), in which students need to rephrase the previous teammate's opinions before contributing new points to the argument.

In an advanced Russian course at Brigham Young University, debate plays a central role in the curriculum (N. Anthony Brown 2009). Throughout the semester, the students participate in parliamentary-style debates on different topics associated with global diplomacy. Language students need time to learn the relevant content and formulate their arguments, so preparation is of key importance. To prepare students, class sessions include time to discuss debate topics and strategies. Students are assigned to read an article associated with the debate topic, write a two-page position paper, and video-record (and receive feedback on) a five-minute persuasive speech. Weekly vocabulary quizzes encourage students to memorize useful terms that will help them participate in the upcoming debate. Students receive color cards with key vocabulary in advance. The yellow cards include connector words; orange cards include target vocabulary from the readings; blue cards include words and expressions that help bridge ideas; and pink cards include idioms and socioculturally appropriate language (see Chapter 6).

Reflection

1. The Brigham Young University curriculum is an example of the integration of debate in an advanced-level course. How would you scaffold activities to prepare students for a debate at the beginning or intermediate level?
2. How could you encourage students to debate in online or virtual spaces?

INTERACTION THROUGH ONLINE MEDIA

In today's globalized world, networking technologies have transformed the ways in which we interact. We have social networking sites, video-conferencing, and online chats where students can communicate with speakers of the target language and become members of different discourse communities. As Kern notes, "The Internet now brings the world of the Other to their desktop" (2014, 340). Hanna and de Nooy affirm, however, that "we have *deceptively* easy access to our linguistic other" (our emphasis; 2003, 72). Although each online environment may have certain practices that are understood globally, there are other conventions, such as turn taking and argumentation, that may vary across cultures and subcultures. Misunderstandings of these practices may lead participants to feel like outsiders in the discourse community—often without understanding why. We need to guide L2 students so that they can optimize their interaction in online spaces. We cannot just throw them into the deep end of the pool; we need to teach them how to swim. In this section, we present models that encourage interaction through online discussion forums, social networking, augmented reality, and gaming.

Discussion Forums

Ramos states that "the media do not simply reflect the world; they represent it and, in doing so, they fail to include all of the components of multifaceted realities" (2001, 34). Critical media literacy encourages engagement with multiple media sources from various viewpoints. The teacher's role is to guide students to analyze critically how the facts are (or are not) presented in various news sources and how the journalists' use of language constructs meaning, perspective, and the publication's leanings. Following the analysis of several news sources, students engage in thoughtful dialogue. For example, Hanna and de Nooy (2009) integrated online forums from mass-media websites such as those of *Le Monde, Libération,* and *Le Figaro* into a third-year French course at the University of Queensland, Australia. The goals of this course were to teach argumentation and debate conventions and to familiarize students with a multiplicity of perspectives on current events. Online discussion forums were chosen for a number of reasons:

- Language and culture are inseparable in online forums.
- The forums provide access to current events and cultural content.
- Students participate in authentic, real-world tasks in forums.
- Forums show how debates about international issues (for example, the environment) vary across the globe.
- Teachers can intervene with advice or recommendations at critical moments.
- Students can receive feedback from other forum participants (not just the teacher).

- Students who are more reserved in class can have a voice online.
- The record of exchanges can be logged and accessed at a later time for in-class discussion and analysis.

Source: Hanna and de Nooy 2009, 155–56.

The online news forums were chosen to showcase diverse political leanings, use of language, and candid or rigid presentation of facts. The forum participants were members of the same "discourse community" (for example, speakers of French) but often came from various origins and cultural backgrounds. To spark discussion, the forums raised thought-provoking questions—for example, "Do you think it reasonable or not to restrict public freedom in the name of the fight against terrorism?"

To prepare students, Hanna and de Nooy designed a number of tasks to familiarize them with forum conventions:

Activity 4.5. Online Forum Familiarization Tasks

Task 1: Familiarity with Forum Conventions

1. Homework: Choose one current event topic and examine how it was presented and debated on four different news forums. Pay attention to political leaning, message length, moments of digression, formality, linguistic accuracy, and identity positioning. Post your analysis on the group wiki on [the learning platform] BlackBoard.
2. Read through your fellow students' observations on the wiki. Post two or three comments on their postings. Be prepared to discuss the various observations in class.

Task 2: Positionality and Argumentation

1. Workshop in class: Find examples of English, Australian, or American learners of French on the forums. Why are certain participants more successful than others? Which strategies do they use? When is it appropriate to present oneself as a language learner? And in which contexts is this positionality counterproductive?
2. In pairs, draft a response to a message on the news forum [teacher chooses one news forum and topic]. The messages will be compiled into a wiki on BlackBoard but not posted on the news forum. Various examples will be analyzed in class for positioning, argumentation, style, etc.

Task 3: Technical Skills

1. Homework: Choose a pseudonym for this project. Think carefully about how this pseudonym may be perceived and what it will reveal about you. Register online to participate in the forums.

Source: Adapted from Hanna and de Nooy's project description (2009, 158–65).

For Task 1, Hanna and de Nooy (2009, 158–60) reported that students noticed variation in register, argument quality, and response length in the online forum postings. Students also paid close attention to how participants used rhetorical questions. They were surprised by the wide range of viewpoints expressed, which raised awareness that there is not just one "French perspective." In the second task (160–64), the learners looked at how the forum participants used various expressions to present and position themselves. For example, in place of "I am . . . ," they stated, "As a woman, . . ." or "Although a vegetarian, . . ." In class, the teacher organized workshops using participants' contributions to the forums as samples for investigation. Students analyzed language use (for example, use of connectors) and linguistic functions (for example, expressing agreement, articulating arguments). In a collaborative examination, the class pinpointed and explored moments of conflict and misunderstanding within the interactions. The assignments for the course included five online news forum contributions, which required students to read other forum contributions, post coherent arguments about current events, and interact with forum members.

Social Networking

In online forums, students interact with an authentic audience. "Twitter and the City," a third-semester Spanish course at Columbia University, engages students with Spanish language and culture by treating New York City as the classroom. Students use Twitter to "captur[e] the presence of Spanish in the city, whether it be visually (announcements, advertisements, linguistic landscape, etc.), aurally (conversations, recordings, other forms of oral interactions, etc.), or culturally (exhibits, lectures, cultural and social events, concerts, movies, etc.)" (Charitos and Van Deusen-Scholl 2017, 26). By collecting tweets and their accompanying hashtags, geotags, photos, and videos, students curate linguistic and cultural resources and become members of a shared discourse community. They communicate their ideas in real time during field excursions, and in the Twittersphere, they interact by posting, replying to, and commenting on relevant tweets. Charitos and Van Deusen-Scholl state that "the city can be the crucial arena for asking questions about language practices as well as the appropriate place where one can examine how the evolving types of interactions between space and language might fundamentally inflect a city's history" (15).

Gaming and Augmented Reality

Fourth-semester Spanish students at the University of New Mexico interact with the local Spanish-speaking community through an augmented reality (AR) game, Mentira: an interactive digital experience within a real-world environment. For example, students take photos of the Spanish-speaking community with their phones, and the images that they capture are overlaid with digital words in Spanish labeling the places. They can then activate a Spanish audio description of each place. Through added visual and auditory information, AR can alter and enhance an individual's experiences in the real world, including transforming interactions with others.

Mentira integrates tasks in a student-driven design that encourages collaboration, exploration, and Spanish language use. In addition to the local Spanish-speaking neighborhood, the game immerses students in Spanish language and culture through authentic dialogue, photos, visual art, and short movies:

> It is set in a Spanish-speaking neighborhood in Albuquerque, NM, and plays out much like a historical novel in which fact and fiction combine to set the context and social conditions for meaningful interaction (in Spanish) with simulated characters, other players, and local citizens. While playing Mentira, learners must investigate clues and talk to various non-player characters (NPCs) in order to absolve their own family, proving they are not responsible for a murder in a local neighborhood. In a core component of the game, players are required to visit the local neighborhood in order to collect additional clues and, ultimately, solve the mystery by determining the responsible party.
>
> Source: http://www.mentira.org/overview.

As described, the game's narrative oscillates between reality and fiction. The game lasts three to four weeks and has two phases. During the first phase, students play independently to become familiar with the murder mystery story line and characters. During the second phase, students visit the Spanish-speaking neighborhood in groups and investigate the murder by interacting with local citizens. To solve the mystery, the groups follow directions to key locations, interpret and discuss clues with fellow team members, and interact with the game's fictional characters. The students then return to class to discuss clues, share information with other groups, and formulate opinions about the guilty party. Research suggests that language learners who play AR games interact on a variety of levels (Thorne and Hellerman 2017). To complete tasks, learners interact with their immediate surroundings and fellow group members as they interpret the various texts and subtexts within the game.

In fact, Sykes and Reinhardt (2013, 33–34) believe that multiplayer online games are inherently interaction driven, since a community of game players needs to work together, collaboratively or in competitive teams, to achieve goals. Game design typically provides players with real-time feedback, and discussions often occur on message boards or in chat rooms where players share advice and strategies as well as fan art and videos. Players also engage in complex decision making as they interpret a variety of texts, including visuals, sounds, and narratives. Moreover, language play emerges when players experiment with the voices of their role-played characters. Sykes and Reinhardt list the parallel attributes of effective digital game design and effective language pedagogy: (1) tasks and goal orientation, (2) interaction, (3) real-time feedback, (4) context and narrative, and (5) motivation and engagement.

> **Reflection**
>
> 1. How can games engage language learners in authentic discourse?
> 2. How can well-designed games encourage interaction through both tasks and texts?
> 3. What can we learn from interactive game design that we can apply to the language classroom?

As socioculturalists have affirmed, language learning is both a social and a cognitive process, and languages are acquired to a great extent through social interaction. It is therefore of key importance to offer students ample opportunities to participate in and manage conversations in meaningful, relevant, and appropriate ways. Through engagement in authentic discourse, comprehensible and meaningful input, collaboration and feedback, and language play, students can hone the skills they need in order to know not only what to say but also how and when to say it. Tasks that encourage group problem solving and joint decision making and texts that infuse cultural relevance offer students opportunities, both online and in the classroom, to participate in meaningful interactions.

5 · Grammar

DEFINING "GRAMMAR"

What does it mean to use "correct" grammar? Does it mean that you are well educated? Does it mean that you are smart? Does being distracted by poor grammar mean that you are elitist? Defining the notion of grammar is complicated. As Katz and Blyth explain,

> It is perplexing that the term "grammar" means different things to different people depending on their perspectives and backgrounds. In other words, students, instructors, teacher trainers, and linguists all use the word "grammar," but they usually are referring to a range of concepts and constructs. Linguists even use the term differently among themselves, depending on whether they consider their research to be theoretical or applied and whether their approaches and analyses are based in cognitive/psychological or syntactic/pragmatic frameworks. As a consequence, people often end up talking about dissimilar issues using comparable terminology, thus dooming discussions about grammar from the onset. (2007, 3)

Grammar is often considered to be a set of prescriptive rules that describe what one should and should not say when speaking and writing a language. Canale and Swain define "grammatical competence," a component of communicative competence (see Chapter 2), as "knowledge of lexical items and of rules of morphology, syntax, sentence-level semantics, and phonology"

(1980, 9). The problem is that grammars do not exist in a vacuum. Whether the grammar mavens like it or not, languages (and especially spoken languages) are constantly evolving.

Many subtle changes are currently occurring in English, especially in the spoken language. For example, the expression "there's" now regularly replaces "there are" as well as "there is" in spoken English:

"There's a cat on your porch!"
"Actually, there's two of them out there."

Similarly, "it's" is also followed by plural nouns, as in "It's my parents who don't like you, not my sister." This construction has actually existed for quite some time. Likewise, "that" has replaced "who" in many contexts, as in "It's my parents that don't like you." The relative pronoun "whom" is all but dead in spoken English, except in formal contexts: "It's Mary who(m)/that/Ø [null pronoun] I saw last night." Although many of us may wince at some of these sentences, it's pretty much all of us that generate them (or similar ones) without even realizing it.

Native speakers are notoriously unaware of what they actually utter (as opposed to what they think they say). The grammars that we have in our heads may not correspond to the rules that we (think we) know about our first language. At the same time, we may make a concerted effort not to use certain grammatical structures (or lexical items) when speaking (remember Krashen's "monitor"—see Chapter 2). For example, we may decide not to use expressions that are literally shoved in our face every day (or figuratively, to be more accurate). We might also choose to expunge the word "like" from our vocabulary, except as a verb. We might vow never to use "impact" as a verb. These choices may be more about vocabulary than about grammar, but there are syntactic/morphological examples as well: that's a whole nother issue. Lexical innovation is more readily embraced than are grammatical changes (Knud Lambrecht, personal correspondence): "bad" grammar can be stigmatizing, whereas new words, when created by members of the group who have status, are cool. Note that language learners do not have this prestige, and their linguistic innovations are rarely considered acceptable.

> **Reflection**
>
> 1. How would you define the word "grammar"?
> 2. What does "correct grammar" mean to you? Do you think that it might mean something else to other people? Are there times when correct grammar does not sound natural?
> 3. Do you think that you use proper grammar in your first language? And in your second or third language(s)?
> 4. Do you pay attention to your grammar when you are speaking your L1? And your L2? Is there a difference? How about when you are writing in your L1 or your L2?
> 5. Did you study grammar formally in school? Did you ever diagram sentences, for example? Can you explain the difference between a phrase and a clause? Can you explain why it is grammatically incorrect to say "That's between my brother and I"?

If the natural evolution of languages challenges the permanence of grammatical rules, why is it important for second language learners to polish their grammar? For one thing, incorrect grammar can be a distraction. When language learners produce utterances that contain a lot of mistakes, their message may be lost or at least blurred. Instructors need to help learners speak and write language that will not dilute their message. By using correct grammar in the L2, learners also demonstrate to native speakers that they have made an effort to study the language, which may reflect what native speakers deem to be respect not only for the language itself but also for the target culture. Native speakers sometimes seem to hold second language learners to unfair higher standards, for example correcting learners who use slang and colloquial structures.

This chapter focuses on effective approaches to teaching and learning grammar. Since the advent of CLT, teachers have received mixed messages regarding the role of grammar in their classrooms, including whether it should be taught at all. Many CLT instructors have felt shamed into eliminating grammar explanations from their classes; they do not want to be seen using old-fashioned pedagogical techniques. Adult learners, on the other hand, often express frustration that grammar is not more of a priority. As Robin (2002) explains: "Ten-year-olds don't want the big picture, but college students are more likely to demand an analytical treatment of the morphological system of the target language. It behooves instructors to play to the best styles of each learner. A few charts and basic manipulation drills on each point does take away from valuable time that might otherwise be spent in communicative activities. But this kind of basic structural hand holding appeals to many learners, especially older ones, who find more chaos than solace in a less structured environment." Below, we argue that there are better solutions than manipulation drills for helping adult learners learn grammar. However, Robin's point is well taken and important: even though some esteemed researchers believe that attaining first and second languages are similar processes, learning a language in a classroom as an adult is simply not the same experience as acquiring a second language as a child.

> **Reflection**
>
> 1. How well do you know your first language's grammar? Do you feel qualified to explain it to learners? Why or why not? Are you more comfortable explaining your L2 grammar?
> 2. Ask two friends who are native English speakers to speak with each other, naturally, about a mundane topic, and tape their conversation. Transcribe it, and then analyze how or whether the language they use differs from formal, written English.
> 3. Look at the text messages that you have on your phone. Do they represent spoken or written English?

TRADITIONAL GRAMMAR INSTRUCTION

Many language teachers genuinely enjoy analyzing the grammar of the language that they teach and feel passionate about sharing their insights with students.

> **Perspectives**
>
> As someone who teaches mostly at the elementary level, I have always preferred teaching grammar to teaching anything else. I am a grammar nerd and proud of it! Students need a solid background in gram-
>
> Continued . . .

mar to master the language. I love being able to anticipate students' questions; I'm able to put everything together nicely into detailed charts and corresponding activities. Give me a grammar quiz to grade, and I don't mind doing that one bit. But ask me to grade a set of compositions . . . there is nothing that I dread more. I have found great textbooks that have excellent grammar activities; we go through them in class after students have prepared them at home, and I can see that students have really learned something. And you know what? My students love studying grammar too. It makes me so happy when I can answer their questions and help them learn.

1. Why do you think that this instructor enjoys teaching grammar so much?
2. Why does this teacher prefer grading grammar quizzes? Do you feel the same way?
3. Why do you think that this teacher's students enjoy studying grammar so much?
4. Why might this teacher feel like an expert in teaching grammar but not as confident when it comes to other areas of L2 pedagogy?

GT and ALM students usually acquire strong metalinguistic knowledge of the target grammar; they do not find themselves adequately prepared, however, to do much of what is considered essential in many situations today: communicating their thoughts and ideas to native speakers and cultivating cultural insights. Honing students' translingual and transcultural competence, the expressed goal of the 2007 MLA report (see Chapter 2), involves a balance of attention to both grammatical form and communication. In addition, as Rios-Font points out, true translingual competence is unlikely to be achieved without the attainment of a high level of linguistic proficiency first (2017, 25).

The 3 Ps

Grammar has traditionally been taught in three stages, abbreviated as "the 3 Ps":

- Presentation: The instructor presents explanations of the grammar point, followed by examples containing the target structure (note: this technique represents a deductive approach).

- Practice: Learners practice the structure in targeted, usually decontextualized, exercises that focus on accuracy.
- Production: Learners produce the structure within a specific context.

Both GT and ALM use the 3 Ps approach, although there are some differences. In particular, GT explanations tend to be longer and more in-depth than the ones found in ALM books and classes, and GT exercises tend to be translations or fill-in-the-blank manipulations. In ALM, the practice and production activities consist of a series of drills that follow a specific format and order.

Drills

Mechanical drills are intended to teach students about the pattern of a given grammar point. They usually consist of substituting one element of a phrase or clause and then making the corresponding required changes. Mechanical drills require two features:

- there is only one correct response
- the learner does not need to attend to meaning

Source: Lee and VanPatten 2003, 121.

The following is an example of a mechanical drill:

Directions: Complete the sentence, modifying the adjective accordingly.
Model: Rafael es alto → Claudia es _____ (answer: alta)
(Rafael is tall → Claudia is tall)

The main criticism of mechanical drills is that students do not need to have any idea what they are saying to complete them. They may not even need to know the target language at all; it is just a matter of figuring out the pattern. The activity above, for example, could just as easily be done using completely made-up adjectives.

Meaningful drills follow mechanical drills. During this stage,

- the learner is expected to attend to meaning
- there is only one correct response
- the answer is already known to the person asking the question (the teacher)

Source: Lee and VanPatten 2003, 121.

The following is an example of a meaningful drill:

> Description: Describe the people or objects in the following photos by providing the correct form of the adjective.
> Models: Es alta? (Is she tall?)
> > No, es pequeña. (No, she is small.)
> > Su ropa es blanca? (Is her dress white?)
> > No, es negra. (No, it is black.)

In this activity, students need to be able to understand the vocabulary in order to provide the correct answers. There is never any doubt, however, regarding the teacher's intention in asking the questions. She is not interested in obtaining information from the students: everyone looking at the pictures already knows the answers.

Communicative drills are the production stage of the 3 Ps. Here the learner is expected to communicate information that is not already known. The following is an example of a communicative drill:

> Description: Working with a partner, ask questions and provide information about the following people and things, using the model provided.
> Model: tus gatos/simpático (your cats/nice)
> > Student A: ¿Tus gatos son simpáticos? (Are your cats nice?)
> > Student B: Sí, son simpáticos. (Yes, they are nice.)
> > > or No, no son simpáticos. (No, they are not nice.)
> 1. Tu madre/alto (your mother/tall)
> 2. Tus hermanos/rubio (your brothers/blond)

There is no way to ensure that students will communicate the truth when they participate in these kinds of drills (do they even have cats or brothers?) or whether they will simply go through the motions, focusing on making the adjectives agree with their subjects. However, the information being shared is previously unknown.

It might be argued that drills are more engaging than traditional fill-in-the-blank-type activities, such as those found frequently in GT textbooks. Fill-in-the blank exercises seem to have weathered the changes in methods, however, and remain a mainstay, especially in workbooks, where even today one might find this kind of activity:

> Mi madre es _____ (bonito), y mi padre es _____ (guapo).
> Son _____ (alto) y _____ (moreno).

(My mother is _____ [pretty], and my father is _____ [handsome]. They are _____ [tall] and _____ [dark haired].)

Can it be argued that these exercises reflect communication? Probably not, but one might say that they help students produce correct adjective agreements by developing their metalinguistic awareness. At the same time, it is hard to imagine a real-life situation in which students would be asked to fill in a missing word. Imagine, for example, walking down the street in San Juan and having a native speaker stop you and ask you to fill in a blank with a missing adjectival ending.

It may not be obvious at first glance, but the drills and the fill-in-the-blank activities mentioned above are not designed to *teach* students a grammar point—their goal is to *verify* that students have mastered the grammar point in question. They are like practice exams, which may not be the best use of class time. Students can always practice and receive feedback outside class by using paper workbooks with answer keys or online workbooks with interactive feedback features. Some researchers would say that such exercises are not useful, however, because acquisition does not require this type of metalinguistic feedback. Teachers may intuitively believe, however, that drills and fill-in-the-blank exercises are helpful for reinforcing the work that students do in class. Students may also find the confirmation that they receive when providing correct answers to be motivating.

Lee and VanPatten are among those who assert that drills and fill-in-the-blank activities are ineffective, even outside class: "Our position is that homework should be an extension of the class. . . . Outside assignments should be consistent not only with the lesson objectives but with the general philosophy of communicative classrooms" (2003, 92). In their *Foreign Language Annals* article "The Evidence Is IN: Drills Are OUT," Wong and VanPatten (2003) argue that empirical research has shown that mechanical drills are useless. In their provocative response "Apples and Oranges Are Both Fruit, but They Don't Taste the Same: A Response to Wynne Wong and Bill VanPatten," Leaver, Rifkin, and Shekhtman (2004) accuse Wong and VanPatten of overgeneralizing their findings and not understanding that Russian, in particular, is different from languages like French, Spanish, and German and that drilling is an effective method for teaching more difficult languages (the so-called LCTLs: less commonly taught languages). Comer and deBenedette (2011), however, who also happen to be applied linguists in Russian, take their Russian colleagues to task in the article "Processing Instruction and Russian: Further Evidence Is IN." In support of Wong and

VanPatten's claims and basing their response on empirical studies, they state that it is time for LCTL researchers and teachers alike to develop materials that reflect findings in the field, particularly in the area of processing instruction (PI), VanPatten's proposed replacement for drilling: "Creating such activities requires instructors and materials designers to think differently about how form and meaning interact, and it requires instructors to think about ways to manipulate language input that force learners to attend to the meaning(s) inherent in grammatical forms. As challenging as it may be to create such new materials in languages where they have as yet been little used, the evidence from PI research shows the benefits of this approach to input in instruction" (665). Clear from this animated debate is that many researchers, in addition to teachers and students, have strong stances on grammar instruction.

Reflection

1. Do you remember drills from your own language learning experience? Did you enjoy doing them? Why or why not? Do you feel that they helped you?
2. What is the most effective use of class time? What should be done outside class?

GRAMMAR IN CLT

When the pendulum swung and CLT replaced ALM as the predominant approach, grammar pedagogy faced an existential crisis. All of a sudden, there was no clear role for grammar in language classes. Some researchers went so far as to argue that it had no role in the communicative classroom at all. Garrett explains that "the claim that the teaching of grammar is of limited use (or even counter-productive) in teaching communicative competence is the cause of considerable uneasiness in the field today. . . . 'Grammar' is clearly a thorny issue" (1986, 134). Katz and Blyth (2007, 226–27) note that the instructors' editions of communicative textbooks often state that students should learn grammar on their own at home, although these same textbooks contain grammar practice activities (sometimes derived from previous approaches, including drills of all kinds, fill-in-the-blank exercises, etc.) to be completed in class.

Lee and VanPatten's influential methods book, *Making Communicative Language Teaching Happen* (1st ed., 1995; 2nd ed., 2003), provides a concrete framework for teaching language, including grammar, communicatively. The authors recognize that the heavy burden of ALM teachers, whose major responsibilities consist of conducting drills and correcting errors, can lead to a state of mind that has been called the Atlas complex: teachers carry the pedagogical world on their shoulders and are thus simultaneously proud of and burdened by their role as conveyors of expertise, transmitters of knowledge, and overseers of learning (2003, 8). Lee and VanPatten propose a very different classroom environment, in which teachers are architects and the students builders (2003, 68).

Lee and VanPatten (2003, 117–29) identify several "misconceptions" about teaching grammar, framed in terms of the following beliefs:

- Belief 1: That's the way I learned, so . . .
- Belief 2: Drills are effective tools for learning grammar.
- Belief 3: Explicit explanation is necessary.

The best way to counter these beliefs is to ask teachers whether their classmates were as successful as they were in the language classes that they took. The rationale is that maybe individuals who decide to become language teachers are particularly adept at learning languages. In addition, numerous studies, as well as what most of us know anecdotally, show that very few students become completely fluent in a language simply through taking language classes. Learners usually need to participate in an immersion experience to achieve true proficiency. Often, individuals who claim that a certain pedagogical approach worked for them also admit that they have spent time abroad.

Reflection

1. What do you think about the idea of students learning grammar entirely on their own at home? Is it feasible?
2. Reflect on the three beliefs cited by Lee and VanPatten. Why do you think that many teachers possess these beliefs? What is the source of these beliefs?

INPUT PROCESSING

At the core of Lee and VanPatten's (2003) book is the notion of input processing, which includes structured input and output. The underlying notion is that learners should not be expected to produce a given grammatical structure until they have already internalized it. This philosophy contrasts sharply with ALM's focus on drilling and automatization through practice. Lee and VanPatten provide the following guidelines for developing structured input activities:

- Present one thing at a time.
- Keep meaning in focus.
- Move from sentences to connected discourse.
- Use both oral and written input.
- Have the learner do something with the input.
- Keep the learner's processing strategies in mind. (154)

In addition, they provide a model that illustrates how input moves along a path to output:

INPUT → INTAKE → DEVELOPING SYSTEM → OUTPUT

They differentiate between input and intake as follows: "Whereas input is the language the learner is exposed to, intake is the *language that the learner actually attends to and that gets processed in working memory in some way.* Thus, not all input—no matter how comprehensible or meaningful—automatically makes its way into the learner's head" (31). Lee and VanPatten do not describe the developing system with much detail in their book, but the concept is straightforward: this is the place where learners store and internalize intake until they are ready to begin producing the structures themselves (output). Structured input and structured output activities are designed as alternatives to all three types of drills, as well as replacements for fill-in-the-blank and other traditional grammar exercises.

Structured input activities are a type of "focus on form." According to Doughty and Williams, "Focus on form entails a prerequisite engagement in meaning before attention to linguistic features can be expected to be effective.... The learner's attention is drawn precisely to a linguistic feature as necessitated by a communicative demand" (1998, 3). The goal is to establish a form-meaning connection. In other words, the learner links a particular grammatical form with its intended meaning. For example, in English, the "ed" suffix indicates past tense. Therefore, if learners hear

"I watched the Red Sox game yesterday," they will know that the event took place in the past. Lee and VanPatten (2003, 138) point out that teachers need to be careful when creating form-meaning connections, however. If the goal is to focus students' attention on the "ed" ending so that they know that the even took place in the past, it is important not to include lexical items that also indicate the past, such as the word "yesterday" in the above example: if the students see this word, they will not need to focus on the verb morphology to know that we are talking about the past.

Structured Input

Binary Options

Lee and VanPatten propose an activity type called "binary options" to lead students to make form-meaning connections. To complete these activities, learners must focus on a particular grammatical form/morpheme. In addition, they must demonstrate comprehension of the snippets of discourse in some nonlinguistic way. The following example is adapted (only the names are changed; the instructions and format are identical) from Lee and Van-Patten (2003, 144) and is an alternative to the adjective pedagogy provided in the 3 Ps discussion above:

Activity 5.1. Kanye or Beyoncé?

Is the speaker referring to Kanye or Beyoncé? Listen to each sentence and the adjective in each sentence in order to decide to whom s/he refers. Then decide whether you agree or disagree with the speaker's statement.

1. a. ___ Kanye ___ Beyoncé
   b. ___ I agree ___ I disagree
2. a. ___ Kanye ___ Beyoncé
   b. ___ I agree ___ I disagree
3. a. ___ Kanye ___ Beyoncé
   b. ___ I agree ___ I disagree

Sentences heard by learner:

1. Es dinámica. (She's dynamic.)
2. Es comprensivo. (He's understanding.)
3. Es reservada. (She's reserved.)

Note that Spanish is a "pro-drop" language, which means that it does not always require a subject pronoun. Therefore, in this activity it is not immediately clear whether the subject of each sentence is masculine or feminine. It is only the *a* or *o* at the end of each adjective that denotes the gender of the subject; this is the form-meaning connection that students must make. As Lee and VanPatten (2003, 144) point out, it is also important to include the agree/disagree segment, so that students will not just listen for the adjectival ending to complete the activity.

Input Flood

The binary options activity above is a perfect example of structured input because of the saliency of the form-meaning connection contained in the adjective agreement. Unfortunately, it is not always easy to make form-meaning connections in such a clear and easy manner, and the other types of structured input activities that Lee and VanPatten propose do not truly achieve this goal. The following three activity types are more aptly called "input flood." They are still useful to lead students to internalize certain grammatical forms, but they do so more implicitly.

Supplying Information

Lee and VanPatten provide the following activity as an example of "supplying information" (2003, 161). We have adapted it to focus on verbs in the past, a topic that we revisit later in this chapter, and we have slightly changed the instructions.

Activity 5.2. Did He or Didn't He?

Step 1. Break into two groups. Select someone from the class whom you all think you know well. That person should sit alone until Step 3.

Step 2. Write that person's name in the first blank below. Then complete each statement with information that you believe to be true.

During spring break, _____.
    1. traveled _____.
    2. played _____.
    3. tried _____.
    4. watched _____.

Step 3. The person returns to the group and listens to the statements, letting classmates know which ones are true and which are false.

As in the binary options activity above, students are not required to produce the target structure (verbs in the past). The goal is for them to hear/say the construction repeatedly so that it becomes part of their developing system. It is at this point that the form-meaning connection should occur. Unlike in the binary options activity above, however, here students do not contrast one form with another.

Note that in input flood activities, it is important to draw students' attention to the targeted grammatical structure. If we want to make the grammatical form in question—in this case the "ed" ending—more prominent, we can employ a technique called "input enhancement" to make students aware of it. Input enhancement typically consists of using boldface or a different color to highlight a particular form.

Selecting Alternatives

Another input flood activity type advocated by Lee and VanPatten is called "selecting alternatives." Here is an example adapted from Lee and VanPatten (2003, 162):

Activity 5.3. How Well Do You Know Your Instructor?

Select the phrase that you think best describes your instructor as a graduate student. Afterward, your instructor will tell you if you are correct or not.

1. As soon as s/he got home from classes, my instructor . . .
   a. read a trashy novel.   b. took a nap.
   c. worked out.   d. made a cocktail.
2. When s/he was in a bad mood, my instructor . . .
   a. worked even harder.   b. criticized everyone in sight.
   c. ate chocolate.   d. hit the bottle.

The goal here is for students to internalize the irregular forms of past-tense verbs. Again, students do not form the verbs themselves; they just receive input.

Surveys

Another type of input flood activity is a survey. Lee and VanPatten explain that

> typical survey tasks includ[e] the following:
> - Indicating agreement with a statement
> - Indicating frequency of an activity
> - Answering Yes or No to particular questions
> - Finding a certain number of people who respond to an item in the same way (2003, 162)

For example, students could be asked to circulate around the room to find classmates who have done various things from the following list during vacation (again, the focus is on the past). Note that this activity contains follow-up questions to collect additional information.

Activity 5.4. Survey

Find classmates who have done the following things. Find a different person for each item.

Model: Have you eaten in a fancy restaurant?
      Name of the restaurant:

1. Traveled in a foreign country
    Name of the country:
2. Watched a terrifying movie
    Name of the movie:
3. Sang in a public space
    Where?
    Badly or well?

Ordering and Ranking

In ordering and ranking activities, students hear or read a list of items containing the target structure and either put them in chronological order or rank them by importance. For example, students could hear a list of events that took place on a particular evening (maybe based on a short film clip that they have watched) and would need to arrange them in the proper sequence. Surveys and ordering and ranking activities often contain several steps, including gathering information, analyzing it, and reporting back to the class as a whole.

Again, it is important to stress that in all these activity types, the students are never required to produce the target structure. Note that in all the activities above, although students provide output of a sort (vocabulary mostly), they do not supply the target forms. It is only during the structured output phase (described below) that they begin producing the grammar point.

There are two common critiques of structured input activities. The first is that a textbook composed entirely of them may become tedious after a while. Once students have completed a number of binary options, selecting alternatives, and similar interventions, they risk becoming bored, even if the topics themselves are interesting. In addition, it is fair to ask if some of these exercises might be considered their own type of drill, since although students are asked to provide information and do something with the input, they can sometimes simply focus on the grammar point without truly engaging with the content in a meaningful way.

Reflection

1. Can you think of grammar topics for which it might be challenging to create structured input activities?
2. Which of the structured input activities above seem the most communicative to you? Why?
3. How do you feel about activities that ask students to imagine the lives of their instructors or classmates outside the classroom?

Structured Output

Lee and VanPatten explain that structured output activities are devised to help students move to the stage of producing the targeted structure themselves. Structured output activities share two critical properties:

1. They involve the exchange of previously unknown information.
2. They require learners to access a particular form or structure in order to express meaning. (2003, 173)

Activity 5.5 exemplifies this type of intervention:

Activity 5.5. Imaging the Future

Work with a partner to describe what you think your life will be like when you're thirty years old, using verbs in the future tense.

Step 1. Fill out a chart with your ideas about your future job, family, living environment, and leisure activities. Contrast your expectations with your impression of what your parents' might have been at your age.

Step 2. As a class, compile a list of the two sets of goals—students' and parents'—on the board and compare them. Are they similar or different? Why do you think that is? How does your generation differ from that of your parents?

Lee and VanPatten (2003, 175) point out that a crucial piece of structured output is having others respond to what one produces. Therefore, it should always include follow-up activities that allow for comparisons, chart or grid making, or probes to ascertain veracity, among other tasks.

INCORPORATING CULTURE IN GRAMMAR ACTIVITIES

A general critique of Lee and VanPatten's input and output exercise types is that they tend to focus too much on students' lives rather than on leading students to make connections to the target culture(s). A broader question is whether every activity (and especially every grammar activity) needs to be linked to culture or integrated into the topic of a particular class. Still, it can be argued that it is a missed opportunity not to infuse culture when possible. Therefore, one might consider how grammar topics that were used in structured input examples above (adjectival endings and the simple past tense) might be taught within a more culturally and textually infused lesson.

For example, when teaching Spanish adjectives, why use Kanye and Beyoncé as binary options when students could analyze self-portraits of Frida Kahlo and Diego Rivera instead? Before the class, students could do some research about both artists to learn a bit about their backgrounds. Such information might be helpful for contrasting the two using adjectives that describe their temperaments or their physical attributes (for the "agree or disagree?" questions). These activities could be part of a larger lesson about the artists; in other words, the instructor might move back and forth between activities that focus somewhat on grammar and those that are more invested in students' interacting with cultural concepts, using authentic texts.

Similarly, if working on the past tense, instead of listing what they did during spring break or imagining a younger version of their instructor, students could be asked to supply information regarding the artists and what they accomplished during their careers (perhaps based on a reading—even if in English—done before coming to class). Otherwise, they could put Frida's major life events in order, or they could decide which life events were hers and which were Diego's. If the instructor wanted to personalize the activity as well, students could be asked to compare their own lives to that of one of the painters: what activities do they share? Or, going back to the adjectives, what kind of personal qualities does one usually associate with artists or with particularly creative people? Even at the elementary level, students could discuss whether certain personality traits tend to be associated with artists (such as passion, narcissism, sensitivity, or dedication) and debate the reasons for these generalizations. Students could also choose two artists from their own culture and compare them to the Mexican artists being studied: Are there similarities/differences? How does their artwork compare? Students could go around the room and conduct a survey to collect the adjectives that their classmates use to describe a work of art that the surveyor had selected prior to class. Spiraling language and content leads to the creation of lesson plans that include smooth and organic transitions between activities. And there is never that awkward moment in class when the teacher tells the students, "OK, now we are going to do some grammar [or culture, or vocabulary]. Open your book to page 5."

Reflection

1. Consider the structured input activities above, and rework each one so that it is couched within a cultural theme related to the language that you teach.
2. Think of a first-semester grammatical construction (other than adjectives or the simple past tense) in the language that you teach. Come up with some structured input and output activities

Continued . . .

> that might work well for this topic, contextualizing them within a relevant cultural theme.
> 3. Consider some texts that might work well to enhance these activities. Texts can be anything from a photo to a video to a written passage.

EXPLICIT INSTRUCTION

Another concern related to using a structured input approach is the lack of explicit instruction (i.e., explanations of grammatical rules). VanPatten and Rothman argue that "learners do not learn rules from the input. Instead, they process particular forms (morpho-phonological units) that are used by internal mechanisms to create a grammar. Rules—if they exist, and they surely don't exist in the classic sense used in instructed SLA research—are by-products of the growth of language in the learner's mind/brain" (2014, 31). Likewise, Lee and VanPatten contend that "the evidence is indicating that explicit information—although we may like it and it makes us feel good about what we are doing—is not necessary for successful acquisition" (2003, 124). At the same time, later in the same book they assert that "after learners receive *a brief explanation* of how past-tense endings work, they might first practice attaching the concept of past time to verb forms in an activity" (our emphasis; 143). Many would argue that a brief explanation is, in effect, explicit information.

A "brief explanation" can indeed be effective for a simple topic such as gendered endings (as in the "Kanye or Beyoncé?" example above). As an alternative, the teacher can use an inductive approach, providing students with data and asking them to figure out the rule themselves. Of course, as experienced instructors know, expecting students to apply adjectival endings appropriately and spontaneously is another story altogether. Lee and VanPatten would argue that their approach leads students to make agreements intuitively when producing the structures themselves; more research should be done to see whether learners do indeed do so when they are not focusing on this grammatical point in isolation.

> **Reflection**
>
> 1. Take a look at the grammar activities that appear in the course materials that you are currently using (or that you might eventually use, if you are not currently teaching). Identify whether they are drills, structured input and output activities, or something else.
> 2. Critique both the grammar descriptions and the activities that you have found. Do you think that they are effective? Why or why not? How might they be improved?
> 3. Try to get a sense of whether the grammar descriptions and activities are consistent. Do they follow the same format? Do they integrate the same pedagogical tenets?

DISCOURSE GRAMMAR

"Discourse grammar" means different things to researchers in the field of linguistics and has not been adopted by applied linguists in a systematic way. We conceive of the term as being linked to the concept of discourse competence (one of the four elements of Canale's [1983] model of communicative competence — see Chapter 2): the ability to combine language structures into different types of cohesive texts. Celce-Murcia and Olshtain state that "it is in discourse and through discourse that all of the other competencies are realized. And it is in discourse and through discourse that the manifestation of the other competencies can best be observed, researched and assessed" (2000, 16). They explain that "using a language entails the ability to both interpret and produce discourse in context in spoken and written communicative interaction" (4). Intrinsic to discourse grammar is the notion of metalinguistic awareness. Simply put, some grammar points cannot be explained or understood through succinct, sentence-level rules. They require the learner to investigate and analyze the environments in which these structures occur.

For example, consider the following grammatical topics in English, and try to come up with brief explanations to differentiate among the various sentences:

Determiners
>I ate the pie.
>I ate some pie.
>I ate some of the pie.
>I ate pie.
>I ate a pie.

Tense and aspect
>I was sleeping.
>I slept.
>I have slept.

Word-order constructions
>I like him.
>Him, I like.
>It's him (he?) that/who/whom(?) I like.
>He's the one I like.

Interrogative expressions
>Where are you going?
>Where is it that you are going?
>You're going where?

Even the most brilliant linguists would have difficulty coming up with "brief" explanations to differentiate among these utterances, because their use in context is so nuanced.

As Harley and Swain's (1984) influential study showed, learners continue to make discourse-related grammatical mistakes even after being immersed in the target language for an extended period of time. Indeed, some learners who have achieved a high level of proficiency in a language, including those who have lived abroad, still make mistakes when it comes to using the kinds of constructions shown above, especially if their errors have never been brought to their attention. Explicit instruction may therefore be necessary for internalizing certain grammatical structures, especially those that depend on the greater discourse contexts in which they are found.

Consciousness Raising and the 3 I's

Consciousness-raising (CR) tasks allow students to engage with complicated, discourse-conditioned grammatical constructions. Ellis defines a CR task as "a pedagogic activity where the learners are provided with L2 data in some form and required to perform some operation on or with it, the purpose of which is to arrive at an explicit understanding of some linguistic property or properties of the target language" (1997, 160). In a similar vein, McCarthy and Carter (1995, 217) propose what they call "the 3 I's" to replace the 3 Ps (see pages 94–95):

Illustration: Learners and teachers examine the data.
Interaction: Learners and teachers discuss hypotheses.
Induction: Learners posit a rule for a pattern or regularity in the data.

In McCarthy and Carter's framework, activities are "characterized by a use of texts rather than invented sentences, by being based on scrutiny of real spoken data, and by including tasks and questions designed to enhance both awareness of language and a questioning approach on the part of learners" (214). Blyth explains that "in a nutshell, the goal is to change the role of the student into that of a language researcher who works to discover patterns and induce rules from authentic data" (1999, 205). Recent studies have found inductive approaches to teaching grammar to be effective (Adair-Hauck and Cumo-Johanssen 1997; Paesani 2005; Haight, Herron, and Cole 2007; Vogel et al. 2011). Salaberry (2010b) provides the following "guided induction approach to grammar instruction," which is a form of CR:

- Lead students to look for patterns in the text.
- Students complete a chart that has them identify the pattern.
- Analyze the structure of the language.
- Expand the universe of data by having students read more.
- Lead students to think critically about the language and the cultural implications.

These types of interventions can be integrated at all levels of instruction, not only in advanced classes. In addition, it is key to identify the grammatical topics that require this kind of focus, as compared to those that can be acquired more implicitly.

One area of discourse grammar that is particularly challenging for students is the notion of tense versus aspect. "Tense" refers to the moment in time when something takes place (the past, present, or future). Aspect is a more complicated concept. Richards and Schmidt define "aspect" as "a term used to denote the activity, event, or state described by a verb, for example whether the activity is ongoing or completed" (2010, 34). They explain that aspect can be either lexical (certain verbs inherently express either ongoing activities or completed actions) or grammatical (specific morphemes will determine whether a particular verb is denoting an ongoing or a completed action or state of being). An example of aspect from the Romance languages is the use of the simple past (*pretérito* in Spanish or *passé composé* in French) versus the imperfect (*imperfecto* or *imparfait*). Students usually have difficulty conceptualizing how these tenses are employed differently in discourse. At the same time, students have to memorize new verb forms for each tense. Learning the morphology of the new verbs is straightforward and should occur first. For the use of the two tenses in discourse, however, a brief explanation is usually insufficient and can be confusing.

CR tasks can be effective, however, for complicated and challenging grammar points. For instance, Blyth (1997) suggests working with a short commercial to help students conceive of the notions of tense and aspect by distinguishing between foregrounded (simple past) and backgrounded (imperfect) information in a given scene. After watching the commercial, students are asked to make a list of all the actions in the scene that must occur in a particular order to remain faithful to its plot (the foreground). Then they are asked to come up with other verbs that illustrate the general state of being in the scene (as well as ongoing background activities that are irrelevant to the plot). This part of the description can be inserted into the narrative in a more flexible way. Note that lower-level students could receive a sheet of verbs in the infinitive and group them into two categories (instead of producing them). As a follow-up input activity after students have categorized the verbs, instructors could pass out a set of sentences (in both the simple past and the imperfect) and ask the students to order them correctly. More-advanced students could be asked to write up their own description of the commercial, using the simple past (for the foreground) and the imperfect (for the background).

> **Reflection**
>
> Find a commercial in the language that you teach that has clearly distinguishable foregrounded and backgrounded elements. What cultural themes in the commercial might also be emphasized?

At a more advanced level, students can participate in a CR task that goes even further in exploring the intricacies of the verb tenses (now including the pluperfect). The following activity (based on similar ones presented in Katz and Blyth 2007, 129–38) guides students to discover the various uses of past tenses in English discourse and then to think about how they correspond to the target language.

Activity 5.6. Analyzing Past Tenses

Instructions: For each underlined verb in the passage below, choose the tense that would be used if you were to translate the passage. Then explain the reason for your choice, using the following criteria:

- finished action (simple past)
- change of state (simple past)
- an activity that continues (imperfect)
- a habitual action (imperfect)
- a state of being (imperfect)
- the past of the past (pluperfect)

Excerpt from "Requiem," by Karen Brennan

1. <u>I woke up</u> one morning and 2. <u>my country was gone</u>. 3. <u>It was strange</u>. 4. <u>It had been there</u> the night before, sparking and hissing, but now 5. <u>it was gone</u>. 6. <u>I could feel</u> its absence in the air, which is a feeling like no other. The garden 7. <u>was</u> still there, the bougainvillea 8. <u>was</u> in some sort of bloom, red blossoms half-opened on thorny stalks. And the house still 9. <u>surrounded</u> me—for the moment, at least. Perhaps 10. <u>it took</u> longer for smaller things to follow suit. All I know is what I'm telling you. 11. <u>I found</u> my slippers—12. <u>the little hole in the toe had not grown</u> larger overnight, thank god, and 13. <u>everything was</u> still in the fridge. It's

not as if 14. <u>some thief had come</u> and 15. <u>stolen food</u>. No, 16. <u>it was</u> only the country, the big picture. 17. <u>I wasn't</u> sure where 18. <u>I was</u>.

Source: See Appendix B or http://scoundreltime.com/requiem/ for the complete text.

Note that studying a passage written in English can help students develop their metalinguistic understanding of tense and aspect in the target language. They can also be asked to translate the passage (or at least the verbs) into the target language as a culminating task. In addition, the grammar exercises above should be embedded within a carefully developed lesson, preceded by activities that set the scene and prepare students for the topics of the text. Following the linguistic exploration (which would include attention to vocabulary and style as well as grammar), students might be encouraged to engage with the deeper meaning and themes of the text and complete focused writing and extension assignments (see Chapters 7 and 8).

TRANSLINGUAL COMPETENCE

In Chapter 2, we discussed the 2007 MLA report's recommendation to cultivate students' translingual (along with transcultural) competence. This notion is somewhat vague in the report, thus allowing for discussion and divergence regarding how it might apply in various contexts. The report states that "students are educated to function as informed and capable interlocutors with educated native speakers in the target language" (3–4). Such interactions require understanding the mind-set of members of the target community, both culturally and linguistically. Jokes, for example, are usually language driven and based on subtleties of grammar or vocabulary. When students understand a joke that they would not have gotten had they not studied the target language, they enjoy an insider status. Exploring humor, and in particular the grammar of humor, is an effective and gratifying way for students to develop translingual competence. This competence, however, may be the most difficult to acquire. For example, consider the TV show *Seinfeld*, which was all the rage in the United States in the 1990s. A website discussed the difficulty of dubbing and subtitling this sitcom for foreign audiences, who often did not understand the humor:

> So, what's the deal with translating *Seinfeld?* In an interview with *The Verge* [https://www.theverge.com/2015/6/24/8809723/jerry-seinfeld-tv

-show-international-translation], Sabine Sebastian, the German translator of *Seinfeld*—herself a *Seinfeld* fanatic—explains a few of the many challenges she faced bringing the show to a German audience. Essentially, these boiled down to linguistic and cultural differences. More than many American shows, *Seinfeld* relied on word-based humor: not only was it full of difficult-to-translate puns and euphemisms, but even the sounds of words or the specific cadence of an actor's speech were part of the humor. It wasn't just the wordplay that was difficult to translate, but the delivery of the lines, the way Jerry, for example, spit out the word "*Newman*."

Source: http://mentalfloss.com/article/67874/why-seinfeld-so-hard-translate.

Teaching students to translate, one of the MLA report's suggestions, is deeply challenging. On the other hand, acquiring translation skills is an effective way to improve translingual competence.

Most of all, grammar needs to be studied in context, with particular attention to the appropriateness of grammatical structures in specific socially conditioned situations. Salaberry (2010a) provides a useful summary of the relevant components, which align with our discussions of discourse grammar and discourse competence, as well as with the goal of achieving translingual competence:

Contextual factors that are part of a definition of language:
1. Mode (e.g., written, oral, by phone, by email)
2. Interlocutors (e.g., age, social class, level of education)
3. Regional variation (e.g., countries, localities)
4. Register (e.g., formal, informal, personal)
5. Genre (e.g., scientific, journalistic, debate)
6. Physical-temporal context (e.g., at the bus station, in the morning on a weekday)
7. Purpose of communication (e.g., to convince, to describe, to chat)

Contextual factor 7 is particularly interesting, because it involves what sociolinguists call "speech acts," which include the speaker's intention: asking, apologizing, complimenting (or responding to a compliment), being polite, or being sarcastic, among others. What an interlocutor from Japan considers polite may be very different from what a Russian deems appropriate, which can cause cultural misunderstandings. Although actions are sometimes sufficient to convey our intentions (bowing, motioning for someone to take your seat, etc.), incorporating sociolinguistically appropriate speech is an important part of grammatical competence. For example, using the conditional instead of the simple present ("I would like" versus "I want") can make a big difference in establishing politeness in many languages, as does choosing appropriate second-person pronouns to refer to one's interlocutor. To explore such differences, we propose some strategies for giving students the opportunity to engage with naturally occurring language in various discourse environments with the goal of cultivating their insights into the appropriate corresponding discourse grammars.

The practice of having students work as researchers can be expanded, especially at later levels of instruction, to asking them to collect and analyze their own data. Depending on the level of instruction and the goals of the particular program, the types of materials and opportunities available to students may vary. In every case, however, students need to understand the contexts of the texts they are using. In addition, they should explore not only the particularities of the setting (formal versus informal, spoken versus written, etc.) but also the characteristics of the speakers themselves (age, social class, gender, education, etc.). In the following sections, we discuss the opportunities for discovering contextualized grammar provided by the study of films, the linguistic landscape, and corpora. Such materials and interventions are at the core of a discourse grammar approach. On a final note, we stress once again that these activities can be blended into text-based explorations that focus on elements other than grammar (e.g., culture, history, or literature).

Films

Bourns explains that "although the conversations in films are not naturally occurring representations of the spoken language (since they are not produced spontaneously), they still provide appropriate models of spoken language for students to explore. While working with short film clips, students come to realize that one reason why they may have had difficulty understanding ... movies in the past (as opposed, perhaps, to ... newscasts or interviews) is that they were not familiar with spoken structures or the spoken lexicon" (2017b, 180).

While watching a short film clip, more-advanced students might be asked to

- note any elements of spoken or informal language that they hear;
- focus on a specific grammar point and identify its use in discourse;
- listen for examples of various speech acts (apologizing, complimenting, etc.) and identify the language used to express them and the situations in which they were used;
- read the subtitles and decide whether the translations are accurate or might be modified; or
- rewrite the scene using different characters (more formal? less sophisticated?).

Reflection

1. Find a film clip that contains informal language in the language that you teach. Then think about how you might structure a lesson in which students would discover grammatical (and lexical) forms that differ from more formal structures that they have studied.
2. What cultural elements in this clip might be interesting to explore?
3. Why might watching a film clip be a better way to study linguistic register than, for example, reading a modern play?

The Linguistic Landscape

Exploring the "linguistic landscape" within a particular culture provides a valuable opportunity for students to hone their translingual and transcultural competence. Landry and Bourhis explain that "the language of public road signs, advertising billboards, street names, place names, commercial shop signs, and public signs on government building combines to form the linguistic landscape of a given territory, region, or urban agglomeration" (1997, 25). Study-abroad programs in particular afford students the chance to analyze the target culture's linguistic landscape. Not only can students collect photos of written language that they find on the streets, in the subway, or elsewhere, but they can also ask natives for their reactions to such photos: for example, do they like the advertisements or find them offensive? Advertisements especially may use language that targets a specific audience (as can the locations in which they are placed, which are important). Does the grammar reflect the desire to catch the attention of younger people, wealthier people, or foreigners?

As Malinowski points out, however, there is another important step to take: "In terms of language learning, . . . students would most profitably not just visit neighborhoods with examples of signs in the target language, taking pictures and noting vocabulary to be studied (*perceived space*), nor would they just conduct walking tours with local merchants, practicing conversation and interviews about their perceptions of change in the identity of a multilingual neighborhood (*lived space*). Rather, they would do both of these and more, also comparing their own experiences and those of others to outside perspectives on local realities in readings, films, maps, and other texts (*conceived space*)" (2015, 109). In other words, students should be encouraged to compare their own data with perspectives beyond those that they have personally cultivated or encountered.

Finally, a great deal of the work on linguistic landscapes includes an exploration of the appearance of foreign language, usually English, in public spaces. The interjection of English in various types of foreign texts is a fascinating topic for students to analyze. In addition, graffiti are particularly revealing, both socially and linguistically, in terms of their intended audience. Being able to understand graffiti is a clear indication that one's translingual competence is strong. Print advertisements, both the ones found in public spaces and those that occur in magazines and newspapers, can also offer insights into grammar used in discourse. Students can be asked to collect all the ads that they can find for a particular product and then to analyze not only the grammar but also the marketing strategies that align with the language and images used. The conversation could extend to whether such a campaign would be effective in other cultures.

Reflection

1. Find some advertising slogans in the language you teach. How might you have students explore their grammar in a discourse-focused way?
2. What elements of the linguistic landscape besides advertisements and graffiti might be interesting for students to explore?

Corpora

There is a preponderance of authentic texts available for advanced students to explore, including corpora of spoken and written language. Concordancing software can also help students target specific structures that might be relevant to their research. When working with corpora, students should be given specific tasks to accomplish. For example, if the goal is to explore spoken language, students can be asked to identify all the structures that are particular to this register (see Bourns 2017b). They can also be asked to provide the written equivalents of the spoken forms that they find (see McCarthy and Carter 1995). In addition, it is interesting for students to explore relationships between speakers as demonstrated by the language that they use. Are they close friends? Acquaintances? Do they speak formally or informally with each other? Does one person have a higher status in the relationship than the other? To investigate such questions, Bourns provides the following instructions for students to analyze a short excerpt from a target language corpus (Kerr 1983):

- Make a list of all the elements of the spoken language.
- Give "standard" or written equivalents of these expressions.
- Find any revealing spoken markers, such as fillers or repeated expressions.
- Evaluate the relationships between the speakers. How well do they know each other, and how can one tell? Are there differences in speaker status (e.g., does one person command more respect that the other, etc.)? (2017b, 185)

Advanced students can also be asked to produce their own corpus by recording and transcribing a free-form conversation between native speakers. Although this is a challenging task, it allows them to take ownership of their learning and be the first to analyze the grammar (and vocabulary and cultural elements) that they find in their data. Finally, such a project allows them to establish and build on their linguistic identity as "informed and capable interlocutors," per the 2007 MLA report.

> **Reflection**
>
> 1. What problems can you imagine occurring within a corpora-based approach to analyzing grammar?
> 2. Can you envision using corpora at earlier levels of instruction? If so, how?

All the activities described in this section stress the importance of encouraging students to work as researchers to discover how grammar functions in authentic discourse environments. The goal is for learners to acquire metalinguistic insights into grammar, even as early as the beginning level. Most important, students need to understand that not all grammar points have the same level of complexity. Whereas some are relatively straightforward, others require a deeper analysis of the contexts in which they occur. It can also be difficult at times for teachers to find effective ways to integrate the study of grammar (and discourse-conditioned grammar in particular) in text-based classes. Some topics are easily incorporated (such as adjectives, which are used to describe, and tense and aspect, which are used to narrate), while others (for example, relative clauses or object pronouns) remain less intuitively connected. Developing curricula that align the teaching of all grammar points with intellectually satisfying and culturally relevant material is a challenge that requires sustained collaboration among the colleagues who instruct at every level within a program.

6 • Vocabulary

WORDS MATTER

The following quotation, provided to us at a workshop by Susanne Rott and cited frequently, sums up the importance of vocabulary acquisition: "The fact is that while without grammar very little can be conveyed, without vocabulary *nothing* can be conveyed" (Wilkins 1972, 111–12). As Guilloteau (2010) points out, language learners can be understood if they make grammatical mistakes, but if they do not possess at least rudimentary vocabulary to express their thoughts or needs, communication will be difficult, if not impossible. The strategic competence theorized by Canale and Swain (1980, 30–31)—the ability to compensate for gaps in one's linguistic repertoire—can be attained only if learners have already acquired a certain baseline lexicon. In this chapter, we therefore recommend that course designers and instructors make a deliberate effort to integrate lexical goals into curricula, lesson plans, and homework assignments.

Perspectives

I remember some humbling moments during my junior year abroad in Berlin. I thought that my German was pretty decent, although I realized throughout my stay that my grammar was a lot better than

Continued...

my vocabulary. I remember attending a reception where I bit into something inedible. I spit it out into a napkin and needed to find a garbage can to get rid of it. I wandered around asking people where I could find "das Trash," which means nothing in German. People looked at me as if I were out of my mind, and I felt completely inept. Another example was when I was talking to my host mother in her kitchen and realized that I had never learned how to say "frying pan." Or "oven." Or "stove." Or "toaster." Those words had just never come up in the conversations in our textbook that we had memorized. She was incredulous, and I was highly embarrassed. I could read and write critical essays about Goethe, but I could not find a garbage can or come up with the word for a frying pan.

1. This person's strategic competence does not seem too great, despite the fact that she was able to read advanced literary works. Why do you think that this is the case?
2. How can students who reach advanced levels of language learning continue to expand their practical vocabulary? How can curricula be designed to help students achieve this goal?

Teaching and learning vocabulary may seem like unwieldy tasks, due to the enormous number of lexical items found in every language. Individuals are even sometimes sensitive to perceived gaps in their L1 vocabulary. The following quotation, from an article about the so-called imposter syndrome, sums it up well: "I'm super insecure about my vocabulary. In fact, I submit my use of the word *super* instead of a more elegant word as evidence of my less-than-sophisticated vocab. I'm especially insecure about this particular shortcoming because I have a journalism degree, two graduate degrees, and I'm a writer. If anyone should have a strong command of the English language it should be me" (https://www.huffingtonpost.ca/sarah-vermunt/imposter-syndrome_b_3595573.html). Language teachers may harbor similar insecurities, especially if they are not native speakers or know that there are particular domains of the target language in which they are weak (for example, some language teachers might admit that they never mastered the vocabulary for trees or the parts of a car). Nonnative teachers sometimes use a trick called "avoidance" to make up for gaps in their lexis: they will deliberately refrain from using a word or expression because they are unsure of its gender, pronunciation, or exact form. Avoidance is an expert employment of strategic competence (and can be used for everything from vocabulary to grammar to pronunciation), so it is not necessarily negative. That said, there is always room for expanding one's vocabulary. Sometimes teachers (even native speakers) learn new lexical items along with their students.

VOCABULARY INSTRUCTION WITHIN PREVIOUS APPROACHES

As we saw with grammar, twenty-first-century instructors tend to avoid techniques that appear to be outdated or traditional. The stigma of "teaching vocabulary," along with a lack of current recommended approaches for doing so, may lead teachers to eschew focusing on lexical items. Methods favored before the rise of CLT, however, offered clear guidelines. During the GT era, students regularly studied long lists of decontextualized vocabulary before reading texts that included the same items. Although students may have learned the meanings of these words, the downside was that there was no emphasis on pronunciation or the integration of this new vocabulary within naturally occurring discourse. In the DM, students learned (mostly) concrete vocabulary through "binding" techniques: the instructor would point to an item or act out a verb and say the word or phrase, and then students would repeat it, focusing on correct pronunciation. The goal was to connect the word to its meaning without including translation in the mix. Students probably learned the term for "garbage can," for example, without any difficulty. Of course, binding works only for vocabulary that has a concrete meaning and can be visualized or dramatized. In the ALM classroom, students would learn vocabulary by participating in vocabulary drills and reciting and memorizing conversations that contained new (glossed) words and phrases. Some ALM books concluded each chapter with a vocabulary list, and most included a dictionary at the end. Although students mastered the vocabulary within the conversations, the downside was that they were not well equipped to express their own ideas. They might be able to describe a tall blond woman, for instance, but not a short redhead.

In the communicative approach, it is generally assumed that students will pick up the vocabulary that they need along the way by participating in activities and tasks. As Vanessa Wei has pointed out to us (personal communication), this belief also exists in advanced "content-based" courses taught by literature professors (see Donato and Brooks 2004).

> **Reflection**
>
> During a workshop for instructors of Spanish at Columbia University in 2017, Aline Godfroid asked participants to respond to the questions below. How would you answer them?
>
> 1. How do you teach vocabulary in your school or program?
> 2. Name one thing that works well about the way vocabulary is taught in your school or program.
> 3. Name one thing you would like to change or improve.

If you ask most language instructors how they learned to teach vocabulary, they will probably pause and then admit that they do not remember that piece from their methods class. As Guilloteau (2010) points out, vocabulary pedagogy has appeared more as an afterthought in most communicative teaching methods books, and strategies for teaching vocabulary are not usually stressed in TA training programs. It is ironic that so little attention is paid to acquiring vocabulary within the communicative approach, since CLT privileges asking students to provide information about themselves, their thoughts, and their personal needs. Developing a working and retainable lexicon should therefore be a priority. At the same time, however, students do not need large, esoteric vocabularies to complete everyday tasks or to communicate basic needs and ideas.

In twenty-first-century approaches to language teaching, vocabulary acquisition is vital for achieving other specific goals. For example, the multiliteracies framework views vocabulary, like grammar, as a tool for engaging with and comprehending deeper meanings of texts of various genres. Vocabulary is always contextualized, and students reflect upon its use within different types of discourse. The motivation for learning vocabulary is strong, since it is essential for understanding the texts. The same is true for CBI, LSP, and FLAC, as well as other content-focused frameworks. In a social pedagogies approach, vocabulary acquisition is instrumental for achieving the goal of creating strong interpersonal connections through interactions, since conversations should be meaningful and not simply transactional. The question is whether students receive enough support to build their lexicons within these approaches.

Studies have shown that, in general, students do not reach superior levels of proficiency after enrolling in university language classes, even for a number of years (Swender asserts that "the majority of undergraduate language majors have achieved oral proficiency levels that cluster around the Intermediate-High/Advanced-Low border" [2003, 520]). Some researchers attribute this deficiency to students' not having acquired enough vocabulary. Hacking and Tschirner report that "it was suggested that a major goal of any curricular reform should include an intentional approach to building receptive mastery of the most frequent 2,000–3,000 words in the first two college years through a mixture of direct vocabulary learning and practice and the use of graded readers and level-appropriate authentic texts, as has been suggested in the literature on vocabulary learning in the field of ESL" (2017, 516). Updating curricular materials to focus on the most frequently used words and expressions is therefore an important, language-specific initiative, and there is still a great deal of work to be done in fields other than English. (At the time of this book's publication, Brigham Young University had begun putting together a website that contains corpora for various languages, and Jamie Rankin had developed an online beginning German textbook, available at https://dddgerman.org, which focuses on the acquisition of the most frequently used words in German.)

> **Reflection**
>
> Look at the vocabulary sections in an elementary textbook for the language that you teach. How is vocabulary presented? Are there long lists of words to memorize? Are words and expressions presented in context? Do you think that this book is effective in teaching vocabulary?

GRAMMAR VERSUS VOCABULARY PEDAGOGY

Many teachers (both native and nonnative) would admit to feeling more confident about their mastery of the target language's grammar than of its vocabulary. We should point out, however, that some researchers do not believe in making a distinction between the structure and the lexis of a language. Michael Lewis is known for his highly influential Lexical Approach framework. He asserts that "language has traditionally been divided into grammar and vocabulary. Crudely, the former consisted of elements of the generative system of the language and the latter was the stock of fixed nongenerative 'words'. Recently, this analysis has been challenged and shown to be seriously misguided from both strictly linguistic and pedagogical points of view (Lewis, 1993; Nattinger and DeCarrico, 1992; Willis, 1990)" (1997, 255). It is indisputable that every word is inherently grammatical, as it belongs to a particular part of speech (noun, verb, adverb, etc.). Learners must therefore identify the grammatical categories into which new vocabulary items fall. Furthermore, students need to be able associate and link related words ("word families") from different categories (see Thornbury 2002, 4–5). For instance, in Spanish one finds the verb *trabajar* (to work), the adjective *trabajador/a* (hardworking), and the noun *trabajo* (work). Students need to know how to conjugate the verb, how to make the adjective agree in number and gender with the noun it modifies, and how to choose the appropriate article to precede the noun.

Words do not exist in isolation. Every word has specific syntactic properties that regulate its use in discourse (the environment surrounding a word is called its "external syntax"). For example, in English the verb "to tell" is what linguists call "ditransitive"—it can take either two grammatical direct objects, as in "He told [her boyfriend] [the ugly truth]," or a direct object and an indirect object preceded by the preposition "to": "He told [the ugly truth] [to her boyfriend]." The verb "to explain," however, cannot be ditransitive; one cannot say "He explained her boyfriend the ugly truth." Nonnative speakers frequently make this error in English, however, because "to tell" and "to explain" are semantically similar. These speakers have overgeneralized the rule for ditransitives (which may not exist in their native language).

Theoretical linguists working in the Construction Grammar framework assert that language consists of grammatical constructions, which are "form-function pairings whose structural and semantic properties cannot, or not entirely, be accounted for in terms of other properties of the grammar of a language or of universal grammar and which therefore require independent explanation" (Lambrecht 2001, 466; see also Fillmore and Kay 1993; Goldberg 1995; Michaelis 2012). In other words, a grammatical construction is not just the sum of its lexical parts—constructions themselves also convey meaning. For example, the "causative" construction in English (subject noun phrase + verb "to make" [conjugated] + direct object noun phrase + verb phrase) inherently implies that something makes something else happen, as in "my professor made me read this book." Although Construction Grammar has not been used as a framework to treat the study of vocabulary, it aligns with the Lexical Approach in that it advocates the interconnectedness of grammar and vocabulary (as well as of pragmatics and pronunciation).

Schmitt explains that knowing a word consists of having insights into its form (spoken and written), meaning, and use in discourse (including the patterns in which it combines with other words) (2008, 334). His emphasis on discourse is especially important for "polysemous" words—that is, words that mean vastly different things depending on their context. For instance, you can break your leg; you can break a date or a promise; you can catch a break; or you can take a break (examples provided by Susanne Rott). You also need to brake for ducklings in the road, "brake" being a homophone with a meaning (and possible etymology) related to some of those of "break" above. Vocabulary is complicated; it can break your spirit.

One way to manage lexical complexity is to analyze language not as discrete words but as what Lewis calls "chunks" (1997, 255). He explains that chunks can contain anything from a single word to an entire utterance. In his manual for teaching vocabulary, Thornbury explains that "there are different types of chunks and different degrees of 'chunkiness'" (2002, 115), including collocations, which are words that are commonly found together ("to waste time"); phrasal verbs, which contain prepositions ("to think through [something]"); idioms, which do not make literal sense ("to kick the bucket"); and social formulae (such as "Bon appétit!"). Thornbury stresses that some chunks are more flexible than others and that "the ability to deploy a wide range of lexical chunks both accurately and appropriately is probably what most distinguishes advanced learners from intermediate ones" (116). At the same time, even advanced speakers of a language can sometimes come out with nonnative-like utterances due to the misuse of a lexical chunk. For example, a French colleague learned from friends that in English, when a conversation is becoming awkward, one can use the phrase "How 'bout those Mets?" as a humorous signal that it's time to move on to another topic. It was even funnier for her friends, she reports, when she instead chimed in with "What is it about these Mets?" during a recent conversation.

Thornbury explains that Lewis's Lexical Approach rests on the belief that vocabulary is learned through frequent exposure and the drawing of students' attention to lexical items; he adds that memorization is also a necessary component of vocabulary acquisition (2002, 116). The memorization piece, or at least the need to devote a significant deal of time to committing lexical items to memory, distinguishes vocabulary instruction from grammar pedagogy, which is more about understanding concepts. Some grammatical topics, however, also require memorization. For example, to conjugate a verb, one must learn the endings by heart and link them to the appropriate subjects. On the other hand, developing an understanding of which past tense would be most appropriate within a particular discourse context is not the same as rote learning. Some researchers, such as Lee and VanPatten (2003), suggest that all grammar and vocabulary is learned implicitly and through copious amounts of input. Conversely, scholarship in the field of vocabulary acquisition has shown that some of the most effective strategies are explicit and intentional. According to Schmitt,

> The scope of the vocabulary learning task, and the fact that many learners fail to achieve even moderate vocabulary learning goals, indicates that it can no longer be assumed that an adequate lexis will simply be "picked up" from exposure to language tasks focusing either on other linguistic aspects or on communication. Rather, a more proactive, principled approach needs to be taken in promoting vocabulary learning. ... Most importantly, students need the willingness to be active learners over a long period of time, for without this, they are unlikely to achieve any substantial vocabulary size, regardless of the quality of instruction. (2008, 332–33)

Teachers may serve as guides, but ultimately students must take responsibility for their own vocabulary acquisition.

INTENTIONAL VOCABULARY LEARNING

Vocabulary items fall into two categories: function (or grammatical) words and content words. Function words constitute a closed set (i.e., new words cannot usually be added to it) of vocabulary items, such as articles, prepositions, conjunctions, and interrogative expressions. These words are usually taught as components of grammatical constructions. For example, when studying interrogative expressions, students need to learn what linguists who work on English call "WH-question" words (what, why, where, etc.).

Advanced learners of a given language have usually acquired all its function words.

Content words, on the other hand, are placed into appropriate slots in already existing grammatical constructions. For example, as mentioned above, the verb "to tell" in English can be inserted into the ditransitive construction. Even native speakers with an excellent command of grammar can lack content words that are specific to given situations, locations, or eras. Therefore, a speaker (native or nonnative) of English who cannot describe a mining expedition may nonetheless have no trouble providing the play-by-play for a baseball game.

The decision regarding which content words to include in a curriculum should be based not only on their frequency within the target language but also on the goals of the various stakeholders (students, teacher, program, institution, etc.). For example, business students may not consider it vital to develop a complex lexicon for literary analysis. Furthermore, those who plan to study abroad should develop a lexicon that will allow them not only to function in the academic world where they will be studying but also to make connections with native speakers. Course developers and teachers should therefore make a concerted effort to include the acquisition of specific vocabulary in their student learning target outcomes for every course.

How can instructors promote vocabulary acquisition? Schmitt states that "overall, it seems that virtually anything that leads to more exposure, attention, manipulation, or time spent on lexical items adds to their learning" (2008, 339). He supports including vocabulary memorization as a course requirement and making students responsible for constructing personal lexicons. In a reference book for teachers, Folse (2004) lists myths that research has debunked about vocabulary acquisition. In particular, he provides a rationale for encouraging students to create and maintain word lists and flash cards (either paper or virtual). Nation (2015) recommends including "extensive reading" assignments in language class curricula to help build students' vocabularies. According to Richards and Schmidt,

> Extensive reading means reading in quantity and in order to gain a general understanding of what is read. It is intended to develop good reading habits, to build up knowledge of vocabulary and structure, and to encourage a liking for reading.
>
> Intensive reading is generally at a slower speed, and requires a higher degree of understanding than extensive reading." (2010, 212)

Nation explains that

> in total, extensive reading should make up around three-sixteenths of the course time.
>
> In a well-designed extensive reading course around two-thirds of this time should be spent on reading material which contains a small proportion of unknown words (around 2% of the running words). Around one-third of the time should be spent reading very easy material containing little or no unknown words with a focus on reading for fluency. (2015, 139)

Folse (2004, 110–20) presents research that advocates having students look up words they do not know in a bilingual dictionary instead of trying to guess their meaning from context. However, if the goal of the reading is not to focus on vocabulary (and students are therefore not required to look words up), it is more effective to gloss unknown words in the margins rather than right after the words within the text or at the bottom of the page.

Beck, McKeown, and Kucan (2013) explain that we acquire most of our L1 vocabulary through spoken input, which is usually clearly contextualized. Written content, on the other hand, is more complicated: "The problem is that it is not so easy to learn word meanings from written context. Written context lacks many of the features of oral language that support learning new word meanings, such as intonation, body language, and shared physical surroundings. As such, written language is a far less effective vehicle for learning new words than oral language" (5). Yet academic institutions tend to value the acquisition of low-frequency vocabulary learned through reading. For example, the SAT and ACT exams require high school students to know the meanings of words that they have probably never heard in discourse. How often do young people hear typical SAT words like "scurrilous" or "penurious"? The rationale is that students who are intellectually curious and who read a great deal will learn these words, and that such students will succeed at the college level. Most students who strive to do well on the SAT, however, do not actually learn these words through reading; they study them deliberately by memorizing uncontextualized lists of words. This technique may not always be effective, since it does not give a feel for how the word is used. Consider "scurrilous," for instance. A learner might jump to the false conclusion that it is related to "scurry," which means "to rush." Even a one-word definition, something along the lines of "scandalous," might be misleading. To understand the true sense of a word, it is important to see it in multiple contexts following its definition, as in this model:

Definition of *Scurrilous*

said or done to ruin a person's reputation

Examples of *Scurrilous* Used in a Sentence

Jeremy got me fired by telling my boss scurrilous lies about me.
In an attempt to ruin the mayor's reputation, the newspaper editor wrote several scurrilous articles on the politician's spending habits.
Your scurrilous remarks are not going to make me stop seeing my boyfriend!
When the judge learned about the scurrilous accusations made against him, he immediately called for his personal lawyer to sue the magazine.

Source: Adapted slightly from https://wordsinasentence.com/scurrilous-in-a-sentence/.

Even though these examples are provided at the sentence level (and not contextualized within a larger text), the learner is able to get a strong sense of the meaning of the word. If she is required to use it in her own sentences as a follow-up activity, it is more likely that she will remember it. She could also be asked to think of a situation in which scurrilous lies about someone led to that person's reputation being damaged. She should review the word regularly, in any case, if she wants to retain it beyond the SAT exam.

Perspectives

I was always interested in expanding my vocabulary, and in high school, I learned a lot of words through reading. I looked up all the words that I didn't know and kept a notebook of them. Unfortunately, I never learned how these words were pronounced, because I had never heard them spoken. I remember being really embarrassed once in college because I mispronounced the word "antithesis" (I pronounced it as the sum of its parts: anti + thesis), and my friends thought that was hysterical. I felt like a pseudo-intellectual.

Continued . . .

1. It has been said that people who mispronounce words are the antithesis of pseudo-intellectuals, since they have learned words on their own through reading. Do you agree? Why or why not?
2. Why is English particularly problematic for learning vocabulary from written texts? Is the language that you teach similar?
3. What strategies have you used (if any) to learn your L2 vocabulary? Have they been effective? Do you still use them?

A semantic map is a figure that groups words related to a particular topic, whereas a semantic set may simply consist of a list of related words (without a drawing). Modern methods books often suggest that students make semantic maps when they learn new words. For example, if ESL students were asked to make a diagram of vocabulary related to baseball, they would put actions of the game in one part of the map; another area would contain materials related to the sport, and another would include game-specific terms (see Figure 6.1).

Folse states that it is a myth that "presenting new vocabulary in semantic sets facilitates learning" (2004, 46). Nation explains that "the research shows that it takes longer to learn words that relate to each other in certain ways than it takes to learn words that are unrelated to each other or that are related to each other in a kind of story line" (2000, 6). That is, studying words at the same time that are too similar in meaning may cause the learner to confuse them, which results in interference (not to be confused with the interference related to transfer errors from one's native language). The following is an example of such interference: a colleague mentioned that she had learned the Arabic words for "eggplant" and "zucchini" together (in a Moroccan restaurant, while looking at a menu), and she can never, to this day, remember which is which (although the two words have nothing to do with each other formally). Another colleague mentioned that she cannot keep the names of two of her husband's college friends straight, despite the fact that they look nothing alike. Every time she has met one, the other one has also been present. One's name is Crowley and the other's is Burde, so even mnemonic techniques are not helpful (both are birds).

Most textbooks commonly present all the relevant vocabulary for family members, food items, or body parts at the same time, but research contradicts the effectiveness of this practice. Nation explains that there is, however, a time for semantic mapping: "Once items have been reasonably well

VOCABULARY

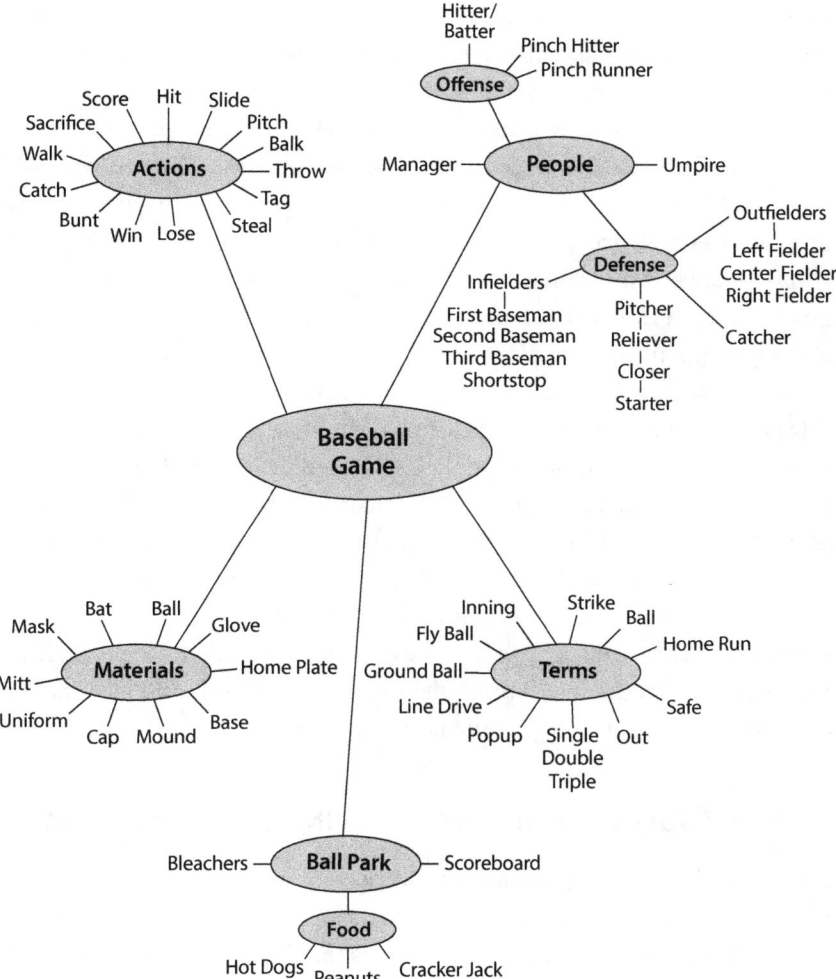

6.1 Baseball semantic map.

established, there is good value in deliberately bringing the items together to see how they differ from each other and where the boundaries between them lie. Seeing items in contrast to each other can clarify their differences in meaning and use, but this contrast should not occur until one or both of them are firmly established. Bringing the items together when one or both have been well established also helps strengthen associations, which may be useful in subsequent use of the items" (2000, 9). In other words, had the colleague above learned the Arabic word for "eggplant" first and then the one for "zucchini" much later, she could have linked the two in her mind afterward as she put together a semantic map of vegetables. At that point, she would not have confused them.

Nation's conclusions seem to support the ALM practice of teaching only the words that are needed for a particular conversation. The problem with many ALM conversations, however, is that they do not always reflect authentic speech. Nation explains that "in addition to the criteria of frequency and avoidance of interference, course designers need to apply a criterion of normal use, meaning that words should occur in normal communication situations, not in contrived, language-focused activities. Using texts, topics, themes, or tasks as the unit of analysis in a course should largely help meet this criterion. On the other hand, using functions, situations, or grammatical features as the unit of analysis is likely to increase the chances of interfering items occurring together. This need not be the case, but without special attention, such occurrences are likely to happen" (2000, 8). The demand for specific vocabulary to achieve particular communicative goals motivates students to learn the appropriate words and expressions. The instructor's or course designer's role is to ensure that students focus on high-frequency words that will enrich their growing lexicons and lead them to acquire greater proficiency in the target language.

VOCABULARY, CULTURE, AND LINGUISTIC REGISTER

Spinelli and Siskin (1992) make the important point that the teaching of vocabulary should be linked to the teaching of culture, since the use of words in discourse, as well as the referents that words denote, is culturally connected. They explain, for example, that textbooks often present "house" vocabulary in a problematic way: "1) the style of the dwelling and/or furniture is culturally generic or oriented toward U.S. culture; 2) little attempt is made to distinguish modern from traditional housing; 3) class distinctions in housing are lacking; 4) geographical location distinctions as they relate to style and price are lacking; 5) explanations of function of rooms/furniture are lacking" (308). DeWaard (2013) provides a similar critique of the Rosetta Stone program, whose photos, used to teach the same vocabulary items across languages, lack cultural authenticity: "There are only four sets of photographs for all the world languages offered: a set for Western languages, a set for Asian languages, and separate sets for Swahili and Latin (Farivar [2006]). If *Rosetta Stone* offers instruction in thirty-one different languages (as of the time of the writing of this paper), it is clear that these four sets cannot begin to be culturally relevant for all of them" (67).

Lord (2015) also criticizes Rosetta Stone for teaching vocabulary, as well as grammar, in isolation. She explains that

> what language instructors know, but stand-alone companies fail to realize, is that in our classes, regardless of delivery medium, we teach our students much more than the simple words and phrases offered by a self-paced stand-alone experience. Not only do we teach culture and pragmatics (which RS does not even attempt to include), but we also provide our students with an understanding of the elements of successful negotiation of meaning, with strategies to assist in real-life communication and breakdowns thereof, and, crucially, how to put all those words and phrases together to create new meaning. Language is so much more than isolated words, and the ability to put them together, to know how to use language—and how to learn language—are invaluable aspects of the learning process. (403)

A colleague tells the story of a recent Uber ride that supports Lord's and DeWaard's assessments. She and a friend were in the back seat and said something to each other in Italian. The driver quickly turned down the radio and announced proudly to them, "Io parlo italiano!" (I speak Italian!). She smiled and responded to him in Italian, but he could not understand what she had said. She tried again, slowing down her speech, using very simple expressions, and overenunciating. Nothing. Finally, he admitted that he had been studying Italian using an app and had been assured by its verification tests that he had attained a pretty high level of proficiency. In fact, he had learned random words in isolation, along with a few stock phrases (such as "Io parlo italiano," which perhaps he should have learned in the negative). Unfortunately, he was unable to understand any of the vocabulary or grammar that he had studied when these expressions were found in an authentic context.

Learning vocabulary items using apps is not an ineffective technique per se; however, learners should study vocabulary that is relevant to what they would like to express and then use it within culturally rich contexts. For example, if a particular unit's focus is on identity, students should compile a vocabulary list that will enable them to express their own sense of self, as well as their perception of others. Perhaps the teacher will provide an initial list of vocabulary for students to learn; it would be linked to a text that students would study. The target vocabulary would include words and phrases of high frequency. Students would later, especially in preparation to create their own texts, be encouraged to fill in the gaps in what they would like to express by adding self-chosen lexical items to their lists. For instance, certain students might need the words "immigrant" or "bilingual" to describe their identity. Most of all, vocabulary must be recycled throughout the course of the semester so that students will remember it. If students see a word only once or twice and then move on, never to use it again, it will be lost.

Reflection

Research some of the vocabulary apps that are currently available to language learners. Do some seem better than others to you? Which one(s) do you think might be useful for your students? Why?

Bourns (2017a) describes an advanced language course that focuses on the idealization of the city of Paris and the French language versus how both have evolved in the twenty-first century. The first half of the semester focuses on texts that demonstrate the glorification of the city and language, as well as nostalgia for what they once were and a pervasive resistance to change. The second half of the semester treats the current city and language and uncovers their modern reality. The spoken French language in particular has diverged from the written form to the point where some linguists have declared them to be separate languages. During the first half of the semester, to prepare for the second, students study between eight and ten words and expressions every week that are found mostly in spoken (or extremely informal written) contexts. The instructor presents four to five contextualized words at the beginning of every class, and students are asked to integrate them into their growing list of slang. The class reviews the words regularly through analyzing discourse snippets that contain them (often in the form of graffiti or social media posts). To recycle vocabulary, the instructor provides students with groups of words that they have previously seen and asks them to decide which one does not fit with the rest of the list (a "one of these things is not like the others" kind of activity, à la *Sesame Street*). For example, in this class, students might find the following word groups:

con   débile   nul   branché

(the first three words are variants of "stupid," while the last one means "with it")

bled   mektoub   toubib   pote

("village," "destiny," "doctor," "friend"; the first three words come from Arabic)

Note that the reason a word does not belong may not have to do with its meaning; it could be, as in the second activity, due to its language of origin.

In the second half of the semester, these expressions appear repeatedly in various film clips and extended readings. Students realize that one of the reasons that they have had such difficulty understanding French films in the past is that they did not know the vocabulary (or grammar, which is also studied) of spoken, informal language. In learning that spoken French is a particular register of the French language (and one that is inappropriate when, say, writing an essay for a literature class or interviewing for a position with a French company), students glean valuable insights into the complexity of spoken and written languages, which is an important goal of the class. In addition, if they master the vocabulary (and grammar) of spoken French and use it appropriately in discourse, it is less likely that Francophones will answer them in English during future interactions.

Contextualized Vocabulary

The "one of these things" activity can be done at any level of instruction. For an elementary class, Spinelli and Siskin (1992) present another effective activity type. After reading a document about making tacos, students are told, "You have been invited to a Mexican friend's home for a taco dinner. As you go to your friend's house, you mentally rehearse how to prepare and eat a taco. Number the following steps to indicate their logical order" (309–10). A more output-focused activity is a dictogloss, which Katz and Blyth describe as "a consciousness-raising activity with a metalinguistic goal [that] calls for students to listen to a short text read aloud several times and then work together in small groups to reconstruct the text as faithfully as possible. Students are encouraged to discuss and justify their linguistic choices with each other. When all the groups have finished, the teacher compares the various reconstructed versions with the original in order to determine whose text is most faithful. The point of the activity is to prompt collaborative metatalk that focuses on various targeted items within the text" (2007, 45). Although typically used to focus on discourse-level grammatical phenomena, dictoglosses are also effective for reviewing and reactivating vocabulary.

Spinelli and Siskin explain that students should engage with vocabulary in a way that encourages them to cross back and forth between their own and the target culture. For example, when learners are studying food, Spinelli and Siskin propose a word-association activity (based on Omaggio 1986, 18) that asks, "What ideas, feelings or occasions do you associate with the following food items? (ham/chicken soup/cookies/beef stew/pie)." They also suggest that students can then brainstorm what comparable food items might mean to the target community (Spinelli and Siskin 1992, 313). To push this activity to the next level, students could conduct some research themselves. They could compare their own cultural norms with the those of the target culture (through interviewing native speakers). For instance, if chicken soup is a comfort food for Americans, it would be interesting to discover what people from other cultures eat to find solace. Furthermore, students could verify whether the idea of comfort food even exists in the target culture.

To study vocabulary at the discourse level (perhaps at a slightly higher level of instruction or supported by ample scaffolding from the instructor) and to focus on the idea of cultural practice, students could watch several film clips that take place at a dinner table in a home or restaurant. Their task would be to determine whether there are certain formulaic sayings that speakers use consistently (such as how they wish each other a pleasant meal, how they ask for something to be passed to them, or how they decline more food). Students should compile a list of expressions and then search online to determine whether these conventions are common or whether they are particular to the data collected.

At all levels, it is useful to have students work with texts of various types to explore both vocabulary and grammar. Again, it is important not to bombard them with vocabulary items that are too closely linked at first, since interference might occur. So, for example, when food is the subject matter, an activity that asks students to choose items from an extensive menu would be more effective at the end of a unit rather than early on. One idea for learning food vocabulary at the earliest levels of instruction is for students to collect advertisements for restaurants in the target culture. For instance, they could look for ads for McDonald's in the language they are studying and then analyze the vocabulary used. Since there are photos of the food, as well as expectations of what one might eat at McDonald's, students could use the visual cues to complete their task. One could argue that McDonald's is not a culturally authentic choice, but the fact that it exists in so many places throughout the world is an interesting reality. The next step might be to compare the McDonald's advertisements with others from the target culture (perhaps for more culturally unique dining venues). Collecting their own advertisements and curating them either on their own or as a class project gives students agency and materials for which they need corresponding vocabulary to discuss their ideas and impressions. In addition, if they are business students (and even if they are not), analyzing how food is marketed in other countries is a valuable cultural learning experience.

Exploring literary texts, short or long, intricate or simple, allows readers to engage with vocabulary in meaningful ways. Below is an excerpt from the literary text "Requiem," which we used in Chapter 5 as a model for teaching tense and aspect. Following the text, we provide a progression of activities designed to help students interact with and learn the vocabulary within the story. These tasks can be done at any level of instruction (although obviously some of the vocabulary that appears in this text is fairly advanced), and they may be seamlessly woven into a lesson that aligns with grammar and also focuses on broader ideas (such as the themes of alienation and nostalgia).

Activity 6.1. Contextualized Vocabulary

Excerpt from "Requiem," by Karen Brennan

I woke up one morning and my country was gone. It was strange. It had been there the night before, sparking and hissing, but now it was gone.

I could feel its absence in the air, which is a feeling like no other.

The garden was still there, the bougainvillea was in some sort of bloom, red blossoms half-opened on thorny stalks. And the house still surrounded me—for the moment, at least. Perhaps it took longer for smaller things to follow suit. All I know is what I'm telling you.

I found my slippers—the little hole in the toe had not grown larger overnight, thank god, and everything was still in the fridge. It's not as if some thief came and stole food. No, it was only the country, the big picture. I wasn't sure where I was.

The sky didn't let on. It was as if the sky knew but wasn't saying anything. I kept looking up. There were no clouds, I can tell you that. I wished there were clouds, truly. They would have given me hope.

As it was, I felt hopeless. I wandered around my home, checking to see. Already I was feeling nostalgic. Yet here was everything in place. The half-full coffeemaker, the slippers, etc.

It was then that I remembered the mouse. Where had the mouse gone? I'd put out a trap and the trap was still armed with a piece of cheddar cheese. No one had nibbled it. I was anxious about the mouse. I didn't want any more disappearances.

Mouse! Mouse! I called, ridiculously, hopefully.

Source: See Appendix B or http://scoundreltime.com/requiem/ for the complete text.

Tasks

1. Use a dictionary to look up the words that you do not recognize in the passage above, and make a list, along with translations into your native language.
2. Compare your words to the following list. Is there overlap?
    sparking
    hissing
    bougainvillea
    in bloom
    blossoms
    thorny
    stalks
    trap
    nibbled
3. Find examples of each of these words in sentences from other texts, and write the sentences below. Are the words used in the same way as in "Requiem"? If not, how do they differ?
4. Find and underline the following phrases in the text, and look them up in a dictionary. Provide translations or definitions for them, and then create your own sentence for each one:

for the moment
to follow suit
the big picture
to give hope (note: this expression appears in the text above as "given me hope")
5. Find three examples of each expression used in other texts, and list them below.
6. Make two lists:
    a. things that the author finds to be the same
    b. things that the author finds to be different
   What generalizations can you make about the two different lists?
7. Choose the word that does not belong in each group (based on the passage), and explain why it does not fit:
    a. hissing   sparking   clouds   nibbling
    b. cheese   slippers   blossoms   coffeemaker
    c. mouse   country   slippers   clouds
   Make up your own word groups using the vocabulary from the story, including one item that does not belong in each.
8. What words from the text do you associate with the following categories?
    a. common household items
    b. a garden
    c. a mouse
    d. country
    e. nostalgia
   What words beyond the text do you associate with each of the categories above? Add them to your list, highlighting them in a different color for each category.

Reflection

1. What strategies for teaching vocabulary do you find included in this sample activity? Can you think of others that might work well? Add them to the activity.
2. Find a short text in the language that you teach, and develop tasks similar to the ones above to help students focus on acquiring the vocabulary contained therein.

Continued . . .

3. After you have read Chapters 7 ("Texts") and 8 ("Writing"), construct prereading, postreading, and writing activities to accompany this text.

A literary text such as "Requiem" can be particularly effective for teaching contextualized vocabulary because it has the potential to be intellectually or emotionally fulfilling. Beneath this simple story lies a deeper level of meaning, which piques students' interest and inspires them to seek (and eventually commit to memory) the meanings of words that they may not yet know. Learning vocabulary as a tool to explore beauty or to discover eternal truths can be a motivating and profoundly satisfying experience.

7 • Texts

FROM READINGS TO TEXTS

What is a text? A text can be "as short and simple as a single letter, such as 'P' for parking, or a word such as 'Exit' or 'Stop,' or as long and complex as a novel" (Kern 2015, 26). Texts can be watched, heard, or, as Braille, touched. A dialogue within a novel is a text, and so are interviews broadcast on the radio or posted on YouTube. Graffiti on a wall, letters penned on handmade paper, messages on a screen, recited poetry, maps, TV commercials, and feature-length films are texts. Reading their intertwined form, content, and cultural significance is an interpretive act wherein the interaction between reader(s) and text produces meaning.

A text is a form of discourse that conveys meaning in a given situation and for a given audience (reader, listener, viewer) via its intertwined content, register, and (if present) linguistic features. Kern (2008) characterizes text as more dynamic than words and sentences. He studies text as "not just an isolated physical artifact" but rather "as it operates (or is operated upon) in relation to its contexts of use" (371). When a text is considered in terms of discourse, it is defined "not by its linguistic extent but by its social intent" (Widdowson 2004, 8).

We begin this chapter with an overview of the evolving role of reading and the interpretation of texts in language teaching. The chapter closes with a discussion of renewed attention to texts in light of content- and literacy-based approaches. With this theoretical context in mind, we discuss how attention to textual genre and interaction with the text in stages can help students engage with readings, audio texts, images, video texts, and feature films. Strategies that guide students to explore these traditional text types can also help learners navigate newer, socially mediated genres (social networks, video games, etc.). The final portion of the chapter addresses how pedagogical approaches to the interpretation of texts in lower-level courses benefit students who explore texts at even the most advanced levels.

Reflection

Look at the instructional materials, textbook, and/or online program(s) for the course(s) you are teaching. If you have other textbooks for that course level on hand, compare a few.

1. Where and how frequently do texts (readings, images, audio, video) appear in the book or program? Would you say that texts are central or peripheral to each lesson and chapter presented?
2. What textual genres are included (letters, postcards, blogs, want ads, short stories, dialogues, poems, movie reviews, videos)? Do they pique your interest? Are they authentic (produced for native speakers, not for the textbook) or scripted (created specifically for pedagogical use)?
3. What types of activities accompany the texts? Do the activities engage students with form, meaning, or both?
4. Are texts integral to the presentation of new vocabulary and grammar?

THE PLACE OF TEXTS IN A TWO-TIERED SYSTEM

The relatively limited treatment of reading in basic language courses over many decades of the twentieth century may have had more to do with departmental structures than with SLA research. Traditionally, university language departments have designed their curricula in two tiers (see Chapter 11). Among the underlying assumptions of this system are that language and literature belong to distinct disciplines requiring different tools for learning and that students must achieve a certain command of grammar and syntax in their first few years of coursework before moving on to engage with literature and other texts. The chiasmus *learning to read . . . reading to learn* has been widely used over the past decades, and not only in foreign language pedagogy, to situate perspectives on reading and the curriculum (for example, see Chall, Jacobs, and Baldwin 1990). In a bifurcated curricular structure, students *learn to read* (by decoding grammar and vocabulary) in basic language courses, then *read to learn* (by focusing less on language, more on meaning) in upper-level courses.

More recently, researchers have argued that learning to read and reading to learn are mutually reinforcing processes that both take place from the earliest through the most advanced learning levels. No longer relegated to a special section at the end of a textbook chapter, reading a range of text types instead complements interpretive, interpersonal, and presentational communication. These entwined modalities function as part of a dynamic, interactive, collaborative process that promotes learning through simultaneous engagement with form and content.

To distinguish between linear and multidimensional approaches to reading, researchers refer to top-down, bottom-up, and interactive processes (Adair-Hauck and Cumo-Johanssen 1997; Paesani, Allen, and Dupuy 2016, 141–42). In a linear approach to reading, learners construct meaning from the bottom up, moving their focus from letters to words to phrases. Top-down processes are more holistic and discourse oriented. They encourage readers' active participation in constructing meaning through predictions and hypotheses. Interactive processing involves a multidimensional mix of bottom-up and top-down strategies that learners may practice both autonomously and collaboratively.

LITERACY AND MULTILITERACIES

Literacy, in the context of foreign language learning, means more than an ability to read and write. Kern maintains that because it emphasizes them "in their social contexts of use," a literacy-focused approach "frames reading and writing as complementary dimensions of written communication, rather than as utterly distinct linguistic and cognitive processes" (2000, 3). According to Kern, who aligns with Halliday's (1978) notion of "language as social semiotic" and Kramsch's (2006) "symbolic competence" (the use of semiotic practices both to make and to convey meaning), language is always interpreted within a sociocultural context. Since "literacy" refers to both cognitive and social knowledge, it depends as much on readers as on texts. Informed by the theoretical and practical implications of a literacy-based approach, some scholars advocate a framework that builds upon what the New London Group (1996) calls "a pedagogy of multiliteracies." As Paesani, Allen, and Dupuy (2016) demonstrate, a multiliteracies approach involves engagement with a tremendous scope of textual genres, including, but not restricted to, literary works.

GENRE AND SELECTION OF TEXTS

What makes one written text more accessible to language students than another? Are short prose passages easier to read than novels? Are want ads more literally decipherable than poems? These questions reflect practical concerns for teachers using a literacy-based approach, or what Maxim calls "textually oriented pedagogy" (2006, 23). Scholars characterize textual genre as "a staged, goal-oriented, purposeful activity in which speakers engage as members of our culture" (Martin 1984, 25), as "recognizable and yet dynamic" (Byrnes et al. 2006, 89), and as having "a set of communicative purpose(s) identified and mutually understood by members of the professional or academic community in which it regularly occurs" (Bhatia 1993, 13). Berg and Martin-Berg (2001) recommend fairy tales and legends for intermediate-level courses because students already have exposure to the structural and stylistic elements of these genres (even if the texts are used differently) in their L1 reading.

The genre of a text does not necessarily determine its difficulty, nor does the word count or the topic, yet these features have to be considered when selecting foreign language texts that will motivate students to read and help them learn. The relative difficulty of different genres depends to some extent on the type of grammar and vocabulary used. A first-semester student studying a Romance language would feel more comfortable working with the present tense than with multiple past tenses, for example, but grammar structures alone do not determine a text's accessibility.

Drawing on research by Halliday (1993), Gee (1998), Bhatia (2002), and other studies related to discourse and the L2 curriculum, Byrnes et al. (2006) propose a sequence of genre-based learning tasks organized not according to grammatical structures but in terms of discourse style. The sequence reflects a move in reading and writing from the personal to the public sphere (94). By codifying textual genres within a framework of discourse styles (designated as primary, "blurred," and secondary), Byrnes et al. address the variable difficulty of given text types: a cartoon, a poem, a personal narrative, or a TV ad may be appropriate for beginning, intermediate, or advanced students, depending on its discourse style.

Activity 7.1. Finding Textual Genres for Your Course

The following table offers suggestions for text types and genres that could be used in a curriculum that reinforces, from semester to semester, the themes of individual and national identity. These categories are of course fluid: some poems work well for beginning students, others for more advanced learners. Add genres to each level based on the texts that you use or would use in your courses. Cross out and replace the suggestions in the cells that would not apply well to the language you teach. Then fill in the second row with text types related to a theme of your choice.

Table 7.1. Sample Genres for Investigating Themes at Different Class Levels

Theme	Beginning Level	Intermediate Level	Advanced Level
individual and national identity	cartoons (simple) comic strips graffiti national IDs online chats opinion polls passports photographs postcards postage stamps posters print ads	blog posts interviews journal excerpts online chats poems songs TV ads	blog posts graphic novels interviews journals memoirs online chats op-eds plays poems political cartoons political pamphlets, signs, etc. talk shows TV ads
[theme]			

> **Reflection**
>
> 1. Think about or discuss which genres in the table above would work best at given levels and why.
> 2. What are the advantages of using authentic texts for the language you teach? Are there disadvantages? What challenges are specific to the language you teach? How do they affect your choice of genres and texts? Which genres would work best in elementary courses? Intermediate? Advanced?

SEQUENCED INTERACTION WITH TEXTS

Schema theory, a cognitive learning model proposed by the experimental psychologist Frederic Bartlett in 1932, gained traction in ESL and foreign language settings in the 1980s. This theory, which takes into account the systematic organization of knowledge in the brain, says that "comprehending a text is an interactive process between the reader's background knowledge and the text" (Carrell and Eisterholdt 1983, 556). As Rumelhart explains, "According to schema theories, all knowledge is packaged into units. These units are the schemata. Embedded in these packages of knowledge is, in addition to the knowledge itself, information about how this knowledge is to be used. A schema, then, is a data structure for representing the generic concepts stored in memory" (1980, 34, cited in Lee and VanPatten 2003, 218). Therefore, reading comprehension involves much more than mastery of grammar and vocabulary or skillful decoding of language. Students will understand L2 texts more easily if they activate their background knowledge, or schemata, before they begin reading, listening, or viewing. Then, in a global phase, they should skim and scan the text for general information related to, for example, genre, topic, and tone. After this segment, students can read more closely for specific information, and finally they can express their own ideas in writing or speech about the text they have just explored.

Schema theory and literacy-based learning have inspired scholars to develop various models of reading, listening, and viewing in stages (e.g., Swaffar and Arens 2005; Maxim 2006; Hedgcock and Ferris 2009). A multiliteracies paradigm (New London Group 1996) refers not to schemata but to Available Designs, a concept that takes into account both readers and text in the production of meaning. The PACE model (Adair-Hauck and Donato 2002, 2015), developed as a whole-language approach to teaching grammar and vocabulary, resonates with many of the stage-based models for reading, listening, and viewing developed in the late twentieth and early twenty-first centuries. The strategy involves teaching new grammar and vocabulary in the context of an authentic written or audio text, in a series of four stages: interactive *Presentation* of the text; *Attention* focused on a specific language structure featured in the text; *Co-construction* of how the featured language element is formed and how it functions, via guided observation, hypothesizing, and analysis; and an *Expansion* activity, which allows students to express themselves, to create their own meaning with the grammar or vocabulary they have just discovered via the sample text. Though texts are essential to the PACE model, this system is designed primarily to focus on form delivered in rich, authentic context, but not necessarily to develop reading or interpretive skills per se.

Although paradigms for approaching texts in stages have been devised on the bases of different emphases and pedagogical philosophies, each addresses the need for students to connect with the text before, during, and after a relatively uninterrupted reading, viewing, or listening experience. With these frameworks in mind, we propose the following five-stage model for interpretation of any text type at any level. The stages represent shifting distances between the text and the reader. The borders between stages are otherwise quite permeable. Students indeed always focus, interact, engage, and create when dealing with texts, but with varying degrees of depth and balance. Instructors should select the activities that best foster learning in terms of course goals. Sections can then be fine-tuned and expanded to promote the presentation and practice of new grammatical or lexical items, although the grammar and vocabulary are here conceived of as tools for interacting with the text. Whether students carry out the activities in class or at home, we recommend an in-class follow-up at each stage.

Preview

The preview usually takes place in class, guided by the instructor, in small groups or as a whole class. Its purpose is to prepare students

Continued . . .

for the content, form, and genre they will encounter and to activate background experience and knowledge of the topic and genre that they will bring to the text. Out-of-class activities include reviewing information that students already have (from movies, readings, or images they have already encountered dealing with a specific theme) and gathering basic contextual information (e.g., through internet searches for the name of a film director, writer, or artist; for examples of the genre in the target language; or for related cultural or historical information).

Interact

Guided-whole-group, small-group, and individual activities give students a sense of the text through skimming and scanning for a few key items. These activities allow students to make predictions about tone and content based on certain textual features. For longer texts that students will read, view, or hear on their own, outside class, have them interact first in class, to build interest in continued engagement.

Focus

In the focus stage, students read, view, or listen at their own pace with few interruptions, in or out of class as time allows, directed via questions or note-taking tasks, the latter perhaps done with collaborative annotation software for longer texts (see Blyth 2013). Guided note-taking and comprehension questions help students understand the text as a whole: the plot or story (if there is one), what happens, who is speaking to whom, the tone, the purpose, and the perspective. These activities can also be designed to present or practice grammar or vocabulary. Be sure to not overwhelm students as they read, listen, or view: if there are several tasks to perform, allow for several readings or viewings, or divide the tasks among students.

Engage

Engagement is grounded in the analysis and discussion of more nuanced topics, such as theme, tone, or perspective. It includes a focus on grammar in context and more in-depth interaction with genre

Continued . . .

elements. This stage can take place in class or in an online forum, in a blog, etc.

Create

Students draw upon what they have learned about the textual genre, the topic, the themes, and the linguistic forms to express their own meaning, compare texts, consider broader contexts, explore related works, state opinions, and generate their own texts or projects.

Reading Written Texts

The following sequence of reading activities is designed for a print advertisement in English that has both visual and written components. This ad for Campbell's soup appeared in the *Saturday Evening Post* on January 6, 1945, toward the end of World War II (see Figure 7.1). The suggested questions and activities could be adapted to suit individual, collaborative, in-class, or online formats. Students would not necessarily perform all the activities or answer all the questions suggested for each stage; activities would also be fine-tuned to reinforce the specific themes, grammar, and vocabulary being treated in a particular course. Here we focus on the themes of personal and national identity.

Activity 7.2. Five-Stage Reading Activity for a Campbell's Soup Print Ad

Preview (small-group or whole-class activity)

- What kinds of food do you associate with home and comfort?
- Why do people serve precooked food (canned soups, frozen dinners, etc.) at home?
- On TV and in print today, what kind(s) of people do you see in advertisements for soups and other prepared foods that are served at home? Singles? Families? Which family members?
- What is a housewife? The term used to be widely used, but it is less popular today. What other terms can replace it? Can you think of TV shows, movies, or other media that depict the stereotypical image of a "happy housewife"?

7.1 Print advertisement for Campbell's soup from the *Saturday Evening Post*, January 6, 1945. Ad used with permission granted by the Campbell Soup Company.

Interact (small-group or whole-class activity)

- Looking at only the picture of the woman, can you guess approximately when the ad was produced? How can you tell? Have you seen similar ads? Where?
- Who is saying, "Just a good plain cook—that's me"?
- Describe the woman in as much detail as possible. What does the physical depiction of the woman suggest about her social class, her style, her lifestyle, her personality? Does she conform to the stereotype of the happy housewife?
- What product is being advertised?
- Based on the picture of the woman, who are the ad's target buyers?
- Skim the ad and make a list of its elements, besides the picture of the woman and the tag line, "Just a good plain cook . . ." How many images are there? How many blocks of text?

Focus (individual task in class or at home)

1. Read the blocks of text in the ad (see Figures 7.2 and 7.3). As you read, make a list of words (nouns, adjectives, verbs) associated with the woman in this ad.
2. In addition to the woman featured, which two people are quoted?
3. Name two things the woman likes to cook.
4. True or false?
   a. The woman is a good cook.
   b. The woman spends eight hours each day in the kitchen.
   c. The woman grew up eating Campbell's soup.
   d. Once the war is over, the woman will stop using canned soup.
   e. The vegetable soup is vegetarian.
5. Circle the word in each pair that best reflects the mood or message communicated by the pictures and the written portions of the ad:
   comfort/fear   simplicity/complication
   optimism/pessimism   straightforward/deceptive
   pride/timidity   strength/weakness
   confidence/uncertainty   energy/lethargy
   hope/despair

... with pride in my fluffy biscuits and deep-dish apple pie. That's why I serve Campbell's Vegetable Soup, too—because it's the kind that always brings a smile from Harry (he's my husband)—and gets him fondly saying, "Thank my lucky stars I married a gal who's got a knowing hand in the kitchen."

And let me tell you, when this war is a thing of the past, and I can spend eight beautiful hours a day in my own kitchen if I want to, Campbell's are *still* making the vegetable soup at our house! It's every bit as good as the finest my mother ever made! Matter of fact, the joke's on me—for when I told Mother so she said, "Goodness, you've eaten Campbell's Vegetable Soup all your life!"

A Rich Stock simmered from fine beef and 15 different kinds of luscious garden vegetables, fixed as fussily and cooked as carefully as you would do, in your own kitchen—that's what makes Campbell's Vegetable Soup rate high with home cooks everywhere!

7.2-3 Details of Campbell's soup advertisement.

Engage (in-class, small-group or whole-group discussion)

1. The ad was published in 1945. Is that approximately the time you guessed? The woman makes reference to "this war." Which war was it?
2. Without using the word "America," the ad appeals to a certain image or self-image of the USA cultivated especially during World War II. What elements of the ad create a sense of American identity and even

patriotism? Consider the layout; objects and people depicted in a positive light; and adjectives, adverbs, and nouns.
3. Does some language in the ad sound outdated today? How would you rephrase it to modernize it?

Create (individual and group tasks; see the rubrics and other strategies for teaching and assessing writing in Chapter 8)

1. In your journal, describe the ad, as if to someone who has not seen it. Then reflect and write about its explicit message and the implicit, or underlying, messages that it communicates.
2. In pairs or small groups: Imagine you are in the advertising business and you are pitching this ad. Write your pitch and present it to the class.
3. The words and image in this ad suggest an everyday story. Dramatize this story for TV, using dialogue instead of prose to sell the product.
4. The woman says that once the war is over, she will be able to spend more time in the kitchen. Though there is no mention of a job, it is likely that readers in 1945 would have understood that this fictional woman volunteered or worked outside the home to support the war effort and that she would return to full-time homemaking after the war. The fictional character Rosie the Riveter became the face of hundreds of thousands of women who worked in factories during World War II. Find J. Howard Miller's poster of Rosie the Riveter. How is she dressed? What is her slogan? What characteristics does she share with the woman in the soup ad (see the vocabulary in Focus #1, above)? Could Rosie's slogan apply to the woman in the soup ad as well?
5. The ad text is written as if the woman depicted were speaking directly to the reader. The language, however, does not always sound natural or like casual, spoken English today. Rewrite the first two paragraphs, staying as close as you can to the original but updating to a spoken register that sounds natural today.
6. Create a new version of this ad for a food product of your era, on paper or digitally. Include a picture, a tag line or slogan, and advertising text.

> **Reflection**
>
> 1. Identify two grammar points and two groups of vocabulary words your students could discover as they explore this text.
> 2. Create specific activities for one of these grammar or vocabulary points (see Chapters 5 and 6 for models).

Reading Visual Texts

Images can play a key role in providing contexts for vocabulary and in helping students visualize words and concepts that may translate easily to English but that look very different in target cultures: bread, hotels, cake, or taxis (Bush 2007; see also Chapter 9). Presented in the prereading/prelistening/previewing phase, images can bridge the space between students' existing knowledge and beliefs and the new material encountered in written or audiovisual texts. Images also stand alone as texts to be "read" using the multistage process proposed above for written texts. Since images do not model language, student interactions have been designed in terms of observation and description, moving from literal to figurative or from objective facts to subjective reactions. Scanlan (1997) divides the reading of photographs into three levels: (1) the literal level (students describe observable facts with the language they already know; the teacher may use guided discussion to introduce key vocabulary that is essential to the basic description), (2) the interpretive-applied level (students make verifiable inferences based on the observable facts [e.g., it is cold outside, or the people are in a small village]; they look for relationships between people and between people and objects; and they speculate about the setting, the age and social status of the people depicted, and their actions and motivations), and (3) the imaginative level (students respond subjectively to photographs, make unverifiable hypotheses, and create interior monologues and biographical information for the people depicted). In their articulation of an approach to "teaching cultural and linguistic competence through the analysis of images," Barnes-Karol and Broner (2010, 422) propose a sequence of interaction with culturally relevant images in previewing, viewing (detailed description), and postviewing (meta-reflection) stages (430).

Scanlan points out that to discuss photographs (and by extension, we

7.4 *America at the Polls*, by Norman Rockwell. Printed by permission of the Norman Rockwell Family Agency. Copyright ©1944 the Norman Rockwell Family Entities.

would add paintings, postcards, and any image with similar contextual, technical, and compositional elements), students will need to know basic terms like *edge, photograph, photographer, camera, foreground, background, setting,* and *black and white* (1997, 352). Attention to compositional elements is especially important if the photograph (or painting) is being presented and analyzed as a work of visual art. If, at lower levels of instruction, students are asked to read and analyze only the content of the image, the vocabulary of placement ("left," "right," "foreground," "background") will help them, but the metalexicon related to the image's creation ("the painter," "the photographer," "the brushstrokes," "the paint") could be saved for a different type of discussion.

Norman Rockwell's *America at the Polls* (1944) interacts with the theme of national identity toward the end of WWII (see Figure 7.4). A writer, painter, and prolific illustrator, Rockwell (1894–1978) is known for his often idealized and sentimentalized depictions of everyday American life. He also took on serious topics, as in his depiction of the now iconic Rosie the Riveter and in *The Problem We All Live With* (1964), an unflinching response to the racist violence inspired by Ruby Bridges's integration into the all-white William Frantz Elementary School, in the American South. President Obama displayed the latter painting in the White House. This background information could be presented in the preview, or students could be guided to find it on their own. For this activity, "readers" will need to know some basic terms: *to vote, polling station/voting station, voting booth, poll workers, to cast a vote*. This vocabulary could be woven into various tasks, including previewing discussions.

Activity 7.3. Five-Stage Reading Activity for a Norman Rockwell Illustration

Preview (teacher-guided whole-group discussion or small-group or individual internet search)

Show or have students find a color copy of the illustration, widely available online.

1. Have you heard of Norman Rockwell? Who is he? When did he live and work? Why is he well known? [*Be prepared to provide additional information or facts if this activity is treated as a whole-group discussion.*]
2. What sorts of subjects did Rockwell paint? [*Show a few well-known works.*]
3. We're going to describe and discuss a painting of an American voting station. Have you been able to vote in a national election? If not, in what election year will you be of legal voting age?
4. Where do people go to vote in your neighborhood? (A school? A church? A library?)
5. Have you seen a voting booth? Not all voting booths are the same. Search for a few images of voting booths in the US.

Interact (small-group activity)

1. What are the first things you notice when you look at the painting? Do certain people or objects stand out?
2. How many people do you see?

Focus (individual or small-group tasks)

1. Make a numbered list of the individuals depicted, from left to right, starting with the woman in red shoes, whose face is mostly out of the frame. Look at their feet to determine the order. Describe them physically, and describe what they are doing, in as much detail as possible: man or woman, voter or poll worker, clothing, actions. How many are waiting to vote? Will they be able to vote soon? How many are in the process of casting their vote? How many have already voted? How many are working at the polling station?
2. What kind of animal do you see? Where is it?

3. Make a list of the objects that you see.
4. What colors do you see? What is the most colorful part of the image?

Engage

1. Does the action seem to take place in a big city or a small town?
2. The building where the polling station is set up is not identified. What could it be?
3. After looking more closely, do you see the same number of people in the painting now as you did at first? Which person is mostly hidden?
4. Do the people waiting appear to be inconvenienced? Bored? Happy? Indifferent? How can you tell?
5. Circle the word in each pair that best reflects the mood or message of the panting:
   efficient   disorderly
   modest   arrogant
   calm   agitated
   clear   confusing
6. Sort the objects that you see into these categories: background objects; objects people are touching/using; objects that could be (but are not being) used.
7. Look at everything that is red. How does the color red direct your viewing?
8. The seven voters represented in the painting illustrate stages of passing through the polling station. Based on their actions, explain what an individual voter would do here: *First, you stand in line . . .*
9. What message does the open voting booth convey to the viewer?
10. This painting was published under the title *America at the Polls*, not *Voters at the Polls* or *Citizens at the Polls*. What is the portrait of "America" conveyed in this painting? How is America characterized (friendly, rude, welcoming, powerful, modest, straightforward, inclusive, urban . . .)?
11. This image originally appeared in the *Saturday Evening Post* on November 4, 1944. What is the importance of this year in American history? Does the year explain to some extent the demographic represented in the painting (more women, no young men)?
12. Both the Rockwell painting and the Campbell's soup ad (see Activity 7.2) were produced during and engage (explicitly and implicitly) with

wartime. In what ways are these responses to the war similar? Think of the visual style, the settings and contexts, and the message.

Create

1. Imagine that you are one of the voters, writing a letter to a family member, perhaps a soldier, far away. Describe the voting experience from this perspective.
2. Describe the scene from the perspective of a reporter for a local newspaper.
3. Rockwell offers a snapshot of certain voters at a certain time in a certain place. In so doing, he conveys a message about the US. What snapshot would you like to offer of a voting station in the US today? Think about geographical setting (city, town), specific setting (a library, a school), the voters (men, women, young, old), etc.

Reading Audio and Video Texts

Although it is tempting to try to understand an audio text in full, it is often logistically impossible to catch every word in real-world situations. Phone messages can be played back again and again, but airport announcements, a song heard on the radio while you are driving, and a tour guide's scripted commentary do not lend themselves to pause and replay. Certain strategies, much like those that bolster reading comprehension, can help learners effectively process the language they hear. The following list is compiled from articles by Goh (1998), Vandergrift (1998), and Cohen, Oxford, and Chi (2005):

Successful foreign language listeners
- resist the temptation to translate word for word,
- focus on semantic cues,
- ask for clarification and attempt to negotiate meaning,
- chunk larger units of meaning,
- use varied strategies depending on context, type of text, type of interaction, etc.,
- make predictions about the listening text, and
- practice "skim listening" by paying attention to some parts and ignoring others.

With daily access to television, movies, YouTube, and other audiovisually designed cyberspaces, students may have more exposure to video texts than to audio texts in their native language, making this medium especially appealing to language learners. Visual cues such as gestures, body language, facial expressions, graphs, charts, and written words also make video texts less intimidating, since they can help students understand language that would be less easily decipherable in pure audio form.

Comprehending a video text may involve simultaneously reading charts and other written material on the screen, noticing facial gestures and body language and movement, and listening to spoken language from one or more voices. Although these multiple audio and visual cues may help students understand the text, this abundance of input can be a lot to encounter at once. For this reason, most models of sequenced viewing begin with a silent phase (see Swaffar and Vlatten 1997).

Activity 7.4. Five-Stage Viewing Activity for a Salvo TV Commercial

Television commercials are easy to work with in class because they are brief (this one runs less than a minute), they tend to present traditional narrative elements (a scene, a situation, characters, actions, and a story), and they are designed to grab the viewer's attention. Since they are pitched at certain buyers, commercials reveal a great deal about the social climate of their era.

Like the 1945 print ad for Campbell's soup (see Activity 7.2), the detergent commercial at https://www.youtube.com/watch?v=gOpCJoZXpZo ("Salvo Detergent Commercial from the Early 70's") depicts a working housewife. In the early 1970s, Salvo ran a series of ads featuring working women suspected (usually by a mother-in-law) of shirking their homemaking duties. Here, when Pam arrives home from work, groceries in hand, she overhears her husband and mother-in-law talking about her.

The suggested activities below could be carried out in class (whole-group or small-group discussion) or at home, depending on course goals. We recommend at least one silent viewing in class to motivate and prepare students to complete the work outside class.

Preview

Think of TV commercials for laundry detergent that feature families. How do these ads present women? As overwhelmed, unhappy, competent, joyful, frenzied . . . ?

162 TEXTS

Interact

1. Watch the commercial with no sound. How would you describe the three characters? What is their relationship to one another?
2. Narrate the main actions that you see, using the present tense. [*If you are working on present-tense verbs with elementary-level students, provide a list of infinitives: to arrive, to listen, to talk, etc.*]

Focus

1. Watch a second time without sound. Circle all the items that you see from the list below.
    a. A bag of groceries
    b. Coffee cups
    c. A coffee pot
    d. A coffee cake
    e. A stove
    f. A refrigerator
    g. A sugar bowl
    h. Laundry detergent
2. Now watch with sound and determine if the following statements are true or false:
    a. The man is Pam's husband.
    b. The husband's name is Harold.
    c. The older woman is Pam's mother.
    d. Pam has trouble juggling her job and housekeeping.
    e. Harold is wearing a new shirt.
    Correct the statements that are false.
3. What is the ad's slogan? Listen again to fill in the words:
    _____, _____ Salvo tablets. Real help for the _____ _____ woman.
    [*"Simple, pure Salvo tablets. Real help for the busy working woman."*]

Engage

1. This commercial was filmed in the 1970s, in the middle of the era of what is now called second-wave feminism. Second-wave feminism was concerned, in part, with finding ways to liberate the traditional housewife. In what ways does this commercial represent

a modernized version of the married woman and the married man? What more traditional ideas are reinforced in the commercial?
2. Salvo tablets are described as "pure" and "simple." This characterization is important for advertising the product, since it cleans and should be easy to use. How are these qualities important for the overall image of the "modern" family depicted in the ad?

Create

1. Tell the story of what happened, starting with the moment just before the action of the commercial begins. Present the information from the perspective of one of the characters. Use the present tense. [*See Chapter 8 for a discussion of techniques for scaffolding writing assignments.*]

    PAM: "So I run out for groceries after work, and when I come home from the grocery store . . ."

    MOTHER-IN-LAW: "So I drop in to see Harold and Pam, and when I arrive, she's not home . . ."

    HAROLD: "So I'm home alone and the doorbell rings. It's my mother . . ."

2. Role reversal: Rewrite the commercial with Pam in the kitchen and Harold coming home with groceries. Then film or perform the skit for the class.
3. Update the ad, and perform it or film it for the class.
4. Both the 1945 Campbell's soup ad and this detergent ad from the 1970s present working women. What qualities do these women share? How are they different? Write a short essay comparing the two.

FEATURE FILMS: CHALLENGES AND BENEFITS

Unless students are majoring in media studies or taking courses on cinema as an art form, they probably do not think of film viewing as a road to literacy. Most of us watch films in our native language simply for short-term entertainment. Students may already realize that they read a work like *The Great Gatsby* differently on the beach than they would in an American literature class, but they may not have had an opportunity to make that sort of critical distinction when it comes to a favorite movie like *Harry Potter and the Prisoner of Azkaban* or *The Wizard of Oz*. While they may have engaged in the close reading of a poem, the idea of lingering on a single, three-minute sequence or taking notes while viewing or rewatching a film that is not a childhood or holiday favorite may be new to them. Moreover, students who have read and analyzed literary texts in high school do not automatically adapt their critical thinking tools from literature to film.

This disconnection may hold true for students' film-viewing experiences in foreign language classes thus far. Films may have been shown as complements to reading; as illustrations of places, objects, and cultural practices; as rewards or breaks from rigorous coursework; or as extra-credit incentives for students to engage further with the language outside class. In such cases, when the film is not deeply connected to the curriculum, a brief personal reaction may be the only follow-up that time allows: *I liked it; I didn't like it; It was too slow; I preferred the book; Sometimes I didn't need the subtitles; They spoke quickly.*

Moving beyond these initial, subjective reactions does not necessarily come easily for students or for teachers. Instructors who understand that they may teach a given poem or short story dozens of times in their careers often balk at the idea of teaching the same film yet again. Similarly, those who have not studied cinema may initially default to "I like it"/"I don't like it" when selecting or discussing films. Years of watching films as a leisure activity, and the pleasure of watching films, should certainly be acknowledged, even when the goal is to move beyond the initial "I liked it" phase. A student's first experience of treating film as a cultural product and as a means of attaining literacy may take place in the foreign language class. Ideally, students should be able to express their emotional and other personal reactions to a movie, and then move on to a more objective experience.

Reflection

1. Make a list of challenges that feature films in the target language present to both teachers and students. Consider content, language, logistics, time, technology, etc.
2. Now make a list of some of the advantages of using feature films in language courses. Do any of your pros and cons overlap?
3. Does the language that you teach present any particular challenges with respect to film?
4. Do you need to be a scholar of cinema to teach films in a language class? Explain.

It is possible that some of the items on your pro list were also cons. For example, films provide exposure to contextualized language, spoken in multiple voices (of men, women, children, adults) and regional accents that might not be heard in the classroom. This diversity offers valuable opportunities to explore language (for both students and teachers), but it can be daunting if students are used to hearing the target language modeled only in the teacher's voice. Likewise, films bring rich cultural information to the classroom that many students and teachers will not be able to experience firsthand, and this encounter can also be overwhelming. To help navigate the linguistic and cultural terrain that feature films offer, it is important to anticipate what students might find useful to know before watching a film, details on which they might get snagged while viewing it, and questions they will probably ask right afterward.

Selection of Films

Film selection should take into account the language modeled, formal and cultural complexity, and the film's relation to course content in general. For students in elementary and intermediate courses, most films will be difficult to understand without subtitles and some may be almost incomprehensible, due to the age of the (restored) soundtrack, the use of dialects that are completely new to students, the speed of dialogue delivery, or particularly advanced and abstract vocabulary. Even native speakers find some films in their language difficult to understand. Although it is not vital that students understand all or even most of the dialogue, if a film's language is completely inaccessible, it can be frustrating or demotivating for listeners.

Reflection

1. Are there any films in the language you teach that you especially like but that might not be the best choice for your class(es)? Why?
2. Think of three films that would motivate your students and help them learn more about the target language and culture.
3. Do you think that students might have expectations for foreign movies based on their experience with American films? What can one typically expect from an American movie? How might

Continued . . .

> you prepare students for the fact that foreign films do not always contain these components?

Sequenced Interaction with Films

Preview and Interact

One of the easiest ways to prepare students to watch an entire film *outside* class is to handle the previewing phase in class. The advantage of using film trailers in the L2 is that they tend to run under three minutes and are widely available online. They also often mix sound, text, and image. Because they are designed to build interest and lure potential viewers, trailers are usually edited to highlight major themes and actions and to engage the viewer in anticipating plot turns.

Brief sequences also provide opportunities for students to anticipate the film's plot, characters, setting, and tone before watching the entire movie. Rather than search the film for the perfect clip, simply start with the first sequence. It may or may not include credits, depending on how the film is composed. It may include much, little, or no dialogue. Try to limit this anticipatory viewing to two to four minutes. Let the length of the sequence determine the time. While students will most likely need to watch the full film with subtitles, this initial clip should be short enough to show without subtitles. Begin with a guided silent viewing. Let the film itself determine the focus. If many pertinent vocabulary words are illustrated, students can skim the images for selected items: a street, a bicycle, an umbrella, a dog, etc. Some sequences lend themselves to being narrated by students. Through silent viewing, students will get the gist of the genre, the time period, the setting, and some of the character types. They may then make predictions about the soundtrack: What style of music do they imagine (jazz, classical, none at all)? What mood (bright, melancholic, brisk)? Are there other ambient sounds (voices, traffic, birds, thunder)? Students can then confirm their hypotheses with a first sound viewing. Focus on language to the extent that is appropriate for their level. With some films, students will be able to determine register (formal, informal) and the tone or mood of the characters speaking. With others, they may be able to fill in blanks or answer comprehension questions. End the viewing with sound by having students make predictions about the film. Will it be funny? Will it be sad? Will there be a love story? Which characters will be important? Will there be a happy ending?

Films inevitably contain cultural references that cannot be covered in detail in class, but the gaps will pique students' interest. Assign internet searches (in class or for homework) that will help students understand such references. For example, Jacques Demy's Umbrellas of Cherbourg (1964) shows a family serving a king cake on Epiphany and placing a crown on the head of the person who finds a charm in her slice. Internet prompts for this film could include locating Cherbourg on a map, finding an explanation of and recipe for king cake, and watching a video demonstration of how to bake this cake. Not only will internet searches help students understand the film in the short term, but just as important, they will gain reading experience by skimming and scanning web articles (preferably in the target language), while relating information from the film to life outside the classroom.

Focus

One of the practical reasons for note-taking while watching films is to create an accessible map of what happened, where, and with which characters. This activity is something all students should do, at all levels. Have them structure their notes according to scene changes: (1) in the café, (2) on the subway, (3) at dinner, and so on. Under these headings, they should jot down the names of characters as they are mentioned or depicted, along with any significant plot points (the mother and daughter have an argument; the teacher is fired), any words they would like to remember, and, of course, any ideas that come to mind as they watch.

This baseline note-taking will help students remember character names and the general flow of action. In addition, it can give them a more specific viewing focus, depending on the sort of discussion, writing, and other extension activities you would like them to be able to handle. Remember that students need to focus on what they see and hear—most likely while reading subtitles too. Do not overwhelm them with tasks. If you will be addressing many facets of the film, assign specific note-taking as a sort of jigsaw puzzle: Students with last names beginning with A–G, for example, should pay special attention to exterior places in the city—subways, streets, buildings, etc. Are they clean, crowded, friendly, menacing? Students with H–M last names, on the other hand, can be asked to pay special attention to relationships among strangers. Who talks to whom? Are these exchanges friendly? Students whose last names begin with N–Z should note interior spaces: kitchens, classrooms, cafés, etc. What sorts of actions and conversations happen in these places? Are they friendly, hostile, personal? And so on. After seeing the film, students will bring their special knowledge to the discussion where these threads of note-taking converge around thematic and cultural questions.

Engage

Sequenced discussions about films help students confirm their basic comprehension before tackling specific information or themes. Co-constructing the plot, student by student, is an effective way to jog their memories and confirm their comprehension while practicing the vocabulary needed to talk about the film. In most languages, students will want to use the present tense, not only to avoid complication but also because it is customary in literary and film criticism to summarize plots in the present. Begin with a simple prompt: How does the movie begin? Then: What happens? With whom? Where? And then? Why? Once students have refreshed their memories, move on to more specific questions (multiple choice, fill-in-the-blank, sequencing of events, etc.) to be sure that everyone has a grasp of the basic information presented in the film. For elementary students (or even more advanced ones), true-or-false statements about the plot can provide a comprehension check, along with model sentences incorporating vocabulary that students will be able to use in discussion.

Students should also have a chance to express their personal reactions to the film, which, after all, is usually the first thing that most people do after seeing a movie in a nonacademic context. The reactions that students express pave the way for more objective discussions. A comment such as "I didn't like the whiny main character" leads to: Why? How do the other characters see her? How does she see herself? Are these different views of the main character important to understanding her motivation and actions? How does her portrayal as not entirely likable reinforce themes or ideas expressed in the film?

Specialized note-taking can be incorporated into whole-group discussion if questions are designed to draw from the information that it collects. In small groups, mix students who have noted different things. That way, each student has different information to bring to the analysis of, say, friendship, urban life, or family life as depicted in the film.

Instructors who use film in elementary- and intermediate-level language courses are sometimes frustrated because they cannot explore abstract themes or political, historical, or cultural messages in sufficient depth. The result may be that they avoid these questions altogether or pitch them at a level that is too advanced for students to handle with the language skills they have acquired so far. Of course, any questions that require extensive background knowledge not covered in the class should be avoided. In most cases, a brief text in English offering the context (historical, cultural, etc.), read outside class, can provide students with some of the content knowledge necessary for participation in a thoughtful discussion about the film (with careful language scaffolding in class). Reviews in English are a good resource, since they address a broad readership and thus reinforce the international interest and relevance of the film beyond the classroom.

Similarly, questions that ask students to support a hypothesis might require linguistic tools that they have not yet encountered. But students do not necessarily need advanced grammar to discuss complex topics. With helpful prompts (sentence completion, either/or questions, lists of options to answer questions that can be expanded upon), beginners can express their thoughts and opinions using grammatical structures they have already learned.

Reflection

Read the following discussion prompt. Identify its features that would make it difficult for students to respond.

Prompt: The film *Manhattan* has been criticized for its romanticized and unrealistic depiction of New York. Do you agree with this criticism? Was it irresponsible for the filmmaker to romanticize New York in this way in the twentieth century?

The above questions contain numerous assumptions about students' background knowledge. In an advanced undergraduate or graduate course focused on New York, students might have already engaged with reading material that would help them understand what constitutes the "romanticized and unrealistic depiction" mentioned in the prompt. For students who have never been to New York, this film may be their first exposure to the city or one of many that have contributed ideas of what it is like. Students who have enjoyed the film have now been told, indirectly, that they are naïve or unsophisticated. In addition, the question of a filmmaker's responsibility is complex. To address these issues, students would benefit from guided note-taking in the Focus stage to prepare them for discussion.

Now compare the prompt below, which builds on students' viewing notes (from the Focus stage) and is scaffolded to lead them to their own hypotheses. How does this revised prompt reward students' linguistic abilities and critical thinking skills?

> What image of New York is projected in the film *Manhattan*?
>
> *As you watch the film*: Take notes on the city of Manhattan. How does it look? What interior and exterior spaces are shown? What monuments do you see? What do people do? [*For beginning students, provide a list of nouns and adjectives that they can circle while viewing.*]
>
> After viewing the film: In groups, make a list of the sequences you noticed in *Manhattan* that feature the city's streets, buildings, parks, and monuments. Select two of these scenes. Describe how New York is depicted in each scene: What does the spectator see (people, objects, actions)? Is the city friendly, dangerous, crowded, clean? Draw a conclusion from these examples about the image of Manhattan conveyed in this film.

This prompt allows students to collect evidence and present it in a narrative mode that leads to a hypothesis. It makes a cohesive move from viewing to speaking, and it rewards students by allowing them to discover and construct their own ideas.

Create

Responding to feature films offers students opportunities for self-expression in a wide range of genres and media. They may write and film an alternative ending, create a trailer, adapt a portion of the film to a different era or region, or compose illustrated timelines of events or life stories depicted.

Some films lend themselves well to supporting language study. Characters speak clearly using a verb tense just studied, or a scene depicts items that correspond to a recent vocabulary lesson. During a busy semester, it is not worth the time to try to find perfect examples of grammar or vocabulary in a given film, though databases of such material are available for some languages. Some films are simply not very cooperative when it comes to modeling grammar. But there are other ways to link films to grammar and vocabulary lessons.

> **Language and Feature Films**
>
> - If a portion of the film clearly models a grammar structure, use it to present grammar in context.
> - Look for possible connections to grammar and vocabulary in visual representation: identification of objects in a room or rooms of a house, physical descriptions of characters and their clothing, a series of actions that students can identify or narrate in a given tense, etc.
> - Use content, characters, ideas, and events from the film as springboards for creative language production (role playing; composing an alternative ending; offering advice to characters using the subjunctive, conditional, or imperative; etc.).
> - Use film context for grammar sections of quizzes and other forms of assessment.

TEXTS IN ADVANCED-LEVEL COURSES

This chapter has focused on teaching with texts in lower-division courses, since new instructors and TAs often begin at the elementary and intermediate levels. But as we have seen, discourse- and genre-based approaches to language learning derive from the theory that a language-literature split is more an administrative construct than a pedagogically justified curriculum design. Although administrators, instructors, and even students might view advanced literature courses as a sharp move away from language courses, it is likely that the sixth-semester literature student was a fourth-semester language student just a summer or semester ago. As Donato and Brooks show in their study of the types of discourse that students practice in foreign language literature classes, "learning language and literature study are mutually constituting and supporting experiences" (2004, 184). Though the study focuses specifically on speaking, its findings suggest that linguistic issues must be addressed at all levels and in relation to all skills.

Advanced students who do not have near-native proficiency also still need help with basic, literal comprehension of novels, short stories, and poems. A language program that focuses on various types of discourse, including fiction and poetry, will go far in preparing students to approach longer texts; more complicated or intentionally hermetic texts, however, will remain a challenge for them. L1 courses can provide some strategies for interpreting literary texts: an introduction to narrative elements, aspects of prosody, or figures of rhetoric, for example. Fecteau found that while students with background knowledge in L1 literature may have an advantage when reading L2 literary texts, "instructors who design courses around FL [foreign language] literary texts should not assume that students who have completed advanced FL courses and have also read literary texts in their L1 will read and comprehend L2 texts with equal fluency and accuracy" (1999, 489). This study also confirmed that students' levels of basic comprehension can vary widely, owing to the linguistic complexity of the text, their background knowledge, or both.

Perspectives

Sometimes I feel like I am a closeted language teacher in a literature grad student's clothing. I love teaching language classes. There is nothing that I find more rewarding than watching the progress that students make from the first day of an elementary class, when they cannot say *anything*, to the end of that same semester, when they are speaking in complete sentences. I also love to see their awakening attachment to the language, the culture, and yes, especially the literature (so maybe my clothing is actually appropriate). I always do my best to integrate short literary snippets into the language classes that I teach, just to share my passion with my students. They seem to love it when I do that.

I look forward to teaching undergraduate literature courses one day. But I'm a little nervous about teaching my first literature course with no prior experience. When I was an undergraduate, I didn't pay much attention to the pedagogical approaches my teachers were using. I know some teachers lectured, while others implemented some group work. The rest of the details are fuzzy. As a result, I really have no model for teaching literature. I'm also concerned that when I go on the job market for an interview and they ask me to teach a literature class, I won't know what to do. I can think of a lot of

Continued . . .

ways to adapt my Language 101 strategies to develop some dynamic, interactive lessons. But at the same time, I don't want to come across as taking literature teaching too lightly or pitching the class at the wrong level. So I'm kind of in a tough spot here.

1. Why do you think that this graduate student is feeling ambivalent?
2. This individual mentions how much she enjoys integrating literature in her language classes. How do you think she does so? Might she already be teaching literature in a way that can carry over to more advanced classes?
3. What suggestions might you give this person?
4. How might you integrate a favorite passage from a literary text into a lower-level class in the language that you teach? How might you then adapt that lesson, using the same text, to a more advanced course?

Some discussion activities traditionally practiced in literature classes reflect the multistage approaches more overtly advocated for beginning and intermediate language levels: a preparation stage, for example reading only the title and first sentence for a general, global comprehension of content and textual features (identification of a narrative voice or persona, themes and motifs, dominant verb tenses, discourse modes such as dialogue and description, presence or lack of metaphors and other figures of style and rhetoric); an eventual zooming in for close reading and detailed discussion; zooming out to relate content and style to related ideas, other works treated in the course, and social and historical context; and an expansion stage in which students express themselves (traditionally in the form of an analytical paper). A more systematic application of the five-stage model introduced in this chapter may help advanced students grapple with the entwined linguistic, cultural, and thematic complexities of upper-level courses, and thus promote critical thinking and the sharing of ideas in writing and discussion.

Preview

Situate the text in historical, geographical, and cultural context. Be sure students understand the basic conventions, including structural elements of the genre (sonnet, fairly tale, novel, political tract, manifesto, etc.). Reinforce topics and themes pertinent to the course or unit.

Interact

One of the easiest ways to spark interaction with a text is via instructor-guided or small-group discussion in class of the title, the first sentence, and, in longer works, the first paragraph (see Berg and Martin-Berg's approach to teaching the first sentence of a short story [2001, 183–88]). Lead students to discover the text's feel, tone, register, and topic. Encourage students to think about where the text is going and how it will get there.

Focus

Guide students' out-of-class reading so that they will be prepared for in-class follow-up. Block out some time for in-class reading, either individually or in small groups. Assign note-taking activities that help students map features of the text and track changes in narrative voice, tone, or setting. If individual students focus on different textual characteristics, each will bring specific expertise to follow-up discussions. In the case of a novel, for example, have three students keep a list of rhetorical figures (metaphors, comparisons) and when they are used, three others record specific settings (indoor, outdoor) or motifs (animals, storms), three others note direct references to everyday activities and practices, and another group of three tracks mentions of historical and cultural events. Whole-group discussion might focus on the development of a given topic, theme, character, narrative strategy, or stylistic feature, informed by all these elements.

Strategies honed in lower-level courses, such as inferring the meaning of new words from their context or reading groups of sentences without stopping to decipher each word, are sometimes effective in upper-level classes as well. But literature courses in particular often require a return to more careful and close reading. Offer strategies to help students navigate abstract, arcane, and historically or geographically specific vocabulary.

- For longer works of fiction, announce which passages will be the topic of close reading in class so that students may prepare to go over them attentively.

- Ask students to keep a list of words that seem important enough to look up; allow them to merge their lists via discussion threads, blogs, shared documents, or wikis.
- Compile an illustrated encyclopedia: Students often need to look up words for places, objects, and historical events mentioned in literary texts. This vocabulary may not be high frequency, but it would have allowed readers of the author's era to visualize aspects of the text and to make familiar social, cultural, and historical connections. In a blog, on a discussion board, or in a shared document, individuals or groups of students post a word they have looked up (referring to an object, clothing, visual arts, the book a character is reading, or a historical event), along with an illustration and the sentence in which it appears. The entries should be in alphabetical order.

Engage

Whole-group and small-group class discussions are perhaps the most familiar modes of follow-up to reading outside class. In the interest of promoting both critical thinking and oral participation in the target language, it is beneficial to sequence discussion activities from concrete to abstract and from literal to figurative. Here are some ways to achieve this goal:

- Give students a chance to express their subjective reactions to the text. Take a few moments to let them say that they liked or disliked it or found it challenging, unconvincing, inspirational, or frustrating. Then move on, but link these reactions to the style and context that you eventually discuss.
- Begin discussion by having students "tell the story" of what they have read. This strategy is effective for poetry as well as for narrative fiction. For poems, establish who is speaking to whom. Does anything happen? Does the poem allow the reader to visualize the speaker or poetic persona in time or space? How? Can we visualize other characters or actions? For narrative prose, establish understanding of the most obvious who, what, where, and when of the text before moving on to a more nuanced discussion. Have each student contribute a sentence to a co-constructed telling of the story. Use prompts to help them remember: *And after that? Where? Then what happened?*
- Ask yes/no questions, which tend to elicit one-word answers, as a

bridge to discussion, as well as to bring in vocabulary that will be useful in the discussion.
- Start with the facts of a text: have students list the most basic units of meaning in each sentence. Then have them rewrite syntactically complex phrases in prose and poetry in brief, declarative sentences to confirm basic comprehension and to illustrate how rhetoric, syntax, and figurative language shape meaning.
- When moving to more in-depth interaction with the text, allow students to express themselves in small groups as a rehearsal for speaking up in whole-class discussions.
- Vary the format and size of small-group discussions. Think in terms of pairs, groups of three, and teams of six or more. Designate discussion leaders and notetakers for extended discussions in teams. Have discussion leaders, each with a different question, move from group to group to gather input from everyone.

Create

Students in advanced language courses often express their reactions to the literary texts that they study by writing essays and analytical papers. There are, however, countless ways to promote creativity and critical thinking at the same time. The sorts of transformational activities advocated in genre-based approaches to learning include close reading, interpretation, and production of meaning. Telling a story from another perspective, staging a dialogue between characters, and writing a journal entry in the voice of a character are among the many creative responses that can be assigned. Digital projects designed to complement the scope and content of the course (virtual museums, interactive maps, etc.) also allow students to expand their interaction with primary texts from new perspectives.

Reading and texts are central to language, literature, and culture courses at all levels, particularly when those courses are recognized as crucial to the larger mission of the humanities. By completing scaffolded activities that foster interaction and critical thinking, students can become more careful and engaged readers. As we discuss in the following chapter, interaction with model texts also prepares students to become more confident and effective writers in the target language.

8 • Writing

TEACHING WRITING AT ALL LEVELS

Persuasive essays, textual analysis, reflective writing, and research papers are longtime staples of advanced courses in literature and culture. Recent decades have also seen increased attention to how and why writing complements language learning when integrated with other tasks in beginning and intermediate courses. Writing has a place at all levels of a program rich in content, attentive to form-meaning connections, and cognizant of the contribution that foreign language programs can make to a discourse-based orientation across and beyond the language/literature curriculum. As a strong background in writing is increasingly valued in a variety of professions (see Allen 2018, 514–16), writing in foreign language courses is recognized as a transferable skill that will benefit students by helping them "build . . . academic, professional, social, cultural, critical, and digital literacies" (Ferris and Hedgcock 2014, 96). Once seen as perhaps the most academic of practices, writing now plays a significant role in the ever-changing realm of technology and social media, particularly in interpersonal communication and self-expression, where the line of demarcation between speaking and writing is less and less obvious.

Discourse- and genre-based approaches to language learning recognize an essential, symbiotic relationship between reading and writing. Moreover, researchers in the field of applied linguistics have increasingly deemed the separation of linguistic communication into discrete skill categories for the sake of language instruction to be artificial in light of real-life language use. Gaming, for example, involves concurrent interpretive and interpersonal communication. Similarly, shared elements of written and spoken communication in various genres of social media make the compartmentalization of speaking, reading, and writing less useful for understanding how language works.

This chapter is organized around questions pertinent to instructors who teach writing at all levels. We first discuss how attitudes, apprehensions, and habits that students and teachers develop with regard to their L1 writing may produce logistical and affective obstacles to L2 writing. Then we move to an overview of how approaches to foreign language writing have evolved in recent years. Through providing model texts, clear writing prompts, guided editing tasks, and assessment rubrics for all course levels, we also explore ways to make the writing process a pleasure, rather than a burden, for students and teachers alike.

PREEXISTING RELATIONSHIPS TO WRITING

Do you enjoy writing? Do you enjoy grading papers? Do your students enjoy writing? Do you know many students or colleagues who experience the sort of passion for writing evoked in the following interior monologue? "To write! To be able to write! It means long reveries before the blank page. . . . To write! It is the gaze hooked, hypnotized by the reflection of the window in the silver inkwell, the divine fever that rises to the cheeks, the forehead. . . . It also means forgetting what time it is. . . . To write! I feel deeply, every now and then, the need, as strong as thirst in the summer, to note down, to describe . . ." (Colette [1910] 1990, 61; our translation). This passage voices Renée Néré's description of the emotional, sensory, intellectual buzz of writing. Colette (Sidonie-Gabrielle Colette), the author who gave voice to this character in *The Vagabond* (1910), was nominated for both a Nobel Prize and the Prix Goncourt. Not all renowned writers enjoy popular or critical success in their lifetime, nor do they necessarily find the writing process quite as exhilarating. Charles Baudelaire, today recognized as one of Europe's most influential poets, earned widespread acclaim only after his death. He also famously found as much pain as pleasure in writing. Baudelaire put off many of his writing projects, often complaining of financial, physical, and affective obstacles. A letter penned when he was sixteen years old expresses a struggle with writing that he never fully won: "This anguish that I feel, putting my ideas on paper, is nearly invincible; and here in school what repugnance I feel having to write out homework" (Baudelaire 1973, 43; our translation). Similarly, more than two years into the composition of his now iconic *Madame Bovary*, Gustave Flaubert lamented that sometimes writing the novel tortured and mortally depressed him. He complained of having spent five days on drafting just one page (Flaubert 1980, 179). At the same time, when other writers write about writing, they invoke control, healing, resilience, and transformation: "A word after a word after a word is power" (from "Spelling," by Margaret Atwood [1981, 64)]).

> **Reflection**
>
> 1. Find two or three statements about writing from poets, novelists, or nonfiction writers. How would you characterize the emotional, practical, or intellectual relationship to writing evoked in these quotations?
> 2. In just one or two sentences, express how you feel about writing. What role does writing play in your life? Consider, for example, personal communication, professional writing, and journal writing.
> 3. In what ways do you think your students will use writing (in the target language) in further study, work, travel, or personal communication?

Writing can be at once challenging, emotionally fulfilling, tedious, invigorating, physically exhausting, and stress inducing. If most students do not enroll in L2 classes to become novelists or poets, they do, for better or worse, already have an established emotional relationship to L1 writing. Some know the unbridled joy of filling pages with words; others freeze before the blank page or screen. Most have experienced both the highs and the lows of meeting writing deadlines. Think of the countless how-to books by and for professional writers (including academics) who have trouble focusing, who experience anxiety around writing, or who consider procrastination their mortal enemy and longtime companion (e.g., Lamott 1994; Rabiner and Fortunato 2002; Silvia 2007; Akbari 2015). Then consider how the challenge of writing in a foreign language might magnify preexisting apprehensions.

Attitudes that students have acquired about writing long before they enter the foreign language classroom create barriers that prove just as daunting as culturally variable conventions of register and syntax, a sticky grammatical structure, or an unfamiliar alphabet. At every stage of the writing task, from the selection of genre and topic through the creation of editing and assessment prompts, instructors should take into account how these scaffolding materials can motivate students to write and to be read. Such support and guidance are equally important in elementary language courses and advanced literature seminars.

Traditionally, much of the research on the teaching of writing in FL courses derives from studies in ESL (see Reichelt et al. 2012). Yet the FL environment presents slightly different challenges. Like all students, those in FL classes arrive with different backgrounds and levels of experience. Along with individual learner variables, academic traditions in the target culture influence how the language is taught to foreigners. For example, Reichelt et al. found that French has a "strong writing tradition," which influences pedagogy outside France (2012, 29), while German curricula "are not heavily influenced by the German writing traditions" (30). Because of the complexity of their writing systems, other languages, including Japanese, tend to focus more on the spoken rather than the written language in the US classroom (32).

THE CHANGING LANDSCAPE OF COMMUNICATION IN WRITING

North American students devote hours each day to writing as a physical, mechanical activity, be it pushing a pen (less and less often), tapping keys, or swiping a screen. Everyday writing tasks tend to be spontaneous, improvised, and unedited. New technologies and social media blur the distinction between written and oral speech, as well as interpersonal and presentational communication. Though technically *written*, text messages function as spoken language, while presenting some writing-specific elements (punctuation, capitalization) according to their own hybrid and quickly evolving rules of grammar. Even the hashtag, first popularized to identify and group written Twitter content (#spanishgrammar), soon represented a more nuanced variety of speech, including expressions of mood or tone (#ironic), intention (#justkidding), and metacommentary (#Imabooknerd). This functionality has migrated from the written form to oral communication, where the spoken word ("hashtag multitasking!"), like its written ancestor, may serve as a basic topic marker or identify a speech act. Immensely popular at the moment, hashtags will most likely take on new communicative meaning in the near future, or even disappear as a trend altogether in the years after this book is published.

A fluidity between oral and written expression is evident across forms of interpersonal communication. In the early days of email, a professional communication once destined to be composed on paper would be transposed word-for-word for electronic delivery. Correspondents were (and often still are) irritated by brief, breezy, informal email messages. More recently, however, busy readers with overflowing email boxes prefer shorter messages that adhere less strictly to conventions such as formal greetings and closings. Whether this relative relaxing of genre rules is fallout from the Wild West nature of social media or a necessary adaptation to time-management needs, the phenomenon reflects the deep connection between communication and culture.

APPROACHES TO L2 WRITING

There are several ways to conceptualize the purpose of L2 writing in the twenty-first century. Writing is one of four skills or modalities (along with reading, speaking, and listening) that were for some time treated separately in language curricula but are now more often seen as interconnected. From a proficiency and performance perspective, writing encompasses both interpersonal communication (texts, emails, letters, postcards, online chats) and presentational communication (storytelling, talks, speeches). A writing task can be treated as primarily a product, mainly a process, or a more or less equal mix of both.

The types of writing tasks that students have been deemed able to handle at various levels of language learning have differed over time as well. A focus on structure, for instance, takes into account the difficulty of grammar, favoring the basics (e.g., present tense) in elementary-level courses and saving more complex usage (subjunctive mood, literary past tenses) for advanced course levels. But if correct manipulation of grammatical structures is all that counts, why write a paragraph when a list of sentences would do? Moreover, judging the complexity of a reading or writing task by structure alone can be deceiving. In English, the present tense is used to review novels and films, to tell jokes, to recount anecdotes, or to write emails and other texts. Yet novels, op-eds, political speeches, and news articles, all more complex forms, can also be written in the present tense, and some emails and film reviews are more challenging to read than others. Instructors must pay attention to grammatical structures and lexical fields when developing appropriate writing tasks for a particular level, but only in conjunction with the communicative function and purpose of the writing, as well as the content itself. In recent decades, approaches to teaching writing have evolved to give balanced attention to form, function, and meaning. Three key terms designate this shifting paradigm in the pedagogy of L2 writing: "product-based approach," "process-based approach," and "genre-based approach."

Product-Based Approaches

Students accustomed to writing essays, reports, and research papers in their native language may already think of FL writing as a relatively formal, labor-intensive, product-oriented academic practice. Teachers also find writing assignments among the most labor intensive to evaluate (Tierney 2013; Jenkins 2015; Millner 2018). One of the obstacles to engaging students in the development of their L2 writing skills is their sometimes emotional and even stressful reaction to writing in their native language. A product-based approach involves assigning a writing prompt to which students respond individually, usually outside class. Most student writers have (at least once) tackled this kind of assignment using a linear approach: drafting the paper from the first sentence through the last in their final order, in one sitting, most likely the night before the assignment is due. It is no wonder that students and teachers have been conditioned to approach these assignments with a certain amount of dread.

Model texts are sometimes used in a product-based approach, primarily to demonstrate correct use of grammatical structures. Product-based writing may even include more than one graded draft. The second (and final) draft incorporates the instructor's often grammar-focused prompts for revision. Evaluation of the assignment takes into consideration both drafts. Although this familiar linear approach is fairly easy to implement, it has been shown to contribute little in the way of improving students' writing or raising their awareness of their own process and skills (Zamel 1982; Magnan 1985; Magnan, Murphy, and Sahakyan 2014).

Implicit in the product-oriented approach are two assumptions about L2 learning that may not be valid. First, the relative isolation of writing tasks suggests that skills or modes are best taught separately rather than as mutually reinforcing. Second, a traditional product-based approach treats writing as a practice performed only individually, with little collaboration or interaction. In programs that emphasize oral production with minimal error correction, the shift to a more reflective mode of thinking about language may seem at odds with the pace of spontaneous (often spoken) language production. For these reasons, many programs, particularly those with a two-tiered framework, offer a grammar and writing course to be taken immediately after the basic language sequence. The unrealistic expectation is that if students focus on writing in this one particular course, they will perfect their skills, thus preparing them for subsequent content courses where writing is required but not overtly taught.

A Cognitive, Process-Based Approach

Attention to process takes into account that successful writers do not simply correct errors when they edit their work. They rethink, rephrase, replan, reassess, and rewrite throughout the phases of composition (see Flower and Hayes 1981; Scott 1996; Adair-Hauck and Donato 2015). In so doing, writers focus on form, but in relation to meaning and purpose and with awareness of a real, imagined, or implied reader. It is important, however, not to confuse the sort of linear approach discussed above with a cognitive writing process. Recognizable features of a process-based approach include, for example, multiple drafts. But as we saw above, draft writing alone does not engage students in a cognitive writing process.

Reflection

Is the following scenario familiar to you? Think about the benefits and drawbacks of this linear, product-based approach, both for the student who is writing and for the teacher who is evaluating the work.

1. Students carry out a prewriting activity in class.
2. Students draft a composition, incorporating the prewriting.
3. Peer editors read the composition in class. They signal errors.
4. Students incorporate the peer feedback and turn in their compositions.

Continued . . .

> 5. The teacher signals errors of form, syntax, style, voice, and register that need to be addressed in the second draft.
> 6. Students then revise and rewrite, paying attention to the flagged errors.
> 7. The final grade is based on both drafts, taking improvement into account.

Writing in accuracy-focused linear stages (prewriting, composing a draft, revising a draft), while in some ways useful, does not automatically foster cognitive processes. Moreover, if students are simply correcting errors signaled by the instructor (and often mis-signaled by fellow students), a linear draft model can become no more than an exercise in prompted error correction at the word or sentence level, with little consideration of context, message, or audience.

How can teachers promote cognitive processes when self-awareness, self-assessment, and self-editing are by definition individual and solitary phenomena? Krueger (2006) advocates identifying and reinforcing basic axes of focus in all stages of the linear writing process, particularly in the writing prompts, self-editing guides, and grading rubrics:

1. *Attention to genre and function.* What is the purpose of this writing genre? What am I trying to accomplish? For example, am I trying to convince, persuade, give instructions, give advice? How can the texts I've read in the target language help me communicate my ideas?
2. *Attention to the reader/audience.* Who is my audience (real or fictive)? How do I reach these individuals? How do I keep their attention? What could confuse or distract them? How can I appeal to my readers, make myself clear, and make them want to read more?
3. *Attention to form.* What grammar should I verify, and with what resources? What vocabulary and structures will help me accomplish the goals of this writing task? What rhetorical devices will help me convince, persuade, express an emotion, etc.?
4. *Attention to content, culture, and context.* Do I make critical connections between the assigned text (poem, painting, film, video) and the writing task? Is my content creative and appropriate? Is there evidence of sufficient research of the content and cultural topic? Do I communicate the content?

The writing topic can have an effect on how eagerly students engage in peer reading or in the thoughtful rereading and revision of their own work. In lower-level courses, due to the limited structures and lexicon that students can manipulate, the writing prompts may be generic and relatively uninspiring: describe a typical school day; write a letter about a vacation; etc. With a few minor revisions, however, even the most basic writing assignment can become a more creative and engaging exercise for writers, peer readers, and the instructor who will assess the work. The following box demonstrates how to build a degree of critical distance into writing prompts by incorporating a shift in tone, perspective, context, or task.

Box 8.1. Adding Critical Distance to a Personalized Writing Prompt

Generic prompt

Describe your typical week in an email to a friend in another county.

A shift in tone

You are writing a humorous blog post to share with friends in the US and abroad. The title is "What I've Been Doing Lately." But your typical week has been dull lately. The challenge: make a normal, uneventful week sound interesting without fabricating events. In other words, make the ordinary seem fascinating.

A shift in perspective

A gossipy friend or relative writes an email to a mutual acquaintance proclaiming that you have it easy, that everything in your life runs without a glitch. S/he uses the description of your typical week as evidence. Write the message from his/her perspective.

A shift in context

Show students a photo or fine art reproduction of an image that reflects the target culture. Write about the typical week of the person depicted. Explain the basic events based on what you see in the picture. Do not explain the link between the events and the image (i.e., do not write, "In this picture we see X"). Instead, let the reader infer the connection via your description of the activities.

> **A shift in task**
>
> *Assign whole-class and small-group prewriting activities.*
>
> Whole class: Brainstorm the activities that a person depicted in a photo or fine art reproduction might perform in a typical week, based on what the person is wearing and doing in the image.
>
> Small groups: Describe the events of a typical week from the point of view of the person pictured. Incorporate the notes from the brainstorming activity. Group A will make these events sound fun. Group B will make these events sound boring. Group C will make these events sound mysterious. Group D will make these events sound important.
>
> Individual writing: Use your cooperatively written description to complete your own draft of this description.

Source: Adapted from Krueger 2001, 21.

The above "shift in task" is especially helpful for engaging students in collaborative writing or writing workshops in which they share their work. Since students start with the same basic content components but then take their writing in quite different directions, they read the work of their classmates not just as a perfunctory task but instead with genuine curiosity and a focus on meaning.

Despite its benefits, a cognitive, process-based approach has not been found, on its own, to be an adequate L2 writing strategy. While it helps learners to become more engaged, confident, aware, and self-reliant writers, its tenets do not address meaning or meaning making (Byrnes 2011). Nor is this paradigm devised to emphasize cultural inclusivity or the potentially social nature of writing (Ramanathan and Atkinson 1999). Ken Hyland points out that "key principles [of process-based writing] which originated in L1 classrooms such as personal voice, peer review, critical thinking, and textual ownership tacitly incorporate an ideology of individualism which L2 learners may have serious trouble accessing" (2004, 20). Some instructors and materials do include textual models in the target language when implementing multiple writing stages, but this principle is not part of the framework. Moreover, the personal growth, self-awareness, and confidence fostered in a cognitive approach are difficult to track and assess from draft to draft or writing task to writing task.

Genre-Based Approaches

While a process-based approach encourages students to be conscious of their writing and to think carefully about the symbiotic relationship between form and meaning in the texts they produce, recent research suggests that this introspection is not enough to gain mastery in a second language; text types and models are essential to the development of writing skills in social, cultural, and discursive contexts. A focus on genre is by definition a focus on discourse. In this approach, students read, think about, and engage with sample texts before and as they write their own. Concentrating on genre and literacy does not preclude the logistics of process writing: the two approaches can work together to provide the input (content, culture), self-awareness, confidence building, and attention to form-meaning connections that students need to become motivated, successful writers in a second language.

Ken Hyland defines "genres" as "abstract, socially recognised ways of using language" and points out that without necessarily being able to identify them, native speakers in a given community will nonetheless understand conventions of familiar genres (2007, 149). He specifies five underlying principles of genre-based teaching:

1. *Writing is a social activity.* To communicate in writing, students must engage with a variety of genres that serve different purposes and intended readers.
2. *Learning to write is needs-oriented.* Teachers must identify the kinds of writing that students will likely use in the L2.
3. *Learning to write requires specific outcomes and expectations.* These should be made clear to students from the beginning.
4. *Learning to write is a social activity.* Teachers and peers play an important role in scaffolding writing assignments.
5. *Learning to write involves learning to use language.* In genre-based teaching, grammar and vocabulary are not studied in order to decode texts; instead, grammar teaching is integrated with the teaching of reading and writing. (152–53)

Text types can be classified in terms of interpersonal and presentational communication modes. Interpersonal writing involves a writer and an expected responsive reader. Text messages, chats, and handwritten and email correspondence are examples of interpersonal writing genres. Presentational writing is composed with an audience in mind, but not with the expectation of an active exchange. Reports, reviews, stories, poems, and various kinds of blog posts are generally written for presentational purposes. The chat that may ensue in a comments section after a news story or a blog post is interpersonal. Whether students write interpersonal or presentational texts, their reading of and engagement with the text types, or *genres*, appropriate to their level are seen as essential to their writing process in a genre-based model (see Chapter 7).

Textual Borrowing

The term "textual borrowing" has been used for some time in its negative sense, to denote the overuse of another writer's words or the appropriation of another writer's ideas without attribution. In the context of writing pedagogy, textual borrowing has nothing to do with plagiarism. Instead, it is the implementation of genre and language conventions encountered in target-language texts. Textual borrowing derives from theories of discourse, textual ownership, and the dialogical nature of speech (Bakhtin 1981), and in particular from Kristeva's characterization of intertextuality: "any text is constructed as a mosaic of quotations; any text is the absorption and transformation of another" (1986, 37). In the process of textual borrowing, students adapt the syntax, structures, and vocabulary of texts they have read to their own writing (see Maxim 2009). Textual borrowing is thus central to genre-based pedagogies, which involve "building learner awareness of the moves associated with specific text types and how these moves are realized linguistically and stylistically" (Allen and Goodspeed 2018, 90).

Writing is a featured expansion activity in discourse- and genre-based pedagogical sequences because it helps students engage with texts and create their own language. In these approaches, students navigate and demonstrate understanding of new information with a focus on content (in the texts studied), discourse (in the ways in which these texts create meaning), and writing (as a means of connecting and showing mastery of language and content). To demonstrate how students may be guided to interact with model texts as they create their own, we have selected passages from Raymond Queneau's *Exercices de style* (1947; first published in English in 1958, as *Exercises in Style*) to serve as templates. This book has stood the test of time in French language and literature classes because of its humor, its focus on expression in different voices and registers, and its examples of how one story can be told and retold in multiple ways. A highly successful experiment in "literary constraint" (also called "constrained writing"), Queneau's book recounts the same seemingly inconsequential anecdote ninety-nine times: a man riding a bus witnesses a brief altercation between two other passengers; later on, he spots one of them at a train station, where another individual is telling him that he should add a button to his overcoat.

Exercises in Style has been translated into many languages (including Chinese, German, Italian, Japanese, Portuguese, Russian, and Spanish) and can be integrated as a model of various registers of spoken and written language, as well as literary and nonfiction genres. The story is recounted in various discourse styles and textual genres (for example, comedy, free verse, sonnet). Certain selections use variations on spoken language, while others explore rhetoric and wordplay. As a result, some ("Apostrophe," "Parachesis," "Prosthesis," "Syncope") are quite a bit more challenging to read than others, due to either their literary and rhetorical complexity or their reliance on recognition of given speech patterns and accents. Others ("Passive," "Past," Present," "Reported Speech") model grammatical form and function (see Paesani 2006, 2009). Since our purpose is to inspire students to write by engaging with model texts, we have selected as examples a few "exercises in style" that demonstrate obvious shifts in style, narrative function, or tone and that would be accessible to students in fourth- or fifth-semester courses (see Appendix C).

Activity 8.1. Discovering Queneau

Students discover and understand the Queneau text through previewing, interacting, focusing, engaging, and creating (see Chapter 7). (Note that guidelines on self-editing, peer editing, and assessment rubrics appear later in this chapter.)

Preview

1. Think of a movie you have recently seen and liked. How would you summarize the plot briefly for a friend? For a six-year-old cousin? For a film professor? How might a person who did not like the film describe it differently?
2. In these descriptions of the plot, did you alter the content? The language? Your narrative voice?

Interact

1. Quickly read the three versions of the anecdote provided in Appendix C. Suggest a title for each. In groups, compare your titles and explain your choices.
2. How do your titles compare to those the author chose ("Notation," "Surprises," "You know")?

Focus

Reread each version of the anecdote, and respond to the following prompts:

1. Do you imagine the story being told in conversation or in written form? In what context?
2. Make a list of examples (words or phrases) to explain your answer.
3. In groups, compare your examples.
4. What impression do you have of the narrator in each version of anecdote? How would you describe him or her?

Engage

This anecdote was written ninety-nine times in the book *Exercises in Style*, as a formal letter, a sonnet, and a dream, in the past, and in the first and third person (to name just a few examples). Think of three more styles in which you could tell the story, and jot down a title for each. Consider different tones, moods, points of view, and genres, from poetry to social media. For each of your titles, make a list of at least five textual elements (specific words, phrases, grammatical features, stylistic features) you could use to reinforce your version of the anecdote. In groups, compare the titles you have come up with, and add to the lists.

Create

Contribute to a crowdsourced "exercises in style" based on the encounter shown in the Salvo detergent TV commercial (Chapter 7).

1. Rewatch the ad and take notes on the actions you see.
2. In small groups, compare and combine your notes. Write, as a group, a text in the style of Queneau's "Notation."
3. Individually and outside class, compose your own "exercises in style" in the three styles you thought of earlier (see Engage above), using the textual elements that you specified.
4. Upload the final version of your "exercises in style" to the course blog.

FROM GOALS TO ASSESSMENT

Backward Design (Wiggins and McTighe 2005) involves articulating educational outcome goals before creating assessment tasks, materials, and activities (see Chapter 10 for a more detailed description). This curricular model provides clarity for student writers and for teachers, who articulate the desired results before assigning a writing task and include this wording in the instructions. Teachers also clarify how students will demonstrate their ability to reach the stated goals, and they provide assessment rubrics that reinforce these goals and the means of achieving them.

> **Reflection**
>
> Read the writing prompt (provided here in English) for an essay assigned in an intermediate-level foreign language textbook. Then examine the three sample essays. Based on the prompt, how would you rank the quality of the three compositions?
>
> Prompt: Three weeks into the academic year, your family wants to know how you are doing. They especially want to hear about your day-to-day life. Write an email to a family member or family members. Describe your room and a roommate or a new friend. Then talk about the activities you like best, using the vocabulary lists in your textbook.
>
> **Sample A**
>
> Dear Mom and Dad,
>   In my room there are books, a carpet, a big window, pencils, and a little bed. There are also lamps. On the wall there are also posters and pictures of you. I also have a roommate, Mark. Mark has brown hair and he is spacey. He is also nice. He lives in Indiana. He likes parties and movies. There are no problems. The room is sunny and pleasant. I like the University. It is big and there are a lot of friends. I like movies and friends!
>
> > Continued . . .

Sample B

Dear Mom,

I love the University! The courses are difficult. But the teachers are nice and intelligent. There are a lot of friendly, fun students. We like to go out all the time to partys and football games.

I like my room. We have a little radio and tow stereos becuz we like the music. Mark, the roommate, likes jazz best, but i love rock. We have a lot of vinyl. Mark is nice, but a little spoiled. He's rich and he likes to slep all the time. He's a student lazy. I'm always hardworking, but I like to sleep on Saturdays.

There are also some problems. The room is not very sunny, and we do not have no carpeting. And I am not a girlfriend. But I talk a lot with good friends and they like to dance. Sometimes we leave for the movies on weekends.

Sample C

Dear Mom and Dad.

I to like theese university. It's very handsome and there are alot of nice student. I to like the campus beautiful. The courses are difficult but the proffesers are fun. I don't have a girlfriend, but i like to go out for football "matchs" and i like to eat "the nachos." The [feminine article] roommate's name is Mark. He is nice. He is brunette and blond. He is from New York.

1. Which writing sample is most grammatically accurate?
2. Which writing sample do you think is best written? Why?
3. How could the prompt be revised to guide students to write better compositions? If two versions of the paper were to be assigned, how could you design a prompt for Version 2 that would push students to expand the form or content?
4. Working with the same general writing topic above, think about how the assignment could be redesigned to help students achieved desired outcomes. Consider the following:
    a. Define the goals of this writing assignment, in terms of content (relation to themes and cultural information already encountered in the course), related vocabulary, pertinent

Continued . . .

grammar structures, and model texts that students have read in the target language. What should students know how to do, and how should they demonstrate that they can do it?
   b. The prompt does not include critical attention to content or culture. How could you redesign it to ensure that students are engaged in thoughtful writing about relevant cultural content? How could a genre-based approach be used? How could you focus students' attention on the social, cultural, and discursive elements of writing an informal email in the language that you teach?
   c. How could you incorporate textual borrowing?
5. Rephrase the writing prompt to provide more guidance to students and to reflect these goals.

Grading, Feedback, and Interactive Rubrics

It would be impractical for teachers to provide formal feedback on every stage of writing. Grading two versions of an essay is a manageable compromise. If students have done some journal writing or in-class composing, alone or in groups, the first version they hand in is not necessarily a first draft. Nor does it have to be a rough draft. In fact, the shorter the paper is, the more care students may put into the first version they turn in. The relative weights of the collected and graded drafts should depend upon how much risk students are encouraged to take at each stage. In beginning-level courses, when students do not yet know what they do not know, it makes sense to allot more points to the final, revised writing assignment. In contrast, according a slightly larger percentage of points to the first graded draft of a paper in upper-level courses encourages students to take ownership of content and form from the very beginning.

Instructors are often unsure what kind of feedback to give on the first draft, and the value of form-focused feedback (signaling of grammatical errors) versus more general feedback on content and organization remains a topic of debate in SLA research (Ferris 1999; Truscott 1996, 1999, 2007). Though grammar correction alone does not seem to improve students' writing, motivated students have been shown to benefit from the consciousness raising provided by form-focused feedback (Fiona Hyland 2011).

There are several ways to assess both form and content in writing assignments, such as a single, holistic grade (A, B, C) or one that reflects a form-content split (50 percent based on form and 50 percent on content, for example). Yet even when explained to students, these methods can seem arbitrary and potentially subjective or unfair. Moreover, a form-content split could send the message that the two are not interdependent. Should writers consider what they say and how they say it as unrelated? And how should teachers define "form" and "content" in such a way that students understand expectations? If form shapes meaning and vice versa, where should a teacher draw the line between the two?

Prompts that articulate the goals of the assignment offer transparency to student writers and minimize ambiguity for the instructors who assess the work. Grading rubrics, posted or distributed with the assignments, show students exactly what they need to do from the outset and provide a checklist of sorts to ensure that they have not missed anything. Once filled in, rubrics clearly identify which portions of the paper are successful and where improvement is needed. They can also help students scaffold a paper's progressive composition by reinforcing changes in content and structure in two or more versions. Finally, rubrics promote self-awareness during the writing process, as well as interaction between the instructor and students, via direct questions about the steps that students took to revise their papers (see Tables 8.1 and 8.2).

The descriptors provided in the rubric in Table 8.2 offer beginning- and intermediate-level students an understanding of the areas that they need to develop. Instructors could underline specific words, such as "creative," or descriptors, such as "some avoidable errors," to pinpoint particular strengths or weaknesses in the prose. This rubric may be used for both the first and the second collected drafts, to encourage students to track their improvement.

Designing a Writing Assignment

The goals of a writing assignment, articulated in the prompt itself, should be reinforced in the assessment rubric. Create an assessment rubric that reinforces the goals you listed for the email assignment on pages 191–93. Here are some categories you may want to include:

Table 8.1. Interactive Assessment Rubric

Students turn in this rubric with the first of two graded versions of the writing assignment. The instructor adds comments and points in the second column and returns the rubric with the paper.

Logistics: paper turned in on time, in the format assigned, according to any policies or guidelines
[Note policy on deduction of points for late work, etc.]

Structure: sentence level, paragraph level, genre level, depending on the assignment (5)
[Reinforce connection to model texts.]

Basic editing: spelling and agreements (subject/verb, noun/gender) (5)

Grammar studied up to this point (5)

Focus grammar (e.g., use of past tenses to tell a story, use of conditional clauses to make an argument, use of imperative and subjunctive to give advice) (10)

Vocabulary, especially that studied up to this point and any pertinent to the paper (10)
[Reinforce connection to model texts.]

Attention to reader: style, readability
Who is your target reader? What is the tone of your paper? How would you like your reader to react? Please reply in the cell to the right. (5)
[Reinforce connection to model texts.]

Content: topic treated in sufficient depth, good use of examples, clear analysis (20)
[Reinforce connection to model texts.]

____ / 60

Table 8.2. Rubric for Beginning- and Intermediate-Level Writing Assignments

	10–9 excellent	8 very good / good
Organization	Content communicated well; writing follows a logical plan, with a clear sense of beginning and closure	Generally good content, although topic may not be fully explored; writing usually follows a logical plan, with some sense of beginning and closure
	10–9 excellent	8 very good / good
Expression	Sentence lengths and patterns vary; excellent and appropriate control and choice of vocabulary; good variety of words used	Sentence lengths and patterns show some variety; good control and choice of vocabulary; moderate variety of words used
	20–18 excellent	17–16 very good / good
Grammar	Excellent control of grammatical structures, spelling, conjugations, and agreement; very few errors	Good control of grammatical structures, spelling, conjugations, and agreement; some avoidable errors
	10–9 excellent	8 very good / good
Content and cultural analysis	Highly creative and personalized; evidence of extensive research of cultural topic	Creative and personalized; evidence of sufficient research to complete cultural assignment

7 acceptable	6 unacceptable
Ideas are often unrelated; adequate content, although repetitious and simplistic; writing often strays from a logical plan, with a weak sense of beginning and closure	Poor ability to communicate and inadequate development of ideas; writing follows a minimal logical plan

7 acceptable	6 unacceptable
Sentence lengths and patterns seldom vary; fair control and choice of vocabulary; minimal variety of words used	Sentence lengths and patterns are repetitious; tone is lifeless and shows no involvement; poor control and choice of vocabulary; definite lack of variety in words used

15–14 acceptable	13 unacceptable
Fair control of grammatical structures, spelling, conjugations, and agreement; many errors	Excessive errors in grammatical structures, spelling, conjugations, and agreement

7 acceptable	6 unacceptable
Fairly creative and personalized; minimal research of topic	Lack of creativity and personalization; insufficient research to complete assignment

- basic grammar and spelling
- grammar and/or vocabulary focus
- personal grammar (for students who are tracking their progress in a journal)
- genre or style focus (elements gleaned from model texts)
- attention to rhetorical and discourse goals (to persuade, inform, entertain)
- attention to genre and its implied readership
- reflective statement regarding something the student improved or that they prefer about this version of the composition (including a sample revision if applicable)
- reflective statement regarding the writing process (anything from the resources used to the physical conditions of writing)
- logistics (will points be deducted for papers that are late or incomplete or that do not respond to the guidelines?)

Self-Editing

Self-editing takes place when students revise their own writing, considering feedback from the instructor and from peer reviewers. More accurate grammar, spelling, and vocabulary can be easy to spot in a revised draft when students have responded conscientiously to signaled errors. Revision at the sentence level is not as easy to track, and the sorts of rethinking and revising skills that students should hone to become better writers cannot be measured. It is possible, however, to underscore the importance of self-awareness in grading rubrics, as illustrated in the examples above. Interactive rubrics can be used to draw attention to self-editing and to log evidence of this work in the form of rewritten sentences and reflective statements about how students have completed this revision.

Peer Reading versus Peer Editing

The literature on first language writing does not always distinguish among peer response, peer review, and peer editing (e.g., Lin and Chien 2009; Ludemann and McMakin 2014). In FL classes, "peer editing" is often used to refer to the process in which students, individually or in groups, read and offer feedback on their classmates' writing. Ideally, the benefits of this task will extend to both the writers (who receive valuable advice for improvement) and the readers (who are exposed to different ways of treating a topic that they too have addressed). If students know that one or more of their peers will be reading a draft of their work, they are encouraged to write for an audience other than just the professor.

It is not surprising that studies have shown that students may be resistant to peer editing (Amores 2007; Zhao 2010; Kaufman and Schunn 2011). Some are embarrassed when their peers point out errors. Those who have devoted a great deal of time to polishing their own work resent providing feedback on mistakes that their peers could have caught. Still others find that their classmates do not have the expertise to identify errors of grammar and vocabulary. Their peers may miscorrect items or not catch true errors.

Still, feedback from readers is invaluable to any writer. So why is it so problematic in L2 courses? Perhaps the idea of peer editing in this context deviates too much from its real-world feedback models. When academic journals and publishing houses solicit evaluations from expert readers, they do not call this process "peer editing." In fact, manuscripts abundant in basic, avoidable errors are often sent back to the writer before a peer reviewer ever sees them. A peer reviewer comments on content, structure, readability, and relevance. A reviewer may flag problems of form but is not expected to point out or correct discrete errors. If students in FL courses offer peer review or peer *responses* rather than peer editing, they participate in a task that is more meaningful for both the writer and the reader. In their article about L2 writing fellows (students who are vetted to help their peers become better writers in the language they are studying), Snyder, Nielson, and Kurzer (2016) emphasize that successful peer tutoring, like peer review, involves social interaction and a conversation about the content of students' papers — not error correction.

Guided peer response can be used for any level of writing. The following activity is designed for relatively short papers, but it can be adapted to other genres and to longer assignments. The peer reading could take place outside class. One advantage of in-class peer reading, however, is that the teacher can answer questions and provide guidance as needed.

Activity 8.2. Peer Review

Reading a Classmate's Persuasive Essay

Reader's name:
Writer's name:
In groups of three, exchange papers so that you do not have your own.
1. First read-through.
   a. Take turns reading the papers aloud at a moderate pace.
   b. Underline any repetitions of words or phrases that stand out and obvious mistakes that catch your attention, but don't linger on these for now.
   c. Write comments directly on the paper you are reading.
2. Silent reading. Now, as you read the paper silently, jot down your responses to the following questions.
   a. What is the main subject of the paper?
   b. What is the writer's opinion or perspective on the subject?
   c. What sentences articulate the thesis or argument?
   d. How does the writer justify his or her opinion and argument? What do you find most convincing?
   e. What do you like best about the paper? Are there specific sentences and specific ideas you find especially strong?
   f. Do you have any advice for improvement in form or content?
   g. How does the paper spark ideas for improving your own writing?

Follow-Up

After completing the tasks above, students share their observations and confer within their groups. Next, as a class, they discuss the purpose of the peer-review activity: in reading aloud, did they hear things (such as unnecessary repetition, bland sentence structure, missing words) that they may not have noticed while reading silently? Students then share the impressive sentences that they have found in their classmates' papers and explain what makes those sentences stand out. Finally, they share responses to question g, to remind them that reading—even reading the work of a classmate—can help them fine-tune their own approach to writing.

> **Perspectives**
>
> I have always loved to write, and I see writing as a solitary activity. The only time I want anyone reading my work is when it is finished. I really hate it when teachers make us work with partners to give feedback on each other's work and to brainstorm topics. I don't want to share my ideas with my classmates, because I don't want them to write about the same things that I do. I want to be original! These are my ideas, not theirs. And although I don't mind giving a classmate feedback on a paper (and showing him where he has made mistakes), I don't need anyone to go through my paper to tell me where I've made errors. I don't make a lot of mistakes, and I've had classmates tell me that things were wrong when I knew that they were right. It's really frustrating. Why do we always have to do everything in groups?
>
> 1. Do you think that this student's perspective is unique, or do you think that most students don't enjoy peer response or editing?
> 2. Do you agree that students should not be forced to participate in the process if they would rather work alone?
> 3. How might the process be adapted so that this student would be more willing to participate?

In-Class Writing Workshops

In-class writing workshops equip students with a draft on which to build their individual assignment at home, so they will not have to begin with a blank page or screen. Moreover, students may consult the teacher as they write during in-class workshops. The instructor thus has a sense of where students are getting snagged, as well as when to pause to demonstrate the use of online dictionaries and other resources. Immediate, in-person feedback from the teacher allows students to revise their work early on. Workshops also permit the teacher to guide students through aspects of process that students may skip on their own if they tend to default to a more linear approach. A writing workshop, which may include a combination of group and individual prompts, might encompass the only stretch of focused, uninterrupted work that students do for the course.

The following handout was created for a fifth-semester course in which students were preparing to write a persuasive essay. They had already interacted with the genre by reading an example in the target language. The guided reading and follow-up discussion prepared them to think about the sort of language and rhetorical structures they would like to use to make their own prose more convincing. Students had brainstormed possible topics for their essays the day before and were now ready to pick one and to think about how to address it.

Box 8.2. Workshop: A Persuasive Essay

Individuals

1. Jot down two to three topics you considered for this essay. Circle the one you have chosen.
2. What question or problem regarding this topic will you address in the essay?
3. Who is the target audience (fellow students, an educated readership well versed in politics) and what is the target venue (a blog, an op-ed) for your essay?
4. How will the venue and readership influence some of your linguistic choices, examples, or content?
5. What opinion, perspective, advice, or urging do you wish to convey?
6. How would you like the reader to "hear" your voice? As knowledgeable, as humorous, as laid-back, as ironic, as empathic . . .
7. Sometimes a thesis does not emerge until you have had time to write through your arguments. If you think you have a thesis, write it down now. You can revise it later.
8. Are there specific words you know you will need to look up in order to write the essay? Make a list here, but don't search for them yet.

Pairs or small groups

Briefly share the information in #1–6 above.
Help your classmate(s) with more ideas for #7.

Continued . . .

> **Individuals**
>
> Free writing. On paper or on your laptop, begin writing the essay, without stopping to look up words or grammar. Just record your thoughts. Mark places where you would like to go back and say more, but move on. You do not have to start at the beginning. Write about any aspect of the essay that is on your mind now. You have [10/15/20] minutes.

Once students have completed the in-class writing workshop's final, free-writing phase, they do a word count to see how much they have been able to write in a short period of uninterrupted time. They may then take notes regarding revisions that they would like to make later, with more time, outside class. In a whole-group discussion, the instructor guides students to generate lists of the vocabulary they have identified as important to their topics. Selecting one or two words (preferably ones that may pose translation problems owing to their cultural specificity, such as "graduation" or "fraternity"), students may use online tools to discover the limits of quick and easy word-to-word translation.

Journal Writing

As the lines from Colette quoted earlier remind us, writing can indeed be a pleasure. The strategies outlined in this chapter have been designed with pedagogical goals, clarity, and practicality in mind. Happily, manageable logistics and sound scaffolding also clear space for writers to find their voices and even enjoy the process. That said, the kinds of writing assignments discussed so far tend to be formal, in that they are carefully constructed and graded. Students can also benefit from FL writing assignments with lower stakes. Keeping a journal, for example, on paper or in a blog or another social media format, can motivate students to express themselves in writing free of the inevitable creative constraints (and stress) that more prescribed genres impose (Peyton 2000). A simple pass/fail grading system emphasizes that the value of these activities lies in the experience, not the product.

WRITING AND UPPER-LEVEL COURSES

As mentioned above, courses with titles such as "Grammar and Composition" and "Introduction to Literature," offered to students who have completed beginning- and intermediate-level language classes, often serve, in theory, as preparation for advanced work in literature and culture. Instructors may presume that by a certain level, students no longer need the sort of pedagogical support for writing that they did earlier in their studies. It is especially easy for teachers in programs with separate language and literature faculty, and correspondingly unrelated curricula, to conceptualize the advanced literature student as different from the language student. Students themselves may or may not compartmentalize their role(s) as learners in this way. But regardless of their talent and experience, upper-level students in "content" courses will also benefit from the sort of scaffolding they have come to expect in language courses — such as the following set of questions, designed by Snyder, Nielson, and Kurzer (2016) for peer tutors working with fellow students on their writing in advanced-level language courses. Like other evaluation systems, theirs focuses on content and encourages a dialogue about the writing rather than a silent reading for error correction. These questions can be adapted to one-on-one peer review and to evaluation rubrics in general.

Box 8.3. Questions for Peer Writing Tutors

1. Assignment: Does the paper meet the expectations of the assignment?
2. Ideas/thesis: Does the paper have interesting things to say? Does it have a probing and controlling thesis?
3. Global organization: Does the order of the points support the thesis? Do the introduction and conclusion set up the thesis and end the paper by answering the "so what"?
4. Paragraph organization: Is each paragraph unified and sufficiently long to make its point?
5. Evidence: Does the paper contain enough appropriate evidence? Is there more analysis and synthesis rather than summary? Is there enough detail supporting the main points?
6. Style and correctness: Do the sentences have variety, and is the

Continued . . .

language elegant and clear? Does the writer follow the conventions of spelling, mechanics, and usage?

Source: Adapted from Snyder, Nielson, and Kurzer 2016, 753.

Reflection

1. Are there some writing genres that are specific to the social or academic culture(s) of the language that you teach? Will students be expected to work within these writing genres if they study abroad?
2. Are any of these genres closely related to the academic context of the language's target culture(s)?
3. Where could you find model texts (not how-to lists) that students may read before producing their own work?

Textbooks for elementary- and intermediate-level language courses often include readings that can serve as models for students' writing: a personal letter, an advertisement, a poem. Advanced classes also offer students the opportunity to explore various written genres and to hone their skills by exploring and imitating model texts. In courses that focus on literary analysis, there can be a disparity between the texts that students read and those that they are expected to write. For example, in a course on the Romantic novel, will students write their own fiction, or will they compose essays analyzing the primary works? Students in a poetry course may be asked to compose their own poems in order to gain insights into rhythm, rhyme, and rules of prosody, and writing fiction can be effective in helping students understand the workings of various genres in an active way that involves critical thinking and personal expression (see Gebhart 1988; Austen 2009). If a final exam or paper incorporates a written close reading of a poem, however, students should have exposure to a model text of that type in the target language before writing their own. Certain critical writing genres are very specifically linked to target-culture academic settings; American students therefore may never have encountered these genres before being asked to produce them themselves. For example, the *commentaire composé*, a highly codified genre of literary commentary well known to students in France, often figures among assignments in upper-level French courses in the US. Like its predecessor, the *explication de texte* (once a mainstay of textual analysis), the *commentaire composé* is the topic of countless legitimate how-to books and websites published in France for teachers and students. Yet finding a single completed example in this plethora can be a tough order. Lists and how-to documents are helpful, but a sample paper would be more useful. Reading and analyzing an authentic *commentaire* allows students to see how key formal and structural elements work, as students create their own meaning within that genre.

The need for sample texts is something to keep in mind even in major seminars and graduate-level courses. Like beginning-level students writing their first email in the target language, more-advanced students preparing to write a twelve- to twenty-page research paper benefit from reading and understanding the architecture of a similar text in the target language. Instructors who ask students for written permission to use their (anonymous) work in the future can build a library of sample texts for future classes. For beginners and more-advanced learners alike, opportunities for creativity and self-expression, along with more objective and analytical composition assignments appropriate to the course level, allow meaningful engagement with texts of all genres and registers from the target culture. In addition, the writing training that students receive in their L2 classes helps them become more confident and effective writers across the curriculum.

9 • Culture

TWENTIETH-CENTURY CONCEPTIONS OF CULTURE IN THE LANGUAGE CLASSROOM

Over the years, scholars and instructors have developed a variety of ways to address culture in the language classroom. Until the 1960s, language instructors emphasized what was later called "big-C culture." Big-C culture encompasses the masterpieces of a given society, including its art, literature, and philosophy. This focus aligned with grammar translation's attention to reading and translating "great" works and authors. "Little-c culture"— "native speaker" behavior, ways of life, and daily practices—came to the forefront of foreign language education in the 1980s when the communicative turn shifted attention to language use in real-life situations. Associated activities aimed to equip students with the tools to interact with native speakers in culturally appropriate ways. However, this model treated language and culture as separate entities and often presented culture, commonly described as "the fifth skill" (following reading, listening, reading, and writing), as something instructors could add to the curriculum if they had extra time.

In 1996, the ACTFL Standards offered a newly articulated classification of culture. To provide a road map for pedagogy in the United States, culture was divided into products, practices, and perspectives. Products include a society's tangible and intangible creations; practices are its behavioral or

Table 9.1. Categories of Cultural Products, Practices, and Perspectives

Products	Practices	Perspectives
Literature	Conversational norms	Notions of individualism
Paintings	Table manners	Family values
Household items	Use of space	Attitudes toward given age groups
Food	Formal versus informal address	Values regarding ownership
Music	Traditions	Values associated with personal privacy
Laws		

interactional patterns; and perspectives are the meanings, attitudes, and values of a specific society's world view (see Table 9.1).

In the revised version of the Standards (2015b), the Culture goal asks learners to "use the language to investigate, explain, and reflect on the relationship between the practices and perspectives" and "between the products and perspectives of the culture studied." Note how the word choice reflects the intention to unite discourse, culture, and critical thinking, as well as to create connections among products, practices, and perspectives. The website of the Center for Advanced Research on Language Acquisition includes a set of modules that help instructors see the relationships among products, practices, and perspectives and the ways in which they intersect. Here is an example linked to aging in the United States: "In the U.S., youth has traditionally been valued more than old age (a *perspective*). As a result, *products* that purport to prolong youth and vitality (e.g., face creams, high fiber breakfast cereals, and fitness equipment) have become an integral part of our culture. At the same time, *practices* that are perceived as prolonging youth and health are encouraged: school children have physical education to promote physical exercise; many invest in running shoes (*products*) or join a fitness club (*product*); some take extreme measures to look younger and have plastic surgery (*practice*)" (http://carla.umn.edu/cobaltt/modules/curriculum/textanalysis/Practices_Products_Perspectives_Examples.pdf). This example follows the Standards-based approach as part of a lesson that does not isolate factual knowledge about a culture's specific products but instead reinforces an understanding of how the products and the cultural practices of a particular society intersect with its cultural perspectives.

> **Reflection**
>
> The ACTFL website contains several Standards-based units, lesson plans, and templates at https://www.actfl.org/publications/books-and-brochures/the-keys-planning-learning. Choose one unit or lesson plan and analyze how it spirals communication and cultural products, practices, and perspectives. Provide specific examples. Are there particular approaches here that you could apply to your own teaching?

The Comparisons Standard also emphasizes culture, calling for students to "use the language to investigate, explain, and reflect on the concept of culture through comparisons of the cultures studied and their own." (ACTFL 2015b). The idea of cultural comparison gained favor in foreign language classrooms in the late 1990s in connection with Michael Byram's (1997) work on intercultural competence, which includes critical cultural awareness as a key feature. The goal was for students to "see relationships between different cultures—both internal and external to society—to mediate, that is, interpret each in terms of the other, either for themselves or for other people" (200), and to show flexibility and open-mindedness when encountering another culture. Instructors therefore developed activities in which students could compare cultures, focusing on similarities and differences (Byram 2003). This approach encouraged students to analyze the values, beliefs, and practices of the target culture and their own. As Kramsch explains, the aim of intercultural education was "to understand the Other on the other side of the border" (1998, 81). In this model, the native speaker often had special prestige as the owner and gatekeeper of the "authentic" culture.

Cultura, a project developed by Gilberte Furstenburg, Sabine Levet, and Shoggy Waryn at MIT in the 1990s, aims to develop students' intercultural competence. The curriculum engages learners in virtual discussions with students from other cultures, using teleconferencing and online discussion boards. Two of this program's main goals are for students to learn to communicate effectively across languages and cultures and for them to understand the central role of culture in people's behaviors and practices. MIT students in a third-semester Spanish class, for example, could be paired with students studying English at the Tec de Pachuca in Mexico. Students from both institutions would start the semester by answering the same set of questions, designed to draw out potential cultural differences with word associations (e.g., what words do you associate with individualism?), sentence completions (e.g., "A rude person . . ."), and reactions to situations (e.g., "You see a student next to you cheating on an exam"). To expose their partners to authentic language, students post in their native language in the program's online forums. Class discussions are then conducted in the target language to analyze and compare the data provided by both groups. Throughout, the instructors guide students to find cultural patterns. Other activities include comparing US and target culture data and images, including foreign films and their US remakes (or vice versa). The creators wanted students to gain "a real insider's view of the culture" and to "put together the cultural puzzle" (Furstenburg 2010, 331).

Reflection

MIT has developed a helpful online educator's guide for Cultura: https://cultura.mit.edu/educators-guide/. It includes the questionnaires and the associated Images, Film, and Newsstand Modules.

Cultura Archived Exchanges

https://cultura.mit.edu/cultura-exchanges-archive
Choose one of the archived exchanges and analyze the cultural similarities and differences in the word association, sentence completion, or situation reaction forum. How would you organize a discussion with your class using these online forums?

Cultura Images Module

https://cultura.mit.edu/educators-guide/images-module
Review the format and organization of the Images Module. Review the suggestions of topics for image selection (e.g., "Show how specific products are advertised in their own culture. Students could choose

Continued . . .

> advertisements for products and compare how those products are presented in their respective cultures"). What other topics would you recommend for comparing images in your courses?

While attention to differences in cultural products, practices, and perspectives can be illuminating, scholars such as Kramsch have questioned the homogeneous conception of "culture." Who are "native speakers," and what exactly are their little-c and big-C "cultures"? Whom do they represent? Do all speakers of a specific language behave similarly in the world? Are the ways of thinking of a particular culture easily defined and categorized in the globalized world? What scale of culture should be taught (national, regional, cyber, global)? What roles do social groups, gender, and ethnicity play in the complex and multifaceted conception of culture? In this chapter we will investigate the difference between twentieth-century, modernist conceptions of culture and twenty-first-century, postmodernist conceptions of culture (Kramsch 2015, 405). We will then offer strategies to help teach culture(s) in a postmodern world.

> **Reflection**
>
> 1. Reflect on the questions raised in the previous paragraph. How would you define a "native speaker"? Why is it difficult to define and categorize a specific culture's "perspective"?
> 2. Whose culture should be taught in the foreign language classroom when there are several to choose from?
> 3. What other elements make it difficult to describe a particular culture?

A POSTMODERNIST PERSPECTIVE ON CULTURE

Kramsch (2015, 405) explains that from the twentieth-century modernist perspective, a language's "cultural context" was often understood as the context or country/countries in which it was spoken. Native speakers were often prioritized as authentic representatives of the target culture. Adhering to clear boundaries and fairly fixed conceptions, the language instructor fostered intercultural understanding by leading thoughtful discussions comparing culture A to culture B. In the twenty-first century, perspectives on culture began to evolve. Mobility, trade, and the media have blurred cultural borders. One can now find Starbucks in Riyadh (complete with separate seating areas and counters for men and women) and popular clothing chains such as H&M and Zara lining the streets of Vienna alongside traditional *Kaffeehäuser* (coffeehouses). Fast-food restaurants such as McDonald's are now popular in Kuwait, to such an extent that they are changing dietary practices across the country. Globalization is shaping cultural practices and perspectives in complex ways across the world. Furthermore, according to Kramsch, cultures of connectivity are transforming social interactions worldwide (406–10). Online communications and social media often promote abbreviated and transactional discourse styles.

The relationship between language and national cultures has also become more fluid. Previously, one may have studied English to interact with Americans or the English, but now people learn English to communicate in Japan, China, and Russia. Spanish, French, and many other languages similarly extend beyond traditional borders. Because English has become a lingua franca in many parts of the world, an understanding of the hybridity of culture must move even further to the forefront. Speaking the same language does not automatically mean sharing a world view. The challenge then becomes twofold: one must balance "the need to acquire 'usable skills' in predictable cultural contexts and the fundamental unpredictability of global contexts" (Kramsch 2015, 409).

Kramsch has defined culture as "membership in a discourse community that shares a common social space and history, and common imaginings" (1998, 10). The emphasis is now on the individual instead of the collective. Kramsch (1993, 233–59) earlier encouraged students to find a "third place": a space between their native culture and the target culture (see Chapter 3). Today, however, she rejects the dichotomous nature of a native culture A and a target culture B. With an understanding that cultures still have unifying factors despite the diversity of their members' perspectives, Kramsch and Whiteside (2008, 664) advocate for *symbolic competence*, or the ability to move within and across languages and cultures. They suggest that this type of variable positioning has a similar premise to that of the MLA report's goals of *translingual* and *transcultural competence*, or the ability to operate *between* languages and cultures. Formerly, foreign language curricula compared the perspectives, practices, and products of fairly fixed societies in an effort to cultivate *intercultural competence*. Today, in contrast, texts, images, and other

Table 9.2. Perspectives on Culture

Twentieth-Century Modernist	Twenty-First-Century Postmodernist
Little c and big C	Symbolic competence
Fixed products, practices, and perspectives	Culture as discourse
Fixed boundaries	Fluid boundaries
Regional, national, and ideological borders	Notions of plurality
Comparisons of culture A to culture B	Contextual, circumstantial, and unpredictable
Set rules of behavior and cultural practices	Multimodal and multilingual
Prioritization of authentic "native speaker"	Cultural mobility
Intercultural competence	Transcultural competence
Dichotomous	Contradictory and dynamic

Source: Adapted from Kramsch 2015, 403–10.

media are often used as springboards for discussion to foster *translingual* and *transcultural competence*. In line with this approach, we provide specific pedagogical strategies and applications in the following sections.

CULTURE, CONTENT, AND CURRICULUM

After exploring the evolution of perspectives on culture, questions may arise about how to teach the complex nature of culture in today's postmodern world. This section showcases a number of key approaches that scholars and instructors have recommended in recent years to help connect theory to practice.

Culture and Content through Narratives

Transcultural understanding may be fostered through the interpretation of multiple cultural narratives associated with the same topic, theme, or event(s) (Kearney 2010). Cultural narratives appear in a variety of forms, from linguistic through visual to audiovisual: fictional stories, first-person memoirs, historical accounts, documentaries, paintings, poetry, songs, and plays are all examples. They can include complementary as well as competing story lines, depending on the source or perspective of the narration. This pluralistic approach allows students to grasp the complexity of events and practices. Thus, conflicts in point of view are not avoided but welcomed. As Graff stated almost thirty years ago, "Culture is a debate rather than a monologue" (1992, 15), and teaching approaches should reflect this perspective.

By exploring conflicts and acknowledging that multiple representations exist, students are able to "imagine themselves and the world differently" (Kearney 2010, 334). Approaching culture via multiple narratives also permits students to conceive of the world in a more realistic and nuanced fashion. Kearney explains that there are several key ways in which narrative approaches can engage students in cultural understanding: they allow students to (1) see how others interpret the world, (2) understand how our points of view determine how we process our experiences, (3) view the world from a different perspective, and (4) understand how their own perspectives may be unfamiliar to others (334). The teacher's goal is therefore to select the narratives carefully, develop activities, and organize discussions that guide students to analyze conflicting perspectives on recurring themes.

The use of cultural narratives in early-level courses raises questions regarding balance, sequencing, and logistics, including these:

- How do we develop students' transcultural and translingual competence while reviewing the necessary vocabulary and grammar to develop linguistic proficiency?
- How do beginning-level students engage in critical language and culture awareness when they have limited linguistic proficiency?

These are important issues to consider in beginning-level courses, where it is tempting to default to a "food, fairs, and folklore" approach (Kramsch 1991, 218), because moving from theory to practice is just too daunting. But teachers sometimes fail to realize that students are often deeply motivated by complexity and only superficially engaged by simplicity. Knutson (2012) describes how instructors often avoid or oversimplify difficult topics in lower-level courses and textbooks because of a desire for new language learners to find the target culture(s) appealing. For example, many lower-level French textbooks include short cultural capsules on the Maghreb, but their presentation often consists of just dry, factual paragraphs about the region and its demographics. For a unit about the Algerian War, Knutson recommends using these textbook descriptions as the springboard to a portfolio project: Beginning students collect photos, images, and short texts in both English and the target language that reflect the various narratives and points of view associated with the war. Over time, students develop a bilingual dossier (or maybe even an academic poster) that requires them to read and write in both English and the target language. The detailed readings in English supplement the interpretation of the visual materials in the portfolio and allow students to understand more fully the complexity surrounding the target language narratives (e.g., graffiti, photos, propaganda) about the Algerian War. (See Knutson 2012 for a detailed description of this project and helpful teacher resources.)

Narratives with complementary and competing story lines are also beneficial in enhancing transcultural understanding in the upper levels of instruction. For example, Péron (2010) uses a multiple narrative approach in her Advanced French course to showcase the complexity of the French World War II experience. Kearney (2012) analyzes the ways in which Péron's curriculum expertly interweaves story lines. For example, she describes the integration of eight narratives in her first fifty-minute observation of the class, ranging from personal anecdotes about the experiences of the teacher's grandfather as a soldier in Occupied France to stories in a collection of memoirs, read for homework, titled *Paroles d'étoiles* (Words of stars). Other narratives were visual, such as photos and a clip of the mass exodus of Jews from Paris in the film *Jeux interdits* (Forbidden Games). Kearney describes this intertextuality: "The class's activities ultimately link narratives about French experiences of WWII with students' more familiar renditions of this historical period, with other cultural narratives about war from their own culture, with the students' personal lives, and with larger existential questions having to do with social inequality, gray areas of morality, and inaction and silence in the face of injustice and persecution" (67). In this case, the use of multiple French narratives allows students to understand WWII from various angles and points of view. Through such a kaleidoscope of perspectives, they can more fully understand the complexity of a target culture's experience during historical periods.

> **Reflection**
>
> In the course that you are currently teaching, think of a final project that would allow students to showcase various narratives and points of view associated with an important cultural event or topic.

Culture and Content through Images

Images are a staple of foreign language, culture, and literature instruction. At the lower levels, they help establish a cultural context or introduce new vocabulary. At the upper levels, visual scaffolding provides support for the discussion of literature, film, historical events, and so on. As discussed in Chapter 7, when students encounter images in the classroom, they can engage in three levels of observation, described by Scanlan (1997) as (1) the literal (descriptive) level, (2) the interpretive-applied level, and (3) the imaginative level. By maintaining discussions at the literal level, teachers risk keeping students in the "culture as fact" zone of understanding, where culture is viewed as a set of fixed products, practices, and perspectives. With careful guidance, on the other hand, it is possible to move students through the various levels of interpretation and encourage a deeper level of cultural understanding.

The Council of Europe, a political organization that focuses on initiatives that support democracy, human rights, and justice, encourages the use of images and other visual media as a point of departure for intercultural understanding. In response to the increasing diversity of the continent's populations, the organization promotes tolerance among individuals from various religious, cultural, and ethnic backgrounds. Its "White Paper on Intercultural Dialogue: Living Together as Equals in Dignity" (2008) suggests that there is a need for tools to help students think critically about their reactions to and attitudes toward other cultures. As a result, *Images of Others: An Autobiography of Intercultural Encounters through Visual Media* (*AIEVM*; available at https://www.coe.int/t/dg4/autobiography/AEIVM_Tool_en.asp) was developed to teach students to examine critically images from cultures around the world and to promote cultural understanding within Europe and beyond.

Although we are often unaware of the power of their influence, visual media can sway our emotions and perspectives and affect our behavior toward other people. *AIEVM* aims to help students interpret the barrage of images that they encounter on a daily basis, including those that may contain hidden messages. To begin, students are asked to choose an image from the internet, television, or a film that is surprising, thought-provoking, enjoyable, or difficult to understand and that contains at least one person who is depicted in a foreign country or a milieu in the students' own country that is culturally different from their own (e.g., where people speak another language or practice another religion). A series of reflection questions then encourages students to think critically about their own identities and those of the person or people featured in the image. These questions are based on the elements of Byram's (1997) conception of intercultural competence (e.g., respect for otherness, empathy), as represented in Table 9.3.

The *AIEVM* image exercise could be particularly effective before or after students discuss an important current event in the target culture(s). For example, students can be asked to gather photos associated with a current event from various media sources and then to reflect on their respective target audiences, contexts, and manners of representing people. Carefully designed prompts or multiple-choice questions can guide beginning learners to complete this activity in the target language. Since each photographer has a different viewpoint, comparing the images side-by-side during class offers students multiple perspectives of the event.

Visual art in particular can engage students in cultural exploration in powerful ways. According to Parra and Di Fabio, visual art "fosters creativity, provides possibilities for making connections, and acts as a window for understanding different dimensions of our world and other worlds and cultures" (2015, 13). Thanks to online resources, visual art has become easily accessible for classroom use, facilitating these connections to other worlds and cultures. Like Scanlan, Barnes-Karol and Broner (2010) encourage examining images at multiple levels. They recommend Bloom's revised taxonomy (remember, understand, apply, analyze, evaluate, and create [Anderson, Krathwohl, and Bloom 2001]) as a guide to designing step-by-step image analysis tasks. Barnes-Karol and Broner suggest that instructors should first spiral the use of everyday language with more academic language about visual art. After students have provided a basic description of the image, they can carefully reflect on its context and its creator's intentions. They can then critically examine how cultural insiders and outsiders may view it. Considering the equivalent of the image in their own culture

Table 9.3. Example Questions from *Images of Others* (AIEVM) Reflecting Byram's Conception of Intercultural Competence

Elements of Intercultural Competence	AIEVM Questions
1. Acknowledgment of identities	1. "Who was shown in the image? (p. 7)
2. Respect for otherness	2. "How did you feel when you first saw the image?" (p. 8)
3. Empathy	3. "How do you think other people from the same group or culture as them would feel about the image?" (p. 9)
4. Communicative awareness	4. "What do you think you could do to make it easier for you to understand each other?" (p. 10)
5. Interpreting and relating	5. "Are they like anyone that you know in your own life?" (p. 11)
6. Knowledge of cultures	6. "Do you think this image is fair or unfair as a way of showing this person's/these people's group or culture?" (p. 13)
7. Knowledge of media	7. "Who do you think was the main audience the image was intended for? Why do you think this audience watches or looks at this kind of image?" (p. 14)
8. Skills of knowledge discovery	8. "Did you try to find out more about the image and how or why it was made?" (p. 16)
9. Critical culture awareness	9. "Try to imagine that you are telling someone you know well about the image. Do you think they would have the same opinions as you?" (p. 17)

Source: Byram 1997; Council of Europe 2013.

also helps students gain perspective and a better understanding of its relevance in the target culture. Barnes-Karol and Broner describe, for example, how the use of multiple images of homes in a beginning-level course can establish a more authentic cultural context:

> When it is time to teach household vocabulary items, instructors can replace the typical textbook drawing of an imaginary home with rooms that correspond to the book's vocabulary list but that is not found in

any culture. Images of urban homes and rural farmsteads, single-family houses and multifamily dwellings, and housing units that reflect the different social classes, geographic realities, or ethnicities that make up the culture create a more authentic context for language learning. . . . Instructors can engage students in learning vocabulary through contact with images of real cultural products, not through artistic renderings of a generic, pan-middle-class house that no one lives in. (440)

Photos of a swath of homes from the target culture(s) offer a much more nuanced idea of the notion of "home" than a generic clip art image does. Similarly, presenting photos only of houses from the students' culture to teach household vocabulary ties their conception of "house" to their own context. Additionally, photos from the target culture can serve as motivation to learn more, since they pique students' interest. Being presented with a diversity of representations allows students to engage with multiple narratives.

Culture and Content through Film

Film is a useful resource for exposing students to rich cultural narratives. It embeds language in a cultural context through visual images and sound, and characters' words and actions on the screen embody social roles and world views. By linking language and cultural content within a visual format, film also shows students how discourse can take on different meanings in different contexts: a word accompanied by particular gestures and facial expressions means one thing in a certain context and something entirely different in another.

Zhang (2011) has developed a sample lesson plan using the Chinese film *Lan zhihe* (*Blue Paper Crane*, 2003) to demonstrate how students can explore cultural perspectives embedded in language. The goals are for students to investigate alternative ways of thinking, explore the use of language in family contexts, and examine how power relations may be embedded in discourse. Zhang provides a series of activities surrounding a three-minute film clip subtitled in Mandarin. This lesson targets intermediate and advanced learners, but the level can vary depending on the degree of scaffolding and guidance provided.

Zhang's clip includes a scene where the character Gan Hong introduces his parents to his new girlfriend, Juhua, at a family dinner. In the preview-

Table 9.4. Expected and Actual Questions in *Lan zhihe*

Students' Predictions	Mother's Questions
"Where are you from?"	"Your accent shows you are not a native of the Haijang city, are you?"
"Where did you attend university?"	"You came to Haijang to work after graduating from university, right?"
"Where do you work?"	"In what unit do you work?"

Source: Adapted from Zhang 2011, 214, 216–17.

ing section, Zhang provides a brief film synopsis (in Chinese or English depending on the course level) and a photo of the family dinner from the clip. Students are asked to examine the photo and imagine the conversation at the table. After discussing the photo in pairs, they share their predictions in a large-group discussion. To begin the viewing activities, students only listen to the conversation at the dinner table, without seeing the moving image. They are asked to listen once or twice for a global understanding of conversational style and turn taking in the film clip (to answer, for example, "Who asks the most questions?" or "What does the mother want to know, and what is she concerned about?" [217]). The next part of the lesson provides the students with the mother's concerns (e.g., the girlfriend's education and profession) and asks them to imagine what she should ask to learn more about the girlfriend. At this stage, they will typically draft questions based on what they assume to be typical or appropriate in their own culture. In the next phase of the lesson, they receive the transcribed dialogue from the film clip with open blanks (a "cloze passage") for the mother's questions. Watching the clip again, with both audio and moving image, the students listen carefully to the dialogue and fill in the blanks. This activity encourages them to pay careful attention to language, question formation, and accuracy. They then compare their predictions with the mother's actual questions (see Table 9.4). *How are the questions different?*

Next, they consider the conversational features of the dialogue (for example, her son's simple answers, the girlfriend's silence, the use of rhetorical questions). *How does the mother use language to express her disapproval? How does the conversation reflect the power dynamics among the mother, her son, and his girlfriend?* Zhang claims that when students were asked to formulate a question about whether Juhua was well suited for her son, they predicted that the mother would simply not ask. In the film, however, she explicitly says, "Don't you think your backgrounds are very different?" Bringing students' attention to such cultural differences can lead to conversations about parental authority. In a follow-up activity, students listen to and analyze another conversation between the mother and the son. In the transcribed dialogue in Chinese, they underline and label the expressions that communicate the mother's values and perspective. Sample labels include "parental authority" and "hierarchy." After marking the dialogue, students break into groups and explain the reasons for their choices. This task further underscores how the mother's use of language reflects her values. As another postviewing activity, Zhang recommends that each group narrate the scene for the class from the perspective of a different character in the film. The clip can be played without sound while students read their narration in Chinese aloud. This activity gives students the opportunity to imagine the scene from multiple viewpoints and see their own narration presented in a visual format.

Reflection

1. Dubreil (2011) shows how multiple full-feature films may be integrated in an advanced language and culture course to showcase the diversity of contemporary culture. Read his article in the L2 Journal: http://escholarship.org/uc/item/86n1q1j2. Analyze how his film selection captures different ideological and narrative viewpoints around similar themes. Then describe how he organizes and structures his lessons to present the complexity of contemporary culture. Choose a theme associated with the language and culture that you teach. Which films would you select to showcase multiple perspectives associated with this theme?

2. In their article "Film as Source Material in Advanced Foreign Language Classes" (2013), Kaiser and Shibahara present activities that use film to foster students' symbolic competence. Read this article in the L2 Journal: http://escholarship.org/uc/item/3qv811wv. In their fourth-year advanced Japanese course, how do the lessons focus students' attention on the use of language, gesture, and context in film? How would you adapt this lesson for beginning- or intermediate-level students?

The interpretation of multiple cultural narratives fosters transcultural understanding (Kearney 2010, 332–35). In a variety of forms, from written to audiovisual, authentic narratives situate language in culture. Their interpretation can encourage a nuanced understanding of important historical events, and characters' words and actions within narratives may reflect social roles, cultural perspectives, and specific world views. Moreover, films, stories, and images establish an intriguing cultural context for lessons that introduce new vocabulary and grammar. By presenting a multiplicity of narratives, instructors can craft lessons that both raise awareness of cultural complexities and reinforce important language-oriented goals.

10 • Synthesis

In previous chapters, we have emphasized the mutually reinforcing nature of the various components of language learning while, for practical reasons, presenting them in discrete chapters. The fundamental aim of this chapter is to show how teachers can spiral language and content to engage students in critical language and cultural awareness through the investigation of multiple (and sometimes conflicting) narratives and perspectives. To achieve this goal, we provide a model unit that pulls together various topics discussed throughout this book: interpreting different types of texts, incorporating targeted vocabulary and grammatical structures, fostering meaningful and relevant interactions (both spoken and written), and developing students' translingual and transcultural competence. Although this unit's subject matter (the 2015 terrorist attacks in Paris) comes from the final weeks of a second-semester French class, its structure, including the scaffolded progression of activities, can be adapted to any language or topic at any level. In most cases we have provided English translations of the activities (instead of the actual activities and their glosses into English). The unit highlights important tenets of curriculum design as advocated by Wiggins and McTighe (2005, 13–34). At the end of the chapter, we also provide prompts and guidelines for creating similar units linked to current issues in other cultures.

BACKWARD DESIGN

Wiggins and McTighe (2005) explain that when developing courses, syllabi, and units, teachers often instinctively use a "forward design" approach, first creating activities and assessment tasks and only later trying to connect them to learning goals. Wiggins and McTighe suggest that teachers use a backward design framework instead, which encourages instructors to (1) articulate learning goals, (2) develop assessment tasks (in alignment with the learning goals), and finally (3) plan learning experiences (in alignment with the goals and assessment tasks). They ask teachers to consider the following questions before planning their curriculum: "What should students know, understand, and be able to do? What content is worthy of understanding? What enduring understandings are desired?" (17). Note that Wiggins and McTighe distinguish between *knowing* (the knowledge and skills that students will acquire) and *understanding* (the "big ideas," fostered by essential questions). One who truly *understands* a topic is able to *explain* it with theories, illustrations, and knowledgeable accounts; *interpret* its meaning and relevance; *apply* knowledge of it to varied contexts; understand *perspectives* and insightful points of view on it; and display *empathy* toward another person's experiences and world view. The unit presented in this chapter integrates these various facets of understanding with targeted linguistic and cultural goals (Mills 2016).

THE 2015 TERRORIST ATTACKS IN PARIS

From January 7 to 9, 2015, a series of terrorist attacks in Paris and the Île-de-France region killed twelve people and left eleven wounded. The victims included several well-known and beloved French cartoonists, who were assassinated at the main office of the provocative and controversial satirical newspaper *Charlie Hebdo* (Charlie Weekly). These attacks, carried out by jihadists who were enraged by *Charlie Hebdo*'s satirization of Islam, ignited a vigorous political debate, both in France and beyond, about issues that are at the core not only of a democratic society but also of a liberal arts education, including the limits of freedom of expression, the role of censorship in society, and the purpose and potential risks of satire. Less than a year after the *Charlie Hebdo* attacks (November 2015), another series of coordinated terrorist attacks took place in Paris—at a well-known concert hall (the Bataclan), the Stade de France (a soccer stadium), and several cafés—killing 130 people and injuring close to 500.

After the *Charlie Hebdo* attacks, two French faculty members and two research librarians at Harvard University began curating a digital collection to commemorate the tragedy. The Charlie Archive at the Harvard Library is a multimedia compilation of manuscripts, printed matter, and digital materials that were produced in the aftermath of the attacks (see https://hollisarchives.lib.harvard.edu/repositories/31/resources/6880 to access sample materials). The collection reflects an array of reactions, ranging from the famous slogan *Je suis Charlie* (I am Charlie) to *Je ne suis pas Charlie* (I am not Charlie). The growing archive now houses donations from France and around the world, including contributions from individuals, professional artists, and major institutions. It has brought together texts of various genres (complementary or contradictory narratives associated with the same topic; see Chapter 9) in both digital and print formats, such as pictures, drawings, cartoons, essays, personal stories, posters, banners, street art, paintings, independent films, and videotaped interviews. It has also gathered several thousand individual web pages that represent different viewpoints (e.g., published articles, blogs, Facebook pages, and Twitter threads).

Reflection

Review the sample materials from the Charlie Archive at the Harvard Library found on page 226 and reflect on how they and their narratives may be accessible to beginning and intermediate language learners.

STAGE 1: ESTABLISH THEMES AND ARTICULATE GOALS

Wiggins and McTighe claim that "the shift [to backward design] involves thinking a great deal, first, about the specific learnings sought, and the evidence of such learnings, before thinking about what we, as the teacher, will do or provide in teaching and learning activities" (2005, 14). Grounded in this framework, questions to guide the development of the goals for the 2015 Paris attack unit include

10.1 Painting: *Cabu*, by Jesse Artiste Peintre. © Arty Jesse Made in Paris. From the Charlie Archive at the Harvard Library.

10.2 Street art: *Not Afraid. Combattre moins, plus aimer.* Translation of French text: "Fight less, love more." Photographed by Nicole Mills. From the Charlie Archive at the Harvard Library.

10.3 Street art: *Nous sommes la France.* Translation of French text: "Muslims, Jews, Christians, and all others. We are France." Photographed by Nicole Mills. From the Charlie Archive at the Harvard Library.

10.4 Poster: *Memorial.* Translation of French text: *Citizen, Honor, Love, Respect, Liberty, Ideal, Hope.* Photographed by Nicole Mills. From the Charlie Archive at the Harvard Library.

- What enduring knowledge and understanding are desired?
- What are pertinent themes and important topics of discussion?
- What linguistic and cultural content (associated with the themes) can contribute to cultivating students' understanding?
- What should students be able to do?

We highlight the following overarching themes and enduring understandings that students explore and attempt to unpack in the unit:

- People's reactions to satirical texts may be conditioned by their cultural values, personal experiences, political views, and proximity to the subject of the satire.
- The notions of "freedom of speech" and "censorship" can mean different things to different people, and these terms may represent culturally created constructs.
- The media play an important role in the processing and sharing of events, and journalists can spin incidents in contradictory ways.
- People's responses to the terrorist attacks in Paris may depend on their personal, cultural, and academic backgrounds and beliefs, as well as how the events affected them personally.

These themes are complex. Students may not be able to express their thoughts and hypotheses in depth and detail in the target language during only their second semester of language study, but they are certainly capable of understanding these topics, interacting with them intellectually, and expressing their opinions using carefully guided prompts and scaffolding support provided in the target language. Through studying texts and participating in activities in English (in addition to French), students have the opportunity to engage with the compelling subject matter in a variety of ways. To complement the unit themes, the overarching goals are for students to be able to

- explore, interpret, and describe the 2015 Paris attacks as expressed through media, art, the linguistic landscape, etc.;
- exchange thoughtful personal opinions and express emotions using targeted grammatical structures (in this case the subjunctive) and varied vocabulary;
- explain diverse perspectives (domestic and international) on the events; and

- engage in meaningful conversations about the attacks with classmates and with individuals beyond the classroom.

STAGE 2: DEVELOP ASSESSMENT TASK

Wiggins and McTighe explain that an important component of the backward design framework is integrating authentic performance tasks that allow students to demonstrate achievement of the desired learning outcomes (2005, 22). According to Wiggins and McTighe, authentic assessment

- is realistically contextualized;
- asks students to complete meaningful tasks;
- assesses students' ability to explain, apply, and interpret a repertoire of knowledge and perspectives effectively; and
- adds the dimension of a meaningful audience.

Engaging in thoughtful and informed discussions of global events and their implications in today's world is a task that is relevant to students' lives. For the unit's final assessment, students participate in a ten-minute informed discussion of the Paris attacks with a classmate, interpreting and analyzing varied perspectives on it, including their own (see Box 10.1). They receive the description of this assessment at the beginning of the unit so that they have a clear understanding of its relationship to the unit's learning outcomes.

Box 10.1. Informed Discussion (Final Assessment for the Unit)

Context

The *Charlie Hebdo* attacks of January 2015 triggered intense political debates about cultural and political matters that frame the notions of democracy and education. These questions and issues cross disciplines within the humanities and beyond, including the fields of history and literature, media studies, government, religion, law, and sociology. The Paris attacks in November 2015 further complicated this discussion.

Continued . . .

Task

You will be asked to engage in an informed discussion with a fellow classmate about the Paris attacks in January and November 2015. In this ten-minute conversation, you will describe the events using facts and examples associated with the event(s) and explain the perspectives provided by various faculty interviewees. Each discussion partner should bring and interpret at least one image/source from the Charlie Archive at the Harvard Library, attempting to understand and empathize with the creator's perspective. Share your own perspective on the events. Themes of your discussion could include (but are not limited to) the following topics: freedom of expression, religion, immigration, multiculturalism, sacredness, terrorism, censorship, respect, and violence. As appropriate, use the subjunctive, the targeted grammatical structure of the unit, to express your opinions, beliefs, and emotions. After the informed discussion, your instructor will ask you follow-up questions about your commentary.

Evaluation

You will be assessed on your ability to

- interpret and describe the Paris attacks in 2015 as expressed through media, art, etc.;
- engage in a meaningful conversation about current events with a classmate/colleague;
- explain diverse perspectives (domestic and international) on the events; and
- exchange thoughtful personal opinions and express emotions using targeted grammatical structures (subjunctive) and varied vocabulary.

In this culminating, interactive assessment task, students have the opportunity to reflect on the transcultural and translingual insights that they have developed; they are able link what they have learned from the unit to their own perspectives. In other words, they are equipped (and encouraged) to grapple with how their own experiences color their reactions to the attacks and their aftermath (for example, as a Middle Eastern person studying in an

American university, as the American child of French parents, as someone who has lost a friend in a terrorist attack).

STAGE 3: PLAN LEARNING EXPERIENCES

Following Stages 1 and 2 (articulating goals and developing the assessment task), the final stage of backward design is determining the instructional approaches, resources, and experiences that will allow learners to achieve the unit goals and complete the performance tasks (Wiggins and McTighe 2005, 191–226). At this point, the instructor envisions what content students should explore and how it should be incorporated in light of established goals. In the Paris attacks unit, students examine several themes: (1) satire and freedom of speech, (2) conflicting perspectives on the *Charlie Hebdo* attack and its aftermath, and (3) the role of social media in sharing reactions to the January and November Paris attacks.

Day 1: Satire and Freedom of Speech

To establish background knowledge for the unit, students begin by reading, for homework, the blog entry (in English) titled "Seven Questions My American Friends Ask about the Charlie Hebdo Shootings" (https://medium.com/@NabilWakim/the-charlie-hebdo-shootings-explained-to-my-american-friends-81f34f3c9c3e). Nabil Wakim, a journalist for the French newspaper *Le Monde* who was working as a fellow at Harvard in 2015, wrote this essay to respond to several key questions that his American friends asked him following the attacks, regarding notions of free speech in France and the *Charlie Hebdo* publication. By highlighting the complexity of the topic, the article prepares students to regard through multiple lenses the images and texts (a collection of written and visual texts, including caricatures, blogs, tweets, and video-recorded oral histories) that they will investigate during the unit. The first themes that they explore are satire and freedom of speech.

In the course's first lesson, students analyze and describe *Charlie Hebdo* caricatures in French. Working with these authentic materials provides students with insights into the catalysts for the attacks. Each caricature (carefully selected for appropriateness and accessible language) is accompanied by a short description (in French) of its context, a short list of vocabulary words that will be useful to describe it, and discussion questions. Relevant vocabulary and grammar activities are interspersed throughout the lesson.

One of the *Charlie* covers used in the course reads, "Aux chiottes toutes les religions" (down the toilet, all religions), the words interspersed with a drawing of three streams of toilet paper, each with the face of a religious leader (a cardinal, an imam, and a rabbi) beside it (one can easily find this image online by searching for the French phrase above). One toilet paper roll reads "Bible," another "Koran," and the third "Torah." All the words on the page are cognates except for "chiottes," which is a vulgar French slang word that literally means "crapper." To prepare students to discuss the drawing, the following vocabulary words (translated into English here) are included in a box:

the cardinal/the imam/the rabbi
toilet paper
scatological humor
religious texts
to compare/a comparison
to throw away
flush the toilet

Students then use these materials to complete a series of activities:

Activity 10.1. Dictionary Searches

Students are asked to look up in a dictionary whatever words from the list they do not know, to provide two sentences that they have found online containing these words, and to write two sentences themselves using these expressions. Most of the words above are cognates (except for "to throw away" and "flush"); however, students probably have not seen or heard the other words before, so this vocabulary is not part of their active lexicon.

Activity 10.2. One of These Words Is Not like the Others

In this activity, students are asked to choose the term that does not fit with the others in the following groups (note that words that they already know from previous units and cognates that they may not have seen before are integrated here as well). Students should also explain how the "intruder word" differs from the others in the list:

1. a cardinal	a professor	a rabbi	an imam
2. the Bible	the Koran	the dictionary	the Torah
3. the toilet	the handle	the sink	toilet paper
4. flush	throw out	get rid of	keep
5. religion	water	toilet	excrement
6. comparable	similar	different	same
7. humor	severity	irony	satire
8. washroom	bathroom	paradise	water closet

Activity 10.3. Word Associations

In this activity, students are asked to make a list of all the French words (from above, but also others that they may already know) that they associate with the following expressions:

Religion
Bathrooms
Scatological humor
Things or ideas that should be symbolically flushed down the toilet

Activity 10.4. Agree or Disagree

This activity asks students to agree or disagree with the following statements or to say that "it depends." Note that these statements have the potential to be particularly helpful, since students may use adapted (or negated) versions of them when discussing the content of the caricatures in later activities.

1. It is common to make fun of religion.
2. It is normal to find religious leaders' faces on everyday objects.
3. Scatological humor is funny.
4. Scatological humor is a sophisticated form of humor.
5. Jokes mocking religion are funny.
6. The Koran, the Bible, and the Torah are sacred religious texts.
7. It is OK to make fun of your own religion but not someone else's.

The goal of the preceding activities is for students to become comfortable with using some of the key words by reading and recalling them, so that they will be primed to engage in a more thoughtful and meaningful way in subsequent activities. The discussion in Activity 10.5, for example, is more open ended, but it is also somewhat structured, as students work together in small groups to analyze their assigned caricature. The task includes helpful phrases (for example, "Here is an image that makes fun of"; "Here is an image that critiques").

Activity 10.5. Analyze a Caricature

Reflect on the following prompts:
1. Describe the caricature.
2. What is caricatured?
3. What is the message that the caricaturist wanted to express?
4. Do you think that the caricature is original? Objective? Insulting?
5. Other impressions?

Model Phrases

Here is an image of . . .
Here is an image that makes fun of / that critiques . . .
The main characters are . . .
It is a question of . . . / It's about . . .
We find that . . .

Source: Created by John D'Amico and Grégoire Menu (spring 2015).

After their small-group discussions, students present their caricatures to the class and compare representations with the help of the instructor.

Students now move from the knowledge phase to the understanding stage as they engage in a thoughtful discussion about satire and free speech. At this point, the lesson can seamlessly integrate relevant grammar—in this case the subjunctive, which is needed for expressing opinions. Students will have already studied the forms and use of the subjunctive before beginning this unit, but some review will be necessary. It is always important to recycle grammar topics in a scaffolded manner, so students complete structured input activities (in the form of input flood) linked to the topic at hand before producing their own reactions. The structured inputs of Activities 10.6–8 allow students to review the forms and use of the subjunctive.

Activity 10.6. Agree or Disagree?

Do you agree or disagree with the following comments related to the *Charlie Hebdo* attacks? For each, express your opinion ("agree," "disagree," or "it depends") and then provide follow-up comments or reactions. [*Italics indicate where the subjunctive would be found in French.*]

1. It is important that satirists *be able to* express themselves, even if they insult other people.
2. It is surprising that people *are willing* to die for their religion.
3. It is sad that people *use* violence to express themselves.
4. I am afraid that there *will be* more terrorist acts in the future.
5. It is necessary that the French government *provide* additional security for journalists.
6. It is essential that extremely religious people *adapt* if they wish to live in a secular country.
7. It is unfortunate that satirists *parody* religion.
8. It is best that a secular country *welcome* and *respect* all religious views.

Activity 10.7. Your Opinion

What do you think of the *Charlie Hebdo* publication? Choose the appropriate answer(s)—sometimes more than one—and then follow up with additional commentary to justify your choice(s).

1. The cartoonists wanted their readers to
    a. make fun of Mohammad in particular.
    b. make fun of all religions equally.
    c. make fun of cartoonists who make fun of religion.
2. Americans are shocked that the *Charlie Hebdo* covers
    a. have such politically provocative images.
    b. have such obscene images.
    c. are so badly drawn.
3. It is regretful that
    a. *Charlie Hebdo* publishes magazine covers that depict Mohammad.
    b. some people think that *Charlie Hebdo* should stop publishing magazines depicting Mohammad.
    c. *Charlie Hebdo* does not seem to respect religion.

Activity 10.8. Complete the Sentences

Complete the sentences with your thoughts. [*Note that the verbs in the subjunctive (indicated by italics) are given; students are not asked to supply them.*]

1. The artists wanted their readers *to have* more _____.
2. It is sad that terrorists *can* _____.
3. It is necessary that we *remain* _____.
4. It is important that future generations *know* _____.

After they have completed the structured input activities, students are ready to move into the structured output stage and express their own, original reactions to the caricatures. To do so, they need to use the subjunctive; therefore, the discussion prompts include this mood (for example, in Activity 10.9, "It is important that . . ."). To help articulate their ideas, students first write down their personal thoughts before sharing these reactions with a partner. A large-group discussion follows.

Activity 10.9. Discussion

Charlie Hebdo overtly mocks politics, religion, etc., sometimes in an aggressive fashion. Give your reaction to the following statement, basing your arguments on the *Charlie Hebdo* attack and making sure to use the subjunctive where necessary:

Satire should have limits.

Begin with one of the following:

- In my opinion, satire should have limits, because . . .
- In my opinion, satire should not have limits, because . . .

Then continue:

It is important that . . .
It is necessary that . . .
I am sad that . . .
I am shocked that . . .
I am frustrated that . . .
I am angry that . . .
I want that . . .

Source: Adaptation of an activity created by John D'Amico and Grégoire Menu (spring 2015).

Day 2: Multiple Perspectives on the *Charlie Hebdo* Attacks

The Charlie Archive includes post-attack oral history interviews with Harvard faculty members from various academic departments, including History, Literature, Government, Religion, and Law. Interviewees responded to the following questions:

1. How did you find out about the attacks on *Charlie Hebdo* and the kosher grocery store in Paris in January 2015 (Facebook, Twitter, TV, newspapers, etc.)? What was your personal reaction to the shootings and the media coverage that followed?
2. In your opinion, what is the degree of caricature and satire that is acceptable? Is there such a thing as a degree of responsibility in the exercise of one's freedom of speech?
3. Did you see the attack on *Charlie Hebdo* as a unique and unrepeatable event or as part of a larger history of attacks on writers and artists for their work?

To explore diverse perspectives associated with the events, students begin by watching one of these faculty interviews. The ten-minute interviews are conducted in English, but students write a brief summary and reaction in French (five to seven sentences). Watching interviews in English (as opposed to the target language) allows beginning language students to gain an understanding of the complexity of the events without needing superior-level language skills. This task also gives students important background knowledge (about history, law, etc.) that they can use to interpret various French texts and articulate their own opinions more clearly in the target language in class. The reactions to the faculty interviews are shared on the class section's social media platform as a preparatory activity for the class discussion.

During the class session, students participate in an interactive, rotating discussion in French. Chairs are set up in two facing rows, and each student exchanges information about the interview they have watched with the classmate across from them, jotting down the main points of their partner's presentation. After seven to ten minutes, they all change partners by moving one chair to the left. By the end of the session, each student has heard the synopses of five or six faculty members' perspectives from across the disciplines. A culminating large-group discussion, guided by the instructor, allows them to compare all the perspectives.

Day 3: The Role of Social Media in the 2015 Paris Attacks

In the following lesson, students analyze the role of social media in the aftermath of the 2015 Paris attacks: how social media influenced the public response and encouraged and disseminated artistic expressions in reaction to the attacks. To prepare, students explore texts from various social media sources, including viral videos, tweets, and Instagram posts. To participate in the discussion, students need to understand the hidden meanings embedded within the viral tweet and hashtag "Je suis Charlie" (I am Charlie). Because beginning-level students often control limited specialized vocabulary, they receive a list of possible descriptions of the speaker (for example, "a political satirist," "a defender of free speech"). By providing multiple options, the instructor is able to scaffold the discussion and develop students' vocabulary and content knowledge with comprehensible input. Because French and English have a large number of cognates, students are able to understand words and expressions that they have not seen before. They can then choose one or more options from the list, and their responses can serve as a point of departure for further discussion.

Activity 10.10. Developing Students' Content Knowledge through Comprehensible Choices

Je suis Charlie (I am Charlie)

Does it mean that "je" is . . .

- a journalist who works for *Charlie Hebdo*?
- a reader of the *Charlie Hebdo* publication?
- a victim of the January 7, 2015, *Charlie Hebdo* attacks?
- a caricaturist from another country?
- a political satirist?
- a defender of free speech?
- someone who opposes jihad?

Source: Created by Christina Svendsen and Cécile Guédon (spring 2015).

A goal of this lesson is to help students understand the diversity of points of view regarding terrorist attacks in general as presented via hashtags on social media platforms, focusing on the January and November 2015 Paris attacks. Activity 10.11 is a preparatory matching task which aims to ensure that students have understood the meanings of the various hashtags.

Activity 10.11. Matching Hashtags

What do these hashtags mean?

#JesuisParis (#IamParis)
#PorteOuverte (#OpenDoor)
#RechercheParis (#FindParis)
#PriezpourParis (#PrayforParis)
#Noussommesunis (#Weareunited)
#unebougiepourparis (#acandleforparis)
#JeSuisMusulmanPasTerroriste (#IamMuslimNotTerrorist)
#Jenesuispascharlie (#Iamnotcharlie)

This hashtag

- honors the victims of terrorism by posting photos of a small candle on the windowsill or the balcony.
- shows solidarity with the victims: we are all Parisian.
- offers prayers for the victims and their families.
- references the *Charlie Hebdo* attacks from January 2015.
- offers shelter to people in the street following the attacks.
- allows friends and family of the victims to find them on Twitter or Facebook.
- asks people to stop conflating Islam and terrorism.
- emphasizes that one can be opposed to the terrorist attacks but unwilling to identify with the content of *Charlie Hebdo* at the same time.

Following this task, students analyze several tweets, constructing the link between the hashtag and the message. They are then asked to write their own tweets that express their point of view in French, integrating relevant hashtags or creating new ones. (See Chapter 8 for guidelines on self-editing, peer editing, and grading written work.)

Activity 10.12. Tweet-Writing Task

Step 1

For homework, find two tweets in French on Twitter related to one of the hashtags discussed in class. Read each tweet, and try to gain a basic understanding of the message. Then carefully analyze their content. Pay attention to how the opinion is presented through structure, emotions, message length, formality or informality, abbreviations, hashtag choice and placement, and word choice. Post your analysis on the class social networking platform (5–7 sentences).

Step 2

During the following class session, compare your collected tweets and hashtags with a partner. Discuss the perspective of each tweet, focusing on how each one expresses an opinion through word choice, length, hashtags, abbreviations, etc.

Step 3

With your partner, choose one of the analyzed tweets posted on the class social networking platform and write a tweet response in French. Feel free to borrow the approaches used in the analyzed French tweets (e.g., word choice, structure, abbreviations, hashtags) to express your opinion.

Step 4

Post your tweet response on the class social networking platform. If you feel so compelled, post it on Twitter as well. You may receive a response from the original tweeter.

Day 4: Perspective and Empathy through Interaction

On the last day of the unit, students have the opportunity to engage directly with a Parisian who was in Paris during the 2015 attacks, via a Skype interview. Students are asked to prepare one or two questions for homework, which the instructor reviews for grammatical accuracy and comprehensibility. To begin the class session, students "visit" the Paris attack memorials and the targeted cafés via virtual reality headsets. The goal is to transport them to the places where the attacks occurred so that they can experience the aftermath through multiple sensory modalities. Next, students talk via Skype with a Parisian who personally experienced the attacks and is now sitting in La Belle Équipe, one of the cafés targeted in November 2015. Since students have already explored multiple texts (for example, caricatures, tweets, images, interviews, blogs) in both English and French, they possess a rich repertoire of content knowledge to guide their discussion. They also have access to a list of helpful expressions to keep the conversation going (for example, "That's true"), to expand on the topic ("I also think that..."), to ask for clarification ("Can you explain?"), to check understanding ("Is that right?"), and to offer support ("I'm sorry to hear about that"; "It must have been very difficult"). Engaging directly with someone who lived through the attacks is a meaningful and unforgettable experience. It allows students to develop even more compassion for the victims, and it provides them with the opportunity to ask questions that may not have been answered in the texts that they have analyzed for class. Finally, it teaches them how to interact respectfully with someone who has lived through a difficult and heartbreaking experience; they need to use the pragmatic and linguistic tools at their disposal to express their sympathy, solidarity, and support, thus tying together all the themes and linguistic tools that they have studied. Ultimately, it is likely that they will experience a strong sense of empathy as a result of this interaction.

Reflection

1. Review the guiding principles of effective L2 pedagogy in Chapter 1. They include (among others) the use of authentic language and texts; the scaffolding of tasks; the promotion of interaction, critical thinking, and self-awareness; and the expansion of classroom boundaries. Highlight how these principles are integrated in this chapter's unit, citing specific examples.
2. Were the facets of understanding (explanation, interpretation, application, perspective, and empathy) targeted in the lesson? If so, how?

Perspectives

Consider the testimony of an instructor who used the materials above to teach this unit:

> Before the *Charlie Hebdo* unit, I was interested to see this subject included in the course but initially apprehensive, for several reasons. It seemed to be a very sensitive and complex topic to treat appropriately with second-semester students. Would the unit (and my instruction) communicate clearly and respectfully the context as well as the weight of these tragic events? Could these events be

Continued ...

treated in a nonsuperficial way with language learners? I was hesitant because it was very difficult for me to talk about as well, and I didn't know if I wanted to engage myself with my students on it. I didn't know if I was capable pedagogically or if they were capable linguistically. I was also worried that the complexity of the issues at hand would not be successfully communicated, leading students to a very simplified vision of what happened and what it means. I worried about the effect on the classroom environment as well. It was quite a shift from the usual tone in the classroom, which I try to keep playful, light, and high energy. These concerns, however, seemed to be more in my head than a real problem. The students were ready and eager to discuss something more weighty and serious. Some of the things that I was most worried about actually turned out to be the most interesting and productive. The lesson design allowed students to take critical positions on the #JeSuisCharlie movement, as well as express opinions about the meaning of free speech (in the target language!). The class discussions demonstrated very clearly how the students were critically engaged in these issues, how this unit was not in any way a superficial exercise (on the contrary), and how much they reflected on these questions.

1. Do you sometimes avoid teaching certain cultural topics because they seem too serious or complex? Do you have concerns about teaching weighty issues in the language classroom? Do you think that students might have a similar reaction? Explain.
2. What are the benefits of teaching cultural conflicts and issues?

DESIGNING A UNIT PLAN

Using the following guidelines for developing a unit plan for any language or level, you can synthesize what you have learned about language pedagogy in a practical yet creative format. Following the tenets of backward design, your unit plan should include

- clearly defined language- and content-oriented goals (Stage 1),
- a creative authentic assessment task (Stage 2), and
- one representative lesson (Stage 3).

The unit should integrate the context-based instruction of language and culture/content; encourage the use of interpretive, interpersonal, and presentational communication; and guide students toward a critical understanding of its "big ideas." It should also use your language of instruction to target students and should integrate the key principles of effective L2 pedagogy in the twenty-first century (see Chapter 1).

Stage 1: Define Unit Themes and Goals

To define unit themes and goals, follow these steps:

1. Choose a current event in your target culture(s).
2. Gain background knowledge about the event by consulting coverage from various media sources (newspapers, magazines, blogs, newscasts, etc.). In the research process, set aside texts (photos and other images, articles, video clips) that are relevant and accessible to students at your level of instruction.
3. Outline key events and themes associated with the event.
4. Draft a list of unit goals associated with the targeted themes. Reflect on the facets of understanding (explanation, interpretation, application, perspective, and empathy) and their connection to the themes and goals. To articulate objectives (e.g., grammatical, functional, cultural and content oriented, analytical) that spiral language and content,
   - begin with the stem "The students will be able to . . .";
   - add a verb (search online for "list of action verbs from Bloom's taxonomy" for useful action verbs, such as *analyze, recognize, compare, provide, list*); and
   - end with the targeted product, process, or outcome.

   For example: "The students will be able to formulate proposals [using the conditional tense] to address immigration issues in Germany."

Stage 2: Develop an Authentic Assessment Task

Create an authentic assessment task that targets and assesses students' mastery of your outlined goals. Reflect on a meaningful real-world task that will engage students with an authentic audience. Use the following box to guide the development of the assessment task:

Box 10.2. Authentic Assessment Task

Description

What is the realistic context for the task?
Who is the audience?
What is the structure?

Content and Goals

What are the goals of this assignment? Align directly with unit goals.
What content and resources are necessary to complete the assignment?

Language Focus

What grammatical, lexical, and pragmatic knowledge is required to complete the assignment?
What style should be used (formal versus informal, written versus spoken, etc.)?

Process

Will the assignment be submitted in stages (i.e., part 1, part 2)?
How many versions/drafts? What is the length of the assignment? Due date(s)?

Assessment Criteria

How will the assignment be graded? Which criteria will be used? Review the unit goals to target assessment criteria linked to learning outcomes. Draft a rubric (see Chapter 8).

Source: Adapted from Byrnes et al. 2006, 103.

Stage 3: Create a Representative Lesson

Go through the following steps to create a representative lesson.

1. Refer back to your targeted themes and goals from Stage 1. Create a list of three to four subthemes that your unit could address.
2. Choose one subtheme, and make a list of lesson goals linked to it. Create a title for your lesson (e.g., "What is the future of immigration?").
3. Refer back to the texts you gathered in Stage 1. From this collection, choose a variety of texts associated with this lesson's subtheme that are relevant and accessible for students at your level of instruction.
4. Draft a lesson that carefully correlates with your list of goals and integrates authentic texts. Refer to the principles for effective language pedagogy in the twenty-first century (see Chapter 1).
5. Think carefully about how your lesson builds both language and content knowledge from one phase to the next. Integrate the following elements:
    - introduction and warm-up,
    - scaffolded teacher-guided activities and discussions,
    - interactive group tasks,
    - thematic transitions,
    - conclusion.

11 • Profession

PROFESSIONAL LIFE

For language faculty, new and experienced alike, handling the demands of teaching, research, and administration can feel like a precarious balancing act. It can be difficult to step back and to see how short-term tasks and deadlines relate to the larger professional context. The topics, suggestions, and reflection prompts in this chapter are selected to help readers understand their professional role within and beyond their current teaching assignment. The chapter is geared especially toward those who will soon take on their first faculty position in the US, where they may teach a mixture of basic language and more specialized courses. At the same time, it serves as a resource for experienced instructors who have been deep in the trenches for a while but want to reflect on their professional identity and engage in active professional development.

We begin with a topic that every faculty member will need to address, if not philosophically, then logistically: the two-tiered curricular and personnel model that has characterized most language departments for decades. We then present several ways to collect data for a teaching portfolio. Looking at the bigger picture, we discuss concerns that faculty in language departments and the humanities in general have today. Because our book is focused on teaching, we do not discuss alternative academic careers, which more and more PhDs in language, literature, and culture are pursuing (see Sanders 2014).

THE TWO-TIERED SYSTEM

Even first-time graduate TAs are already—consciously or not—developing a professional identity. Not all freshly minted PhDs land the same type of teaching jobs. Some find an area of specialization within a language department: linguistics, medieval literature, film studies. Others, regardless of their expertise, teach a gamut of language courses along with the occasional literature or culture survey. Not all departments hire a language program director (LPD) with expertise in SLA/applied linguistics. Quite often, faculty whose research focuses on literature or cultural studies also supervise basic language courses, either on their own or in consultation with an LPD, a curricular planning committee, or a department chair. Others have sway over the language curriculum even if their direct involvement is minimal. The department that graduate students get to know could be structured much differently from those they later consider for full-time employment. Many universities do not have graduate students or graduate programs, which means that all their language classes are taught by faculty on various lines (tenure-track, clinical, adjunct), as a team or independently.

At various points throughout this book, we have referred to the 2007 MLA report and its influence on pedagogical reforms. The report's authors articulated the components and implications of a divide in language departments that had been widely recognized for decades but seldom so forcefully discussed in terms of the profession as a whole. Traditionally, an overemphasized schism in departments of language/literature/culture has segregated "language" courses from "content" courses and, perhaps more insidiously, pedagogy from ideas. "Content" courses are sometimes seen as related to a department's intellectual identity, while "language" courses represent a sort of pragmatic necessity. The two-tiered system reveals itself in pedagogical practices and, just as important, in divisions of workload and professional rank and status. Some departments offer tenure-track lines (along with enhanced research support and sabbatical opportunities) to some specialists but not others. With different faculty lines come inequitable teaching and administrative loads.

> **Reflection**
>
> 1. Do graduate students who are preparing to be literature professors need to learn how to teach lower-division courses? Explain.
> 2. Do the same instructors teach all levels of courses in your department?
> 3. Do different ranks correspond to different statuses, workloads, or benefits in your department?
> 4. Some institutions house all beginning and intermediate language courses together in a center or department with its own faculty. What are the pros and cons of separating lower-division courses from higher-level courses in this way?

For many language faculty, the MLA report represented a turning point in discussions about the structure of modern language departments in the US. SLA specialists who had long argued for more attention to content in language courses and more focus on language in upper-level literature and culture courses could now cite the report to make their case to administrators who had not been supportive in the past. In the decade following its publication, numerous articles related to SLA, FL pedagogy, and the role of languages in higher education cited the report. A timely and political document, it appeared when the fair treatment of adjunct faculty, many of whom were hired specifically to teach language courses, was already a topic of national debate. Moreover, it was published by the Modern Language Association, an organization that, despite its name, was traditionally seen as dedicated more to research in literature than to language pedagogy. The tides seemed to be turning.

On the other hand, a survey conducted ten years later by Lomicka and Lord confirmed what many colleagues had already observed: that transformation on the institutional and departmental levels in response to the 2007 MLA report had been slow at best (see, e.g., Redden 2017). As Lomicka and Lord explained, "The survey results presented here, although preliminary, show that faculty members are aware of the innovations that are needed but are equally daunted by how to implement them" (2018, 119). Though the report ignited a productive discussion, the language/literature dichotomy, long embedded in the academic collective unconscious and nurtured by institutional policies and practices, still holds strong. Oddly, this separation persists even though in many departments the very same faculty teach both language and literature courses and the very same students move not beyond but *through* "language" courses to "content" courses (see Krueger 2001). Furthermore, in what seems like an ironic illustration of precisely the problem the report exposed, the "literature side" of departments did not respond with the same energy or conviction as the "language side": the overwhelming majority of articles published in light of the 2007 report were written by specialists in SLA/applied linguistics.

What is at stake, for faculty, for students, and for programs, if the potential congruity of language and content courses is ignored? In advocating a cohesive approach to designing a writing curriculum for all levels of "language" and "content" courses, Maxim contends that "almost by default, a department that is able to establish common educational goals at all levels of instruction also will no longer be able to justify the traditional division between language and content courses" (2005, 83). Yet despite the success of curricular reform at some institutions, many departments find it difficult to conceptualize the sequence of courses offered, from beginning language to undergraduate topics seminars, as part of a harmonious continuum.

What if we were to focus not on what is different but rather on what is shared by "language" and "literature" courses? As with any other field, FL pedagogy reacts to the dominant ideologies in academia and our broader culture. Language research and literature research, though usually different in method, progress within a shared sociocultural climate, subject to the same zeitgeist, unfolding against the same political backdrop. The neatly programmed truths of ALM gained traction in tandem with similarly paradigmatic structuralist approaches to literature. The earliest waves of proficiency-based approaches took into account learner variables, multiple skills, and the cultural contexts of both the learner and the material studied. In a wide range of poststructuralist approaches, literary scholars became attentive to the role of the reader as a shaper of textual meaning. Today we find ourselves decades away from the linguistic turn, in a postmethods, postmodern, and postcritical world, where interdisciplinarity and changing modes of interaction with texts resonate in multiliteracy approaches to language learning and in multidisciplinary collaborations in research and teaching at higher levels.

This paradigm shift is not a case of literary theory dictating SLA theory, or vice versa, but rather an example of how teaching and research environments respond to shifts in cultural perspectives outside the classroom. The approaches to language, literature, and culture adopted at a given time have grown with, against, and in reaction to their predecessors. Structuralism no longer plays a dominant role in textual interpretation, yet its emphasis on form and close reading remains relevant. Likewise, the speed, drilling, and memorization at the center of ALM are at odds with learning strategies today, but ALM's valorization of accuracy and practical language still resonates with revised practices. New approaches carry the DNA of their predecessors, but somehow language learning strategies that have helped to move the profession forward are often ridiculed rather than valued once their perceived inadequacies have been revealed.

It seems that philosophical parallels underlying approaches to teaching language and teaching literature have gone largely unnoticed, or at least undocumented. Otherwise, perhaps the language/literature divide would be narrower today. Confronting the problem is especially important at a time when budget cuts to foreign language departments and the humanities generally have been significant enough to make national news. But if a language department does not value its own language courses, how can its faculty convince administrators not to merge or close that department? How can a department chair argue that foreign language is essential to a new, multidisciplinary Global Studies Program if language courses have been devalued in her own department? It is possible that the demise of many language/literature/culture departments today is directly connected to or has at least been bolstered by this internal divide. Although universities deeply support initiatives that stress interdisciplinarity, the integration of technological resources, and effective assessment tools, administrators do not necessarily associate these proposals with FL departments, perhaps because the work behind them has been conducted by untenured colleagues who do not have a strong voice in or influence on institutional matters. In fact, language/literature/culture departments are inherently models of interdisciplinarity, but they too often deny their implicit connection of disciplines, rendering themselves vulnerable to downsizing by repressing the inherent, dynamic continuity of their faculty, students, and course offerings and by cultivating an outdated and impractical internal polarity. Reinforcing the convergent evolution of language, culture, and literature studies would benefit students, departments, and the humanities as a whole.

Fallout from the two-tiered system also manifests itself in a hierarchical curricular sequencing of skills. Most speaking and grammar practice takes place in lower-level courses, and reading and writing are favored in advanced courses. But this paradigm is shifting. Over recent decades, SLA scholars have prioritized the need for a smooth transition from beginning to advanced courses. They have reached across the language/literature divide via conferences, articles, textbooks, teacher education, and daily practice, incorporating reading, writing, and discussion strategies to prepare students for further coursework. They have also infused language courses with content (especially culturally rich texts in the target language).

In response to the MLA report, the "content side" of language/literature/culture programs may have been slower than the "language side" to react and to revise itself pedagogically, or at least it may have been quieter about consciously doing so, yet many literary scholars show genuine concern for students' motivation and emotional connection to course materials. Interactive and cooperative learning models abound, though they are not necessarily so named: for example, without mentioning schemata, instructors of upper-level courses present new material in context and activate students' prior knowledge before asking them to engage with unfamiliar subject matter. On the bright side, a portion of the traditional language/content divide may boil down to a lack of shared terminology.

The traditional bridge course (offered in the fifth or sixth semester of a language sequence and usually devoted to grammar and composition) was conceptualized as a capstone to language study, a last chance for students to master grammar while giving them a taste of what awaited them in upper-level literature classes. The idea of isolating and putting a time limit on grammar mastery in this way was never justifiable, and it seems especially untenable now. Because certain languages are no longer regularly taught in high schools, some college students will start learning a foreign language at a later cognitive and social stage of life than some of their peers. Moreover, most students now come to college with little or no formal study of grammar in their native language; the acquisition of a foreign language grammar is thus even more challenging. Inevitably, students must focus more on linguistic forms as they enter advanced courses. Can we afford *not* to be attentive to language skills in our upper-level content courses?

> **Reflection**
>
> 1. For new teachers: What do you expect to be your biggest challenges as you begin language teaching? For experienced teachers: What are the biggest challenges you face while teaching? Have the challenges that you face changed over the years?
> 2. Does your department offer bridge courses? If so, how are they structured? Who teaches them? Are these classes offered on a variety of topics, or is it mainly one course that is regularly offered?
> 3. Interview the faculty in your department to see who has read the MLA report. For those who are familiar with it, ask them (a) if they agree with its recommendations and (b) whether they think it has made any kind of impact on their department and why or why not.

ESTABLISHING A PROFESSIONAL PROFILE

For a first-time teacher working toward an advanced degree, the job market can seem a long way off. It is not too early, however, to think about how to present oneself as an active member of a professional field. Being aware of one's professional profile from the beginning, while gathering materials and experience along the way, will ease the pressure of preparing for the job market when the time comes. Composing a working CV that includes participation in teaching workshops is a good way to start. Attending guest lectures and professional development programs at any of the many foreign language resource centers (CLEAR, COERLL, CERCLL, CARLA, etc.) provides opportunities for learning, sharing knowledge, and networking. STARTALK offers professional development seminars for those teaching critical-need foreign languages. Many talks from applied linguistics conferences are available online. Moreover, some universities offer professional development certificates from their language centers or centers for teaching and learning. The field has a number of professional journals and organizations; for a list, see Appendix D.

Giving and Receiving Feedback on Teaching

Traditionally, new TAs are observed and observe others; they also receive and give feedback on these observations during their first (sometimes only) year of graduate teaching. Afterward, they can continue to ask colleagues to sit in on their courses and discuss or send constrictive criticism, and they can ask to observe others as well, in the spirit of collecting effective teaching strategies and classroom management techniques. Even the most experienced and creative teachers glean new ideas when they observe a colleague's class. In preparation for the job market and future teaching, it is helpful for TAs to visit upper-level courses taught by experienced instructors.

The Teaching Portfolio

Many award, grant, and job applications require a teaching portfolio. New teachers should think of the portfolio as a work in progress and begin gathering materials early on. Components include

- a reflective statement on teaching (sometimes called a statement of teaching philosophy; abbreviated as "teaching statement" in this chapter);
- documentation of teaching experience, including examples of original, innovative materials (a list of the courses taught, with course descriptions, sample syllabi, sample assignments, etc.);
- video clips of teaching at various course levels (now often used in lieu of teaching demonstrations when Skype interviews replace on-campus visits);
- evidence of teaching effectiveness (reports from peers and supervisors who have observed classes, unsolicited feedback from students and alumni, quotations from teaching evaluations);
- samples of students' (anonymous) work (acquired with students' documented permission to use the material);
- a summary of professional development (participation in workshops, certificate programs, and local and national conferences);
- a list of contributions to the teaching profession (papers, publications, websites that other teachers can consult, etc.); and
- a list of honors and awards related to teaching.

> **Reflection**
>
> Search online for two portfolios posted by colleagues in your field.
>
> 1. What sections does each contain?
> 2. Do you prefer the look or format of one or the other? Why?
> 3. Is one easier to navigate than the other?
> 4. Which materials in the portfolio give you a good idea of the colleague's approaches and skills?

The Teaching Statement

Whatever their area of expertise, new TAs often begin their teaching careers as instructors in the elementary- or intermediate-level language classroom. Similarly, TAs who are now teaching lower-level language courses (and have never had the opportunity to teach advanced classes) will be assigned upper-level (sometimes even graduate-level) courses when they take on their first faculty positions. During interviews, they will need to articulate plans for courses they have not yet had a chance to teach, as well as highlight the ways in which language teaching has prepared them to handle new teaching situations.

A teaching statement is unlike a cover letter in content and tone. The cover letter must be revised to respond to the specifications of each job ad. It must also convey a great deal of information as efficiently as possible. As a result, a cover letter does not easily reveal as much of the applicant's distinctive voice as the teaching statement. The obvious purpose of the teaching statement is to communicate how and why one teaches—something instructors may know instinctively and demonstrate every day but do not always express in carefully crafted prose. It should be a critical discussion of how teaching practices reflect beliefs and goals. Drafting the statement for the first time can be a challenging task. It is a good idea to begin early on, perhaps while taking a pedagogy course. A teaching statement can be required for award and grant applications, as well as for self-assessment dossiers, promotions, and job applications. The document will evolve over the years, and it will need to be adapted to specific situations, but even the earliest versions can help teachers articulate what truly matters to them and how they align pedagogical frameworks with instructional and curricular practices.

> **Reflection**
>
> Imagine that you are reading teaching statements submitted with applications for a tenure-track job that involves teaching language, literature, and culture courses at all levels. Most of the applicants are newly minted PhDs or ABDs with a scheduled defense date. All have taught basic language courses as TAs for at least one semester. A few have had the chance to teach upper-level content courses, while others have not. Why would certain teaching statements rise to the top?
>
> Now search for two teaching statements written by colleagues in your field or in a field very close to yours. Highlight the sections or phrases that impress you. In a different color, highlight any aspects of the statements that are less compelling. Think about these aspects:
>
> 1. Did the writer avoid jargon?
> 2. Are there enough concrete examples to illustrate the ideas?
> 3. Do you think this statement would be most effective for self-assessment, in a promotion dossier, in a teaching portfolio, as part of a job application, or in some combination of the above? Explain why.
> 4. Imagine you are on a hiring committee that has just read thirty-five application dossiers. What about this philosophy statement stands out? Can you complete the following sentence? This is the candidate who _____.
> 5. Based on your reaction to these samples, draft a list of best practices for writing a statement to submit with your own job applications.

For employment purposes, a teaching statement presents a candidate as qualified to take on new teaching responsibilities thanks to transferable experience and knowledge, as well as an overarching self-awareness that is articulated as why and how one teaches. As a point of departure for writing it, think about the cohesiveness of language and literature teaching that has been emphasized throughout this book and about the skills you have acquired that will serve you in any teaching context. A teaching statement provides the opportunity to demonstrate not only your knowledge of your field and of pedagogical frameworks but also your joy of teaching.

> **Reflection**
>
> Before writing your teaching statement, answer the following questions (some adapted from O'Neal, Meizlish, and Kaplan 2007).
>
> 1. What have you learned about teaching while working with elementary- or intermediate-level students that could be carried over into upper-level courses? Consider preparation and lesson planning, grading, in-class activities, and specific skills (especially reading, writing, and speaking).
> 2. What motivates you to learn about languages, cultures, and literatures?
> 3. Why do you teach?
> 4. What do you believe or value about student learning? What are your goals?
> 5. If you had to choose a metaphor for teaching and learning, what would it be?
> 6. How do theories of SLA align with your teaching?
> 7. How do your research and disciplinary context influence your teaching?
> 8. How do you use multiple pedagogical approaches in your teaching?
> 9. What is your approach to evaluating or assessing student performance?
> 10. Think of a teacher who inspired you. What do you admire about that teacher?
> 11. How do you inspire students? What sort of positive feedback have you gotten from students (in person, in messages, on evaluations) regarding your teaching? Recount an anecdote regarding a conversation or classroom interaction with a student that was meaningful to you.

What candidate qualities do search committee members look for in a teaching statement?

- *Strong writing skills.* Like everything else in a grant or academic job application, the teaching statement is a writing sample. It is helpful to read it out loud, to double-check for flow, spelling, and grammatical accuracy, and to ask a friend or colleague to read it.
- *Awareness of the audience.* Keep it concise. The teaching statement should be one to two pages long. Speak in the first person. Capture the reader's interest with a first sentence that represents you and your voice. Some writers begin with an anecdote or vignette and others with a clear statement about their teaching. In most cases, multiple readers with divergent areas of expertise will review your dossier; in some cases, not even one SLA specialist will be part of this group. How will you explain your work to and keep the attention of a professor of French medieval hagiography, an expert in Spanish Caribbean literature, a film scholar, and a linguist?
- *Effective teaching.* Remember that in an academic job application, you are being judged as both a scholar and a teacher, even if some documents in your dossier focus more on one or the other aspect of your academic profile. An eloquent teaching statement underscores (without necessarily stating as such) the symbiotic relationship between a candidate's teaching and research.
- *Attention to students.* Yes, this statement is about you, but that includes how you value and guide your students. Be sure to show that you are attentive to their learning, not just your teaching.
- *Adaptability.* If you are looking for your first job, present yourself not as a current graduate student but instead as a potential colleague. Let the reader know your context and experience but avoid dwelling on details that are specific to your course or department. Consider how your experience teaching a beginning language course can translate to effective teaching in a wide range of courses at various levels.

Perspectives

I was about to complete my PhD program and applied for a tenure-track position that involved teaching language and an occasional literature course at a university seeking a new faculty member whose "energy, knowledge, and talent [would] revitalize the program and

Continued . . .

attract more students to the major." I connected with colleagues during my interviews, impressed the audience with my on-campus job talk, and captivated students and faculty observers with the sample class I taught. Although I was not a specialist in applied linguistics/SLA, my role as a new faculty member would be to supervise and organize the first- and second-year language courses under the supervision of the director of language programs (DLP). I happily accepted the job offer and arrived on campus ready to share my knowledge and creativity. In a private conversation at the start of the semester, the DLP told me that I was hired to "come in and innovate," and I couldn't wait to get started. Little did I know, she didn't tell any of my colleagues that she was looking to make changes. I was so naïve. Shortly after the semester began, I noticed that faculty seemed resistant to some of the practical suggestions I had made. Several colleagues objected to the idea of adopting a new textbook, while others were concerned about the proposed ratio of speaking to reading to writing in beginning courses. I found myself devoting a great deal of time to departmental politics and diplomacy and very little to curriculum reform. I came to realize that some of my colleagues were resistant to change and the DLP was trying to use me as a catalyst for change. I had no idea that my new position would be so complicated!

1. How could the DLP have handled this situation better?
2. What steps might the new faculty member have taken to win over colleagues and get them on board? How might this person have involved them more in the process?
3. Why are colleagues sometimes resistant to change? Why can change feel threatening, especially in today's academic environment?

LANGUAGES AND THE HUMANITIES

A web search for the terms "higher education," "foreign languages," and "budget cuts" or "downsizing" reveals a relationship between endangered language programs and the humanities in general. In recent years, professional online and print media (*Chronicle of Higher Education*, *Inside Higher Ed*, *ADFL Bulletin*, etc.) have reported extensively on the dwindling valorization of the humanities in the US. The argument for downsizing is that courses in history, philosophy, literature, and the arts do not provide skills directly applicable in the workforce and should therefore be the first to go when governments, school districts, colleges, and universities tighten their budgets. More surprisingly, perhaps, a number of Americans, even university administrators, believe that the widespread use of English around the world makes learning a second language unnecessary, even for international professions (see Chapter 2).

Opponents of these arguments have rallied from different, though not mutually exclusive, positions. Zietlow (2017) reports that "the inability of too many Americans to learn or speak anything but English constitutes a foreign language 'emergency' that could end up harming the economy and impairing U.S. foreign policy." Fryer (2012) argues that Americans fall behind Europeans in global leadership because they lack "soft skills" not honed in business schools; above all, they are deficient in cultural empathy, a sensitivity acquired through, for example, living in a foreign country and speaking the language. From a cognitive perspective, defenders of language learning cite studies showing the positive effect of multilingualism on brain development and learning (see, for example, NEA Research 2007; ACTFL n.d.).

From a more pragmatic perspective, proponents note that while a modern poetry course does not offer lessons in coding or biology, it does equip students with skills in communication, cultural awareness, writing, analytical thinking, and critical thinking. These will make future computer programmers and medical doctors better job candidates, colleagues, and practitioners. For example, Shapiro et al. find that studying literature is "an essential element of medical education" for a number of reasons: "The method of close reading . . . contributes intellectual inquiry, emotional awareness, sociocultural context, and a countercultural perspective to questions regarding medical professionalism. Narrative and storytelling broaden and make more complex the ethical context of care provided by students and faculty. They assist learners in rigorously and feelingly examining, in specific evocative contexts, what it means to be a doctor in relationship with patients and families within a framework of larger social dynamics and discourses" (2015). Others argue that the focus on utility, marketing, and money is shortsighted at best. Instead, they maintain that the humanities—reading and literature in particular—have intrinsic value that should be better articulated and more carefully cultivated in pedagogical practice. In *Why Read?* (2004), Edmundson contrasts higher education's focus on consumerism with the inspiring, life-altering benefits of a liberal arts education. In his view, administrators alone are not to blame for the demise of the humanities. Too many scholars of literature are teaching a "dissociation of intellect and feeling" (45). Students spend too much time collecting facts about a poem (its critical and historical context, for example) and not enough time wondering what it says and what it means today. Because information is quickly and easily accessed now, "the result is to suspend reflection about the differences among wisdom, knowledge, and information" (15). Edmundson's observations on the power of reading resonate with the notion of language and literature study as a transformational experience: "What's missing from the current [pedagogical] dispensation is a sense of hope when we confront major works, the hope that they will tell us something we do not know about the world or give us an entirely fresh way to apprehend experience. We need to learn not simply to read books, but to allow books to read us" (46).

Felski has further explored the question of why we read and how we teach reading in the humanities. In *The Uses of Literature* (2008), she promotes "an undogmatic openness to a spectrum of literary responses" (18) and proposes recognition, enchantment, knowledge, and shock as modes of connections, engagement, and interaction with texts. Without abandoning critical theory, she advocates Ricoeur's combining of "a willingness to suspect . . . with an eagerness to listen" to texts (22). She considers the stakes of a "hermeneutics of suspicion" in *The Limits of Critique* (2015). Edmundson and Felski both remind teachers that topics in the humanities can promote an interactive relationship between readers and texts with far-reaching repercussions for the understanding of the present and the past, the familiar and the foreign, the self and others. These concerns also happen to link the too often juxtaposed spaces of language, literature, and culture.

With full days devoted to finding the balance between graduate coursework and teaching responsibilities, it can be difficult to keep up with the larger questions concerning the role of languages and the humanities. Yet today's graduate students and new faculty will influence the future of foreign language studies in North America and beyond. It may eventually be up to any of us to defend a faculty line or to argue for or against blending two language departments that have little in common in the cultures and history that they represent.

> **Reflection**
>
> 1. How would you defend the value of your discipline to others (e.g., students, parents, colleagues in other departments, administrators)?
> 2. Do you think all college students should be required to reach a certain level of competency in a foreign language in order to earn a degree?
> 3. Do you think language should be part of a global studies curriculum? Should language be required for any other majors or concentrations?
> 4. Many specialists in literature, film studies, the visual arts, cultural history, social history, linguistics, and other fields choose to complete their doctorates in a language department. Is that your situation? If so, explain why you picked this route. What about the language department made it seem like a better fit for you than another department related to your specialization?

As we have discussed throughout this book, foreign languages have been taught for centuries in different ways, using different materials. Regardless of which methods or approaches seem the most effective at the time when we are writing or you are reading these pages, we know that the larger context of cultural currents and philosophical turns and the changing needs of students, empirical research, and personal experience will eventually lead us to revise our teaching strategies. We also realize that individual institutions have their own traditions, missions, and goals and that these influences may not always align with prevailing research in language teaching. For these reasons, we have encouraged the questioning of both pedagogical approaches now seen as outdated and, just as important, those currently favored. Empirical research on language acquisition will continue to have a strong impact on pedagogical interventions, especially as the field of applied linguistics continues to advance. The evolving nature of FL pedagogy can be a dilemma for the newly minted and the seasoned faculty member alike. Attitudes regarding language programs may change slowly, in an almost imperceptible philosophical drift whose practical implications gradually surface and lead to a smooth transition. But often, new approaches gain momentum rapidly, culminating in sudden curricular reform with the destabilizing power of a tectonic shift. One of the challenges is determining when and how to implement new teaching paradigms. The philosophically motivated impetus to revise a program can be at odds with the pragmatically sound inclination to leave well enough alone.

It is easy to dismiss reluctance to change as stodginess, pedagogical conservatism, or a lack of interest or knowledge. Most likely, however, clinging to tradition constitutes an act of individual and departmental survival. The humanities in general, and foreign languages in particular, are often first on the chopping block when university administrations cut funding to programs. When a department is unthreatened and running somewhat smoothly, faculty may choose to stick with the status quo and not attract attention. Intradepartmental practices and politics also affect decisions about curricular changes. Instructors become attached to textbooks and readings that they know well and that seem to be effective. Adapting to new materials demands a certain investment of precious time. If a beginning program has finally adopted a textbook that makes the TAs and students happy, why rock the boat? If a colleague is coming up for a promotion evaluation that will favor research over teaching, should she join that contentious course design committee or finish writing her book? (Answer: finish the book.) Freshly hired instructors are often expected to uphold departmental traditions rather than to challenge them, even when employers mention updating the curriculum as a department's goal. There is no one-size-fits-all solution to dealing with differences of opinion among faculty members as to how languages should be taught, but one should be aware that such conflicts do crop up.

Reflection

In Chapter 1, we explained that we do not promote a single method or approach. Instead, we have presented the blending of language and content as an overarching framework, along with ten guiding principles that represent various pedagogical approaches practiced today at all levels: input, texts, critical thinking, tasks, themes, target cultures, motivation, interaction, expansion of classroom boundaries, and self-awareness. We have also emphasized the importance of change and adaptability.

Continued . . .

> 1. Think about how each of the ten principles applies to the course you teach. Are some better fits than others?
> 2. Are there any principles that you would add to or remove from the list, based on your experience and on recent trends in language teaching or education in general?
> 3. What are your predictions for the future of language pedagogy? Where are we headed? How will we get there?

THE BIG PICTURE

For many graduate TAs, a one-semester language pedagogy course and related class visits provide a first and a last formal teacher education experience. Students specializing and going on to careers in cultural studies, film studies, or literature may or may not keep up with applied linguistics research on a regular basis. Yet the skills honed while teaching lower-level classes are valuable in many ways. Exercising time management, promoting classroom discussion, providing meaningful feedback, helping students read and appreciate texts, fostering good writing practices—these techniques will serve teachers well in any classroom.

The construction of a professional identity begins early, with or without conscious effort. By taking time to reflect on the theories and practices that both shape the everyday tasks of teaching and steer national debates, instructors can become more knowledgeable and engaged. This book has focused on the value of navigating the day-to-day logistics of teaching without losing sight of the big picture. We view teacher education not as something to "take care of" in the first year or two of graduate school but as an ongoing pursuit, informed to a great extent by interactions with students and collaborations with colleagues. Language departments bring together specialists in linguistics, applied linguistics, education, literature, cultural history, film studies, and more, all of whom have knowledge and skills to share. We have tried to show that instead of compartmentalizing various familiar components of teaching, all of us in language departments, informed by our respect for and appreciation of others' expertise, can build a continuous and cohesive whole that is much stronger than the sum of its parts.

Appendix A

World-Readiness Standards for Learning Languages

GOAL AREAS	STANDARDS		
Communication Communicate effectively in more than one language in order to function in a variety of situations and for multiple purposes	**Interpersonal Communication:** Learners interact and negotiate meaning in spoken, signed, or written conversations to share information, reactions, feelings, and opinions.	**Interpretive Communication:** Learners understand, interpret, and analyze what is heard, read, or viewed on a variety of topics.	**Presentational Communication:** Learners present information, concepts, and ideas to inform, explain, persuade, and narrate on a variety of topics using appropriate media and adapting to various audiences of listeners, readers, or viewers.
Cultures Interact with cultural competence and understanding	**Relating Cultural Practices to Perspectives:** Learners use the language to investigate, explain, and reflect on the relationship between the practices and perspectives of the cultures studied.	**Relating Cultural Products to Perspectives** Learners use the language to investigate, explain, and reflect on the relationship between the products and perspectives of the cultures studied.	

Continued . . .

Continued . . .

GOAL AREAS	STANDARDS	
Connections Connect with other disciplines and acquire information and diverse perspectives in order to use the language to function in academic and career-related situations	**Making Connections:** Learners build, reinforce, and expand their knowledge of other disciplines while using the language to develop critical thinking and to solve problems creatively.	**Acquiring Information and Diverse Perspectives:** Learners access and evaluate information and diverse perspectives that are available through the language and its cultures.
Comparisons Develop insight into the nature of language and culture in order to interact with cultural competence	**Language Comparisons:** Learners use the language to investigate, explain, and reflect on the nature of language through comparisons of the language studied and their own.	**Cultural Comparisons:** Learners use the language to investigate, explain, and reflect on the concept of culture through comparisons of the cultures studied and their own.
Communities Communicate and interact with cultural competence in order to participate in multilingual communities at home and around the world	**School and Global Communities:** Learners use the language both within and beyond the classroom to interact and collaborate in their community and the globalized world.	**Lifelong Learning:** Learners set goals and reflect on their progress in using languages for enjoyment, enrichment, and advancement.

Source: Printed with permission granted by the American Council on the Teaching of Foreign Languages.

Appendix B
"Requiem," by Karen Brennan

I woke up one morning and my country was gone. It was strange. It had been there the night before, sparking and hissing, but now it was gone.

I could feel its absence in the air, which is a feeling like no other.

The garden was still there, the bougainvillea was in some sort of bloom, red blossoms half-opened on thorny stalks. And the house still surrounded me—for the moment, at least. Perhaps it took longer for smaller things to follow suit. All I know is what I'm telling you.

I found my slippers—the little hole in the toe had not grown larger overnight, thank god, and everything was still in the fridge. It's not as if some thief came and stole food. No, it was only the country, the big picture. I wasn't sure where I was.

The sky didn't let on. It was as if the sky knew but wasn't saying anything. I kept looking up. There were no clouds, I can tell you that. I wished there were clouds, truly. They would have given me hope.

As it was, I felt hopeless. I wandered around my home, checking to see. Already I was feeling nostalgic. Yet here was everything in place. The half-full coffeemaker, the slippers, etc.

It was then that I remembered the mouse. Where had the mouse gone? I'd put out a trap and the trap was still armed with a piece of cheddar cheese. No one had nibbled it. I was anxious about the mouse. I didn't want any more disappearances.

Mouse! Mouse! I called, ridiculously, hopefully.

When your country disappears just like that, while you're sleeping and thinking that everything's just fine, it's hard to believe that, yes, the country has vanished and we don't even know why.

Now everything had settled but newly settled, settled to the point of unfamiliarity as when you watch a horror movie and a thing is almost like the thing you expect to see but not quite, which is the most horrifying of all since it tricks us.

Possibly the country had been vanishing for a long time, in increments, and we hadn't noticed little portions of it flaking off.

In the past, we had possibly been preoccupied.

Had we been looking at our screens instead of the earth under our feet? Well, the earth was still there. But was it the same earth? Would we recognize the old earth? Had we examined it carefully enough in the past? If it was a new earth, was this new earth an imaginary earth? Had we been swallowed up by our computers in some game involving avatars that looked just like us and an earth that looked just like our old earth, but was subtly altered?

Oh where was the mouse?

Everything felt different, as it does when one loses some big thing. There is a hole where the thing used to be. I had that feeling when I lost a sapphire ring in a taxi when I was 16 and I had that feeling when my grandmother died. Things disappear all the time and leave holes. That much we know about life. But an entire country?

This we were not prepared for.

In the past, nothing had been extraordinary, we know. But that was its beauty. In its ordinariness, we flourished. We went to the grocery store, chatted with our neighbors, drove our car under bridges and along rivers and admired all the ordinary views from every window. Sure, we had traveled beyond. But we always returned to the calmness we associate with home, in its beige unextraordinary calmness with our TVs and the moldering vegetables in our refrigerator bins. Was that the problem? Had we neglected things? Had we been inattentive?

And this is the big question and I ask this with a heart full of sorrow. Will we get used to it? Will this new country become familiar, and will we forget the old one? Will we still drive to the grocery store and chat with neighbors, only there will be some shifts that will have changed everything, the shifts barely perceptible to the naked eye? That's what I've come to believe. Even the naked eye will be blind to the shifts. And the disappearance of the mouse will be the first indication.

Mouse! Mouse! I call out. Because I am still remembering. I am still nostalgic. I am trying to plan the time when we tell our children how it used to be, this ordinary country with its banks and voting booths and public schools, with its sewing bees and knitting circles and creative writing workshops and graffiti and miracles—but just as the story of my old country with its rivers and hisses and sparks appears, it evaporates. I am trying to see it, but it cannot be clearly seen.

It is like the recollection of the mouse which, now that I think of it, was never quite visible, never more than my imagination of it, a creature scurrying along the wallboards or shitting on the countertops, a tree's shadow falling through the window or a presentiment of gloom issued from my own sick, nostalgic-crazed, idealistic mind, or a ghost.

Source: "Requiem" was originally published by *Scoundrel Time*, an online literary journal, in 2017. https://scoundreltime.com.

Appendix C

Excerpts from *Exercises in Style,* by Raymond Queneau, translated by Barbara Wright

• • •

In the S bus, in the rush hour. A chap of about 26, felt hat with a cord instead of a ribbon, neck too long, as if someone's been having a tug-of-war with it. People getting off. The chap in question gets annoyed with one of the men standing next to him. He accuses him of jostling him every time anyone goes past. A snivelling tone which is meant to be aggressive. When he sees a vacant seat he throws himself on to it.

Two hours later, I meet him in the Cour de Rome, in front of the gare Saint-Lazare. He's with a friend who's saying: "You ought to get an extra button put on your overcoat." He shows him where (at the lapels) and why.

• • •

How tightly packed we were on that bus platform! And how stupid and ridiculous that young man looked! And what was he doing? Well, if he wasn't actually trying to pick a quarrel with a chap who—so he claimed! the young fop! kept on pushing him! And then he didn't find anything better to do than to rush off and grab a seat which had become free! Instead of leaving it for a lady!

Two hours after, guess whom I met in front of the gare Saint-Lazare! The same fancypants! Being given some sartorial advice! By a friend!

You'd never believe it!

• • •

Well, you know, the bus arrived, so, you know, I got in. Then I saw, you know, a citizen, who, you know, caught my eye, sort of. I mean, you know, I saw his long neck and I saw the plait round his hat. Then he started to, you know, rave, at the chap next to him. He was, you know, treading on his toes. Then he went and, you know, sat down.

Well, you know, later on, I saw him in the Cour de Rome. He was with a, you know, pal, and he was telling him, you know, the pal was: "You ought to get another button put on your coat." You know.

Source: By Raymond Queneau, translated by Barbara Wright, from *Exercises in Style*, copyright © 1947, 1958 by Editions Gallimard and Barbara Wright. Reprinted by permission of New Directions Publishing Corp.

Appendix D
Professional Organizations and Journals

PROFESSIONAL ORGANIZATIONS

African Language Teachers Association (ALTA)
American Association for Applied Linguistics (AAAL)
American Association of Teachers of Arabic (AATA)
American Association of Teachers of French (AATF)
American Association of Teachers of German (AATG)
American Association of Teachers of Italian (AATI)
American Association of Teachers of Japanese (AATJ)
American Association of Teachers of Korean (AATK)
American Association of Teachers of Slavic and East European Languages (AATSEEL)
American Association of Teachers of Spanish and Portuguese (AATSP)
American Association of Teachers of Turkic Languages (AATT)
American Association of University Supervisors, Coordinators, and Directors of Language Programs (AAUSC)
American Council of Teachers of Russian (ACTR)
American Council on the Teaching of Foreign Languages (ACTFL)
Association of Departments of Foreign Languages (ADFL)
Chinese Language Association of Secondary-Elementary Schools (CLASS)
Chinese Language Teachers Association (CLTA)
Joint National Committee on Languages and National Council for Languages and International Studies (JNCL-NCLIS)
Modern Language Association (MLA)
National Arabic Teachers Association (NationalATA)
National Council of Japanese Language Teachers (NCJLT)
National Council of Less Commonly Taught Languages (NCOLCTL)

JOURNALS

Annual Review of Applied Linguistics
Anthropology and Education Quarterly
Applied Language Learning
Applied Linguistics
CALICO Journal
Canadian Modern Language Review
Chronicle of Higher Education
Computer Assisted Language Learning
Contemporary Education
Current Issues in Language and Society
Foreign Language Annals
Foreign Language Learning
French Review
Hispanica
Inside Higher Ed
International Review of Applied Linguistics in Language Teaching
Issues in Applied Linguistics
Issues in Language Program Direction (AAUSC annual volume)
Journal of Second Language Writing
Journal of the Chinese Language Teachers Association
Language, Culture, and Curriculum
Language and Communication
Language and Education
Language Educator
Language in Society
Language Learning
Language Learning Journal
Language Studies
Language Teaching
Language Teaching Research
Language Testing
Modern Language Journal
Pragmatics and Language Learning
Reading in a Foreign Language
Second Language Research
Second Language Research and Practice
Studies in Second Language Acquisition
System
TESOL Quarterly

Bibliography

ACTFL (American Council on the Teaching of Foreign Languages). 1996. "Standards for Foreign Language Learning: Preparing for the 21st Century." https://www.actfl.org/sites/default/files/publications/standards/1996%20National%20Standards%20for%20FL%20L%20Exec%20Summary.pdf.
———. 2001. "A Checklist for Self-Study for Departments of Foreign Languages and Literatures." https://www.adfl.mla.org/content/download/31921/1698564/checklist.pdf.
———. 2012. *ACTFL Proficiency Guidelines.* https://www.actfl.org/sites/default/files/pdfs/public/ACTFLProficiencyGuidelines2012_FINAL.pdf.
———. 2015a. *ACTFL Performance Descriptors for Language Learners.* https://www.actfl.org/sites/default/files/pdfs/ACTFLPerformance-Descriptors.pdf.
———. 2015b. "World-Readiness Standards for Learning Languages." https://www.actfl.org/sites/default/files/publications/standards/World-ReadinessStandardsforLearningLanguages.pdf.
———. n.d. "What the Research Shows." https://www.actfl.org/advocacy/what-the-research-shows.
Adair-Hauck, Bonnie, and Philomena Cumo-Johanssen. 1997. "Communication Goal: Meaning-Making through Whole-Language Approach." In *Collaborations: Meeting New Goals, New Realities—Northeast Conference Reports,* edited by June K. Phillips, 35–96. Lincolnwood, IL: National Textbook.
Adair-Hauck, Bonnie, and Richard Donato. 2002. "The PACE Model: A Story-Based Approach to Meaning and Form for Standards-Based Language Learning." *French Review* 76: 265–76.
———. 2015. "PACE: A Story-Based Approach for Dialogic Inquiry about Form and Meaning." In *Teacher's Handbook: Contextualized Foreign Language Instruction,* edited by Judith L. Shrum and Eileen Glisan, 206–30. 5th ed. Boston: Cengage Learning.
ADFL (Association of Departments of Foreign Languages). 2001. "A Checklist for

Self-Study for Departments of Foreign Languages and Literatures." *ADFL Bulletin* 32: 122–9.

Akbari, Suzanne Conklin, ed. 2015. *How We Write: Thirteen Ways of Looking at a Blank Page*. Brooklyn: Dead Letter Office, Punctum Books.

Allen, Heather Willis. 2018. "Redefining the Role of Writing in Collegiate Foreign Language Education: Toward Design Approach." *Foreign Language Annals* 51: 513–32.

Allen, Heather Willis, and Lauren Goodspeed. 2018. "Textual Borrowing and Perspective-Taking: A Genre-Based Approach to L2 Writing." *L2 Journal* 10: 87–110.

Allen, Heather Willis, and Kate Paesani. 2010. "Exploring the Feasibility of a Pedagogy of Multiliteracies in Introductory Foreign Language Courses." *L2 Journal* 2: 119–42.

Alters, Adam. 2017. *Irresistible: The Rise of Addictive Technology and the Business of Keeping Us Hooked*. New York: Penguin.

Amores, Maria J. 1997. "A New Perspective on Peer-Editing." *Foreign Language Annals* 30: 513–22.

Anderson, Lorin W., D. R. Krathwohl, and Benjamin Bloom. 2001. *A Taxonomy for Learning, Teaching, and Assessing: A Revision of Bloom's Taxonomy of Educational Objectives*. New York: Longman.

Aoun, Joseph E. 2017. *Robot-Proof*. Cambridge, MA: MIT Press.

Atwood, Margaret. 1981. *True Stories*. New York: Simon and Schuster.

Austen, Veronica J. 2009. "The Value of Creative Writing Assignments in English Literature Courses." *New Writing* 2.2: 138–50.

Bakhtin, M. M. 1981. *The Dialogic Imagination: Four Essays by M. M. Bakhtin*. Edited by Michael Holquist. Translated by Caryl Emerson and Holquist. Austin: University of Texas Press.

Barcelos, Anna Maria Ferreira, and Paula Kalaja. 2003. "Conclusion: Exploring Possibilities for Future Research on Beliefs about SLA." In *Beliefs about SLA: New Research Approaches*, edited by Kalaja and Barcelos, 231–38. Dordrecht, Netherlands: Kluwer Academic.

Barnes-Karol, Gwendolyn, and Maggie Broner. 2010. "Using Images as Springboards to Teach Cultural Perspectives in Light of the Ideals of the MLA Report." *Foreign Language Annals* 43: 422–45.

Barthes, Roland. *Critique et vérité*. Paris: Seuil, 1966.

Bartlett, Frederic C. 1932. *Remembering: A Study in Experimental and Social Psychology*. Cambridge: Cambridge University Press.

Bass, Randy, and Heidi Elmendorf. 2010. "What Are Social Pedagogies?" https://blogs.commons.georgetown.edu/bassr/social-pedagogies/.

———. 2011. "Designing for Difficulty: Social Pedagogies as a Framework for Course Design." Teagle Foundation White Paper. https://blogs.commons.georgetown.edu/bassr/social-pedagogies/.

Baudelaire, Charles. 1973. *Correspondances*. Vol. 1, edited by Claude Pichois. Paris: Gallimard.

Beck, Isabel L., Margaret G. McKeown, and Linda Kucan. 2013. *Bringing Words to Life: Robust Vocabulary Instruction*. 2nd ed. New York: Guilford.

Bell, Nancy. 2005. "Exploring L2 Language Play as an Aid to SSL: A Case Study of Humour in NS-NNS Interaction." *Applied Linguistics* 26: 192–218.

Belnap, R. Kirk, Jennifer Bown, Edie M. Dean, Dan P. Dewey, Lucy J. Schouten, Andrew K. Smith, Rebecca K. Smith, and Joshua R. Taylor. 2015. "Project Perseverance and Study Abroad." *Al-'Arabiyya: Journal of the American Association of Teachers of Arabic* 48: 1–21.

Belz, Julie, and Jonathan Reinhardt. 2004. "Aspects of Advanced Foreign Language Proficiency: Internet-Mediated Language Play." *International Journal of Applied Linguistics* 14: 324–62.

Berg, William J., and Laurey K. Martin-Berg. 2001. "A Stylistic Approach to Foreign-Language Acquisition and Literary Analysis." In *SLA and the Literature Classroom: Fostering Dialogues*, edited by Virginia Scott and Holly Tucker, 173–91. Boston: Heinle.

Bernhardt, Elizabeth. 2002. "A Language Center Director Responds." *Modern Language Journal* 80: 246–8.

Bhatia, Vijay K. 1993. *Analysing Genre: Language Use in Professional Settings*. London: Longman.

———. 2002. "A Generic View of Academic Discourse." In *Academic Discourse*, edited by John Flowerdew, 21–39. Harlow, UK: Longman.

Blake, Robert J. 2013. *Brave New Digital Classroom: Technology and Foreign Language Learning*. 2nd ed. Washington DC: Georgetown University Press.

Bley-Vroman, Robert. 1986. "Hypothesis Testing in Second-Language Acquisition Theory." *Language Learning* 36: 353–76.

Block, David. 2003. *The Social Turn in Second Language Acquisition*. Edinburgh: Edinburgh University Press.

Blyth, Carl S. 1997. "A Constructivist Approach to Grammar: Teaching Teachers to Teach Aspect." *Modern Language Journal* 81: 50–66.

———. 1999. "Toward a Pedagogical Discourse Grammar: Techniques for Teaching Word Order Constructions." In *Form and Meaning*, edited by James Lee and Albert Valdman, 183–229. Boston: Heinle.

———. 2013. "eComma: An Open Source Tool for Collaborative L2 Reading." In *Case Studies of Openness in the Language Classroom*, edited by Ana Beaven, Anna Comas-Quinn, and Barbara Sawhill, 32–43. Dublin: Research Publishing Net.

———. 2018. "Designing Meaning and Identity in Multiliteracies Pedagogy: From Multilingual Subjects to Authentic Speakers." *L2 Journal* 10: 62–86.

Borg, Simon. 2003. "Teacher Cognition in Language Teaching: A Review of Research on What Language Teachers Think, Know, Believe, and Do." *Language Teaching* 36: 81–109.

Bourns, Stacey Katz. 2014. "Contrasting *C'est*-Clefts and It-Clefts in Discourse." In *Perspectives on Linguistic Structure and Context*, edited by Bourns and Lindsy Myers, 340–73. Amsterdam: John Benjamins.

———. 2017a. "*Histoires modernes de Paris*: Idealization versus Reality." *French Review* 90: 171–85.

———. 2017b. "Toward an Understanding of Spoken French and Linguistic Register: Pedagogical Recommendations." *French Review* 91.2: 173–89.

Bourns, Stacey Katz, and Charlotte Melin. 2014. "The FL Methodology Seminar: Benchmarks, Perceptions, and Trends." *ADFL Bulletin* 43: 91–100.

Brandl, Klaus. 2008. *Communicative Language Teaching in Action: Putting Principles to Work*. Upper Saddle River, NJ: Pearson.

Brennan, Karen. 2017. "Requiem." https://scoundreltime.com/requiem/.

Brown, Alan. 2009. "Students' and Teachers' Perceptions of Effective Foreign Language Teaching: A Comparison of Ideals." *Modern Language Journal* 93: 46–60.

Brown, N. Anthony. 2009. "Argumentation and Debate in Foreign Language Instruction: A Case for the Traditional Classroom Facilitating Advanced-Level Language Uptake." *Modern Language Journal* 93: 534–49.

Brown, N. Anthony, and Jennifer Bown. 2017. *Teaching Advanced Language Skills through Global Debate: Theory and Practice*. Washington DC: Georgetown University Press.

Bush, Michael D. 2007. "Facilitating the Integration of Culture and Vocabulary Learning: The Categorization and Use of Pictures in the Classroom." *Foreign Language Annals* 40: 727–45.

Bushnell, Cade. 2008. "'Lego My Keego!': An Analysis of Language Play in a Beginning Japanese as a Foreign Language Classroom." *Applied Linguistics* 30: 49–69.

Busse, Vera. 2013. "Why Do First-Year Students of German Lose Motivation during Their First Year at University?" *Studies in Higher Education* 38: 951–71.

Byram, Michael. 1997. *Teaching and Assessing Intercultural Communicative Competence*. Clevedon, UK: Multilingual Matters.

———. 2003. "On Being Bicultural and Intercultural." In *Intercultural Experience and*

Education, edited by Geof Alred, Byram, and Mike Fleming. Clevedon, UK: Multilingual Matters.

Byrnes, Heidi. 2011. "Beyond Writing as Language Learning or Content Learning: Construing Foreign Language Writing as Meaning-Making." In *Learning-to-Write and Writing-to-Learn in an Additional Language*, edited by Rosa M. Manchón, 133–58. Amsterdam: John Benjamins.

Byrnes, Heidi, Cori Crane, Hiram H. Maxim, and Katherine A. Sprang. 2006. "Taking Text to Task: Issues and Choices in Curriculum Construction." *International Journal of Applied Linguistics* 152: 85–109.

Calvino, Italo. 1988. *Six Memos for the Next Millennium*. Translated by Patrick Creagh. Cambridge, MA: Harvard University Press.

Cammarata, Laurent, and Diane Tedick. 2012. "Balancing Content and Language Instruction: The Experience of Immersion Teachers." *Modern Language Journal* 96: 251–69.

Canale, Michael. 1983. "From Communicative Competence to Communicative Language Pedagogy." In *Language and Communication*, edited by Jack C. Richards and Richard W. Schmidt, 2–27. London: Longman.

Canale, Michael, and Merrill Swain. 1980. "Theoretical Bases of Communicative Approaches to Second Language Teaching and Testing." *Applied Linguistics* 1: 1–47.

Carrell, Patricia L., and Joan C. Eisterholdt. 1983. "Schema Theory and ESL Pedagogy." *TESOL Quarterly* 17: 553–73.

Celce-Murcia, Marianne. 2007. "Rethinking the Role of Communicative Competence in Language Teaching." In *Intercultural Language Use and Language Learning*, edited by Eva Alcón Soler and Maria Pilar Safont Jordà, 41–57. New York: Springer.

Celce-Murcia, Marianne, Zoltán Dörnyei, and Sarah Thurrell. 1995. "A Pedagogical Framework for Communicative Competence: A Pedagogically Motivated Model with Content Specifications." *Issues in Applied Linguistics* 6: 5–35.

Celce-Murcia, Marianne, and Elite Olshtain. 2000. *Discourse and Context in Language Teaching*. Cambridge: Cambridge University Press.

Chacón, Carmen T. 2005. "Teachers' Perceived Efficacy among English as a Foreign Language Teachers in Middle Schools in Venezuela." *Teaching and Teacher Education* 21: 257–72.

Chall, Jeanne Sternlicht, Vicki A. Jacobs, and Luke E. Baldwin. 1990. *The Reading Crisis: Why Poor Children Fall Behind*. Cambridge, MA.: Harvard University Press.

Charitos, Stéphane, and Nelleke Van Deusen-Scholl. 2017. "Engaging the City: Language, Space, and Identity in Urban Environments." In *Engaging the World: Social Pedagogies and Language Learning*, edited by Sébastien Dubreil and Steven L. Thorne, 15–36. Boston: Cengage.

Christie, Frances, ed. 1984. *Children Writing: Reader*. Geelong, Australia: Deakin University Press.

———. 1989. "Language Development in Education." In *Language Development: Learning Language, Learning Culture*, edited by Ruqaiya Hasan and J. R. Martin, 152–98. Norwood, NJ: Ablex.

Clifford, Joan, and Deborah S. Reisinger. 2019. *Community-Based Language Learning: A Framework for Educators*. Washington DC: Georgetown University Press.

Cohen, Andrew D., Rebecca L. Oxford, and Julie C. Chi. 2006. "Language Strategy Use Survey." In *Styles and Strategies-Based Instruction: A Teachers' Guide*, edited by Cohen and Susan J. Weaver, 68–74. Minneapolis: Center for Advanced Research on Language Acquisition.

Cohen, Andrew D., and Susan J. Weaver, eds. 2006. *Styles and Strategies-Based Instruction: A Teachers' Guide*. Minneapolis: Center for Advanced Research on Language Acquisition.

Colette. (1910) 1990. *La Vagabonde*. Paris: Albin Michel.

Comer, William, and Lynne deBenedette. 2011. "Processing Instruction and Russian: Further Evidence Is IN." *Foreign Language Annals* 44: 646–73.

Cook, Guy. 1997. *Language Play, Language Learning*. Oxford: Oxford University Press.

Cook, Vivian. 1992. "Evidence for Multicompetence." *Language Learning* 42: 557–91.

Corder, Stephen Pit. 1963. "A Theory of Visual Aids in Language Teaching." *English Language Teaching* 17: 82–7.

Council of Europe. 2008. "White Paper on Intercultural Dialogue: Living Together as Equals in Dignity." http://www.coe.int/t/dg4/intercultural/WhitePaper_InterculturalDialogue_2_en.asp.

———. 2013. *Images of Others: An Autobiography of Intercultural Encounters through Visual Media*, standard version. https://rm.coe.int/images-of-others-an-autobiography-of-intercultural-encounters-through-/168089fc01.

Cummins, Jim. 1998. "Immersion Education for the Millennium: What Have We Learned from 30 Years of Research on Second Language Immersion?" In *Learning through Two Languages: Research and Practice, Second Katoh Gakuen International Symposium on Immersion and Bilingual Education*, edited by M. R. Childs and R. M. Bostwick, 34–47. Shizuoka, Japan: Katoh Gakuen.

Department of Defense. 2011. "Language and Culture: Changing Perspective." https://prhome.defense.gov/Portals/52/Documents/RFM/Readiness/DLNSEO/files/lcwhitepaper.pdf.

DeWaard, Lisa. 2013. "Is *Rosetta Stone* a Viable Option for Second-Language Learning?" *ADFL Bulletin* 42: 61–72.

Donato, Richard, and Frank B. Brooks. 2004. "Literary Discussions and Advanced

Speaking Functions: Researching the (Dis)Connection." *Foreign Language Annals* 37: 183–99.

Dörnyei, Zoltán. 1991. *The Psychology of Second Language Acquisition*. Oxford: Oxford University Press.

———. 2005. *The Psychology of the Language Learner: Individual Differences in Second Language Acquisition*. Mahwah, NJ: Lawrence Erlbaum.

———. 2007. "Creating a Motivating Classroom Environment." In *International Handbook of English Language Teaching*, edited by Jim Cummins and Chris Davison, 719–31. New York: Springer.

Dörnyei, Zoltán, Alistair Henry, and Christine Muir. 2016. *Motivational Currents in Language Learning: Frameworks for Focused Interventions*. New York: Routledge.

Dörnyei, Zoltán, and Magdalena Kubanyiova. 2014. *Motivating Learners, Motivating Teachers: Building Vision in the Language Classroom*. Cambridge: Cambridge University Press.

Dörnyei, Zoltán, and Tim Murphey. 2003. *Group Dynamics in the Language Classroom*. Cambridge: Cambridge University Press.

Doughty, Catherine, and Jessica Williams. 1998. "Issues and Terminology." In *Focus on Form in Classroom Second Language Acquisition*, edited by Doughty and Williams, 1–11. Cambridge: Cambridge University Press.

Dubreil, Sébastien. 2011. "Rebels with a Cause: (Re)Defining Identities and Culture in Contemporary French Cinema." *L2 Journal* 3: 176–200. http://escholarship.org/uc/item/86n1q1j2.

Dubreil, Sébastien, and Steven L. Thorne. 2017. *Engaging the World: Social Pedagogies and Language Learning*. Boston: Cengage.

Dulay, Heidi C., and Marina K. Burt. 1977. "Remarks on Creativity in Language Acquisition." In *Viewpoints on English as a Second Language*, edited by Burt, Dulay, and Mary Bonomo Finnochiaro, 95–126. New York: Regents.

Edmundson, Mark. 2004. *Why Read?* New York: Bloomsbury.

Ellis, Rod. 1997. *SLA Research and Language Teaching*. Oxford: Oxford University Press.

Farivar, Cyrus. 2006. "Rosetta Stone 3.0." *Macworld*, January 19. Available at https://www.macworld.com/article/1048966/rosettastone3.html.

Fecteau, Monique L. 1999. "First- and Second-Language Reading Comprehension of Literary Texts." *Modern Language Journal* 83: 475–93.

Felski, Rita. 2008. *The Uses of Literature*. Malden, MA: Blackwell.

———. 2015. *The Limits of Critique*. Chicago: University of Chicago Press.

Ferris, Dana. 1999. "The Case for Grammar Correction in L2 Writing Classes: A Response to Truscott (1996)." *Journal of Second Language Writing* 8: 1–11.

Ferris, Dana R., and John S. Hedgcock. 2014. *Teaching L2 Composition: Purpose, Process, and Practice*. New York: Routledge.

Fillmore, Charles J., and Paul Kay. 1993. "Construction Grammar Coursebook." Unpublished manuscript, Department of Linguistics, University of California, Berkeley.

Firth, Allen, and Johannes Wagner. 1997. "On Discourse, Communication, and (Some) Fundamental Concepts in SLA Research." *Modern Language Journal* 81: 285–300.

Flaubert, Gustave. 1980. *The Letters of Gustave Flaubert, 1830–1857*. Edited and translated by Francis Steegmuller. Cambridge, MA: Belknap Press of Harvard University Press.

Flower, Linda, and John R. Hayes. 1981. "A Cognitive Process Theory of Writing." *College Composition and Communication* 32: 365–87.

Folse, Keith S. 2004. *Vocabulary Myths*. Ann Arbor: University of Michigan Press.

Fortune, Tara Williams, and Diane J. Tedick. 2008. "One-Way, Two-Way and Indigenous Immersion: A Call for Cross-Fertilization." In *Pathways to Multilingualism: Evolving Perspectives on Immersion Education*, edited by Fortune and Tedick, 3–21. Clevedon, UK: Multilingual Matters.

Freeman, Donald, and Karen E. Johnson. 1998. "Reconceptualizing the Knowledge-Base of Language Teacher Education." *TESOL Quarterly* 32: 397–417.

Freire, Paulo. 1970. *Pedagogy of the Oppressed*. New York: Continuum.

Fryer, Bronwyn. 2012. "Why America Lacks Global Leaders." *Harvard Business Review*, August 23. https://hbr.org/2012/08/why-america-lacks-global-leade.

Furstenburg, Gilberte. 2010. "Making Culture the Core of the Language Class: Can It Be Done?" *Modern Language Journal* 94: 329–32.

Garrett, Nina. 1986. "The Problem with Grammar: What Kind Can the Language Learner Use?" *Modern Language Journal* 70: 133–48.

Gebhart, Richard C. 1988. "Fiction Writing in Literature Classes." *Rhetoric Review* 7.1: 150–4.

Gee, James Paul. 1998. "What Is Literacy?" In *Negotiating Academic Literacies: Teaching and Learning across Languages and Cultures*, edited by Vivian Zamel and Ruth Spack, 51–59. Mahwah, NJ: Lawrence Erlbaum.

———. 2002. "Literacies, Identities, and Discourses." In *Developing Advanced Literacy in First and Second Languages: Meaning with Power*, edited by Mary J. Schleppegrell and M. Cecilia Colombi, 59–175. Mahwah, NJ: Lawrence Erlbaum.

Ghanem, Carla. 2015. "Teaching in the Foreign Language Classroom: How Being a Native or Non-native Speaker of German Influences Culture Teaching." *Language Teaching Research* 19: 169–86.

Gibbons, Pauline. 2002. *Scaffolding Language, Scaffolding Learning: Teaching Second Language Learners in the Mainstream Classroom*. Portsmouth, NH: Heinemann.

Glisan, Eileen, and Richard Donato. 2017. *Enacting the Work of Language Instruction: High-Leverage Teaching Practices*. Alexandria, VA: American Council on the Teaching of Foreign Languages.

Goh, Christine M. 1998. "How ESL Learners with Different Listening Abilities Use Comprehension Strategies and Tactics." *Language Teaching Research* 2: 124–46.

Goldberg, Adele. 1995. *Constructions: A Construction Grammar Approach to Argument Structure*. Chicago: University of Chicago Press.

Golde, Chris M. 2005. "The Role of the Department and Discipline in Doctoral Student Attrition: Lessons from Four Departments." *Journal of Higher Education* 76: 669–700.

Graff, Gerald. 1992. *Beyond the Culture Wars: How Teaching the Conflicts Can Revitalize American Education*. New York: Norton.

Grosse, Christine Uber, and Geoffrey Voght. 2012. "The Continuing Evolution of Languages for Specific Purposes." *Modern Language Journal* 96: 190–202.

Guilloteau, Nancy. 2010. "Vocabulary." Foreign Language Teaching Methods, Center for Open Educational Resources and Language Learning, University of Texas at Austin. https://coerll.utexas.edu/methods/modules/vocabulary/.

Hacking, Jane, and Erwin Tschirner. 2017. "The Contribution of Vocabulary Knowledge to Reading Proficiency: The Case of College Russian." *Foreign Language Annals* 50: 500–18.

Haight, Carrie E., Carol Herron, and Steven P. Cole. 2007. "The Effects of Deductive and Guided Inductive Instructional Approaches on the Learning of Grammar in the Elementary Foreign Language College Classroom." *Foreign Language Annals* 40: 288–319.

Hall, Joan Kelly. 1995. "'Aw, Man, Where You Goin'?': Classroom Interaction and the Development of L2 Interactional Competence." *Issues in Applied Linguistics* 6: 37–62.

Halliday, Michael Alexander Kirkwood. 1978. *Language as Social Semiotic: The Social Interpretation of Language and Meaning*. Baltimore: University Park Press.

———. 1993. "Towards a Language-Based Theory of Learning." *Linguistics and Education* 5: 93–116.

Hanna, Barbara E., and Juliana de Nooy. 2003. "A Funny Thing Happened on the Way to the Forum: Electronic Discussion and Foreign Language Learning." *Language Learning and Technology* 7: 71–85.

———. 2009. *Learning Language and Culture via Public Internet Discussion Forums*. Basingstoke, UK: Palgrave Macmillan.

Harley, Birgit, and Merrill Swain. 1984. "The Interlanguage of Immersion Students and Its Implications for Second Language Teaching." In *Interlanguage*, edited by

Alan Davies, C. Criper, and A. P. R. Howett, 291–311. Edinburgh: Edinburgh University Press.

Hasan, Md. Kamrul, and Mohd. Moniruzzaman Akhand. 2010. "Approaches to Writing in EFL/ESL Context: Balancing Product and Process in Writing Class at Tertiary Level." *Journal of NELTA* 15: 77–88.

Hedgcock, John S., and Dana R. Ferris. 2009. *Teaching Readers of English: Students, Texts, and Contexts.* New York: Routledge.

Heron, John. 1999. *The Complete Facilitator's Handbook.* London: Kogan Page.

Heusinkveld, Paul Rae, ed. 1997. *Pathways to Culture.* Yarmouth, ME: Intercultural Press.

Hoey, Michael. 2001. *Textual Interaction: An Introduction to Written Text Analysis.* London: Routledge.

Horwitz, Elaine. 1988. "The Beliefs about Language Learning of Beginning University Foreign Language Students." *Modern Language Journal* 72: 283–94.

Hsieh, Peggy, and Hyun-Sook Kang. 2010. "Attribution and Self-Efficacy and Their Interrelationship in the Korean EFL Context." *Language Learning* 60: 606–27.

Hu, Guangwei. 2002. "Potential Cultural Resistance to Pedagogical Imports: The Case of Communicative Language Teaching in China." *Language, Culture, and Curriculum* 15: 93–105.

Hyland, Fiona. 2011. "The Language Learning Potential of Form-Focused Feedback." In *Learning-to-Write and Writing-to-Learn in an Additional Language,* edited by Rosa M. Manchón, 159–79. Amsterdam: John Benjamins.

Hyland, Ken. 2004. *Genre and Second Language Writing.* Ann Arbor, MI: University of Michigan Press.

———. 2007. "Genre Pedagogy: Language, Literacy and L2 Writing Instruction." *Journal of Second Language Writing* 16: 148–64.

Hymes, Dell. 1967. "Models of the Interaction of Language and Social Setting." *Journal of Social Issues* 23: 8–28.

Jenkins, Rob. 2015. "Conquering Mountains of Essays." *Chronicle of Higher Education,* June 22. https://www.chronicle.com/article/Conquering-Mountains-of-Essays/231063.

Johnson, Karen E. 2009. *Second Language Teacher Education: A Sociocultural Perspective.* New York: Routledge.

Jones, Robert E. 2002. "'We Used to Do This and We'd Also Do That: A Discourse Pattern for Teaching the Reminiscence Story." *Language Teacher* 26.2: https://jalt-publications.org/old_tlt/articles/2002/02/jones.

Kaiser, Mark, and Chika Shibahara. 2013. "Film as Source Material in Advanced

Foreign Language Classes." *L2 Journal* 6: 1–13. http://escholarship.org/uc/item/3qv811wv.

Katz, Stacey L., and Carl S. Blyth. 2007. *Teaching French Grammar in Context: Theory and Practice.* New Haven: Yale University Press.

Kaufman, Julia H., and Christian D. Schunn. 2011. "Students' Perceptions about Peer Assessment for Writing: Their Origin and Impact on Revision Work." *Instructional Science* 30: 387–406.

Kearney, Erin. 2010. "Cultural Immersion in the Foreign Language Classroom: Some Narrative Possibilities." *Modern Language Journal* 94: 332–36.

———. 2012. "Perspective-Taking and Meaning-Making through Engagement with Cultural Narratives: Bringing History to Life in a Foreign Language Classroom." *L2 Journal* 4: 58–82.

Kern, Richard. 2000. *Literacy and Language Teaching.* Oxford: Oxford University Press.

———. 2003. "Literacy as a New Organizing Principle for Foreign Language Education." In *Reading between the Lines: Perspectives on Foreign Language Literacy,* edited by Peter C. Patrikis, 40–59. New Haven: Yale University Press.

———. 2008. "Making Connections through Texts in Language Teaching." *Language Teaching* 41: 367–87.

———. 2014. "Technology as *Pharmakon*: The Promise and Perils of the Internet for Foreign Language Education." *Modern Language Journal* 98: 340–57.

———. 2015. *Language, Literacy, and Technology.* Cambridge: Cambridge University Press.

Kerr, Betsy. 1983. Minnesota Corpus. Available by request from the creator.

Klee, Carol, and Gwendolyn Barnes-Karol. 2006. "A Content-Based Approach to Spanish Language Study: Foreign Languages across the Curriculum." In *The Art of Teaching Spanish,* edited by Rafael Salaberry and Barbara Lafford, 23–38. Washington DC: Georgetown University Press.

Knutson, Elizabeth. 2012. "Teaching Difficult Topics: The Example of the Algerian War." *L2 Journal* 4: 83–101.

Kondo-Brown, Kimi. 2003. "Heritage Language Instruction for Post-secondary Students from Immigrant Backgrounds." *Heritage Language Journal* 1: 1–25.

Kramsch, Claire. 1991. "Culture in Language Learning: A View from the United States." In *Foreign Language Research in Cross-Cultural Perspective,* edited by Kees de Boot, Ralph B. Ginsberg, and Claire Kramsch, 217–40. Utrecht: Benjamin.

———. 1993. *Context and Culture in Language Teaching.* Oxford: Oxford University Press.

———. 1997. "The Privilege of the Nonnative Speaker." *PMLA* 112: 359–69.

———. 1998. *Language and Culture.* Oxford: Oxford University Press.

———. 2006. "From Communicative Competence to Symbolic Competence." *Modern Language Journal* 90: 249–52.

———. 2009. *The Multilingual Subject*. Oxford: Oxford University Press.

———. 2010. "Theorizing Translingual/Transcultural Competence." In *Critical and Intercultural Theory and Language Pedagogy*, edited by Glenn S. Levine and Alison Phipps, 15–31. Boston: Cengage.

———. 2013. Forward to *Brave New Digital Classroom: Technology and Foreign Language Learning*, by Robert L. Blake, xi–xiii. 2nd ed. Washington DC: Georgetown University Press.

———. 2015. "Language and Culture in Second Language Learning." In *The Routledge Handbook of Language and Culture*, edited by Farzad Sharifian, 403–16. London: Routledge.

Kramsch, Claire, and Anne Whiteside. 2008. "Language Ecology in Multilingual Settings: Towards a Theory of Symbolic Competence." *Applied Linguistics* 29: 645–72.

Krashen, Stephen D. 1981. *Second Language Acquisition and Second Language Learning*. Oxford: Pergamon.

———. 1982. *Principles and Practice in Second Language Acquisition*. Oxford: Pergamon.

———. 1985. *The Input Hypothesis: Issues and Implications*. London: Longman.

———. 2003. *Explorations in Language Acquisition and Use*. Portsmouth, NH: Heinemann.

Krashen, Stephen D., and Tracy D. Terrell. 1983. *The Natural Approach: Language Acquisition in the Classroom*. Hayward, CA: Alemany.

Kristeva, Julia. 1986. "Word, Dialogue, and Novel." Translated by Alice Jardine, Thomas Gora, and Leon S. Roudiez. In *The Kristeva Reader*, edited by Toril Moi, 35–61. Oxford: Blackwell.

Krueger, Cheryl. 2001. "Form, Content, and Critical Distance: The Role of 'Creative Personalization' in Language and Content Courses." *Foreign Language Annals* 34: 18–25.

———. 2006. "An Emphasis on Process from Assignment through Assessment." In *AP® French Language: 2006–2007 Professional Development Workshop Materials—Special Focus: Writing Skills*, 60–67. New York: College Board.

Lambrecht, Knud. 2001. "A Framework for the Analysis of Cleft Constructions." *Linguistics* 39: 463–516.

Lamott, Anne. 1994. *Bird by Bird: Instructions on Writing and Life*. New York: Random House.

Landry, Rodrigue, and Richard Y. Bourhis. 1997. "Linguistic Landscape and Ethnographic Vitality: An Empirical Study." *Journal of Language and Social Psychology* 16: 23–49.

Langton. Diane. 2017. "Time Machine: Famed Illustrator Norman Rockwell Found Inspiration in Cedar Rapids." *Gazette* (Cedar Rapids), December 2. http://www.thegazette.com/subject/news/archive/time-machine/time-machine-famed-illustrator-norman-rockwell-found-inspiration-in-cedar-rapids-20171202.

Lantolf, James P., and Michale E. Poehner. 2014. *Sociocultural Theory and the Pedagogical Imperative in L2 Education: Vygotskian Praxis and the Research/Practice Divide*. New York: Routledge.

Leaver, Betty Lou, Benjamin Rifkin, and Boris Shekhtman. 2004. "Apples and Oranges Are Both Fruit, but They Don't Taste the Same: A Response to Wynne Wong and Bill VanPatten." *Foreign Language Annals* 37: 125–32.

Lee, James. 2000. *Tasks and Communicating in Language Classrooms*. New York: McGraw-Hill.

Lee, James, and Bill VanPatten. 2003. *Making Communicative Language Teaching Happen*. 2nd ed. New York: McGraw Hill.

Lee, Jin Sook. 2005. "Through the Learners' Eyes: Reconceptualizing the Heritage and Non-heritage Learners of the Less Commonly Taught Languages." *Foreign Language Annals* 38: 554–63.

Levine, Glenn S. 2004. "Global Simulation: A Student-Centered, Task-Based Format for Intermediate Foreign Language Courses. *Foreign Language Annals* 37: 26–36.

———. 2014. "From Performance to Multilingual Being in Foreign Language Pedagogy: Lessons from L2 Students Abroad." *Critical Multilingualism Studies* 2: 74–105.

Levine, Glenn S., and Alison Phipps. 2010. "What Is Language Pedagogy For?" In *Critical and Intercultural Theory and Language Pedagogy*, edited by Levine and Phipps, 1–14. Boston: Cengage.

Lewin, Kurt, Ronald Lippett, and Ralph White. 1939. "Patterns of Aggressive Behavior in Experimentally Created 'Social Climate.'" Journal of Applied Social Psychology 10: 271–99.

Lewis, Michael. 1993. *The Lexical Approach: The State of ELT and a Way Forward*. Hove, UK: Language Teaching Publications.

———. 1997. *Implementing the Lexical Approach: Putting Theory into Practice*. Hove, UK: Language Teaching Publications.

Li, Defeng. 1998. "It's Always More Difficult than You Plan and Imagine: Teachers' Perceived Difficulties in Introducing the Communicative Approach in South Korea." TESOL Quarterly 32: 677–703.

Li, Minglin, and Richard Baldauf. 2011. "Beyond the Curriculum: A Chinese Example of Issues Constraining Effective English Language Teaching." TESOL Quarterly 45: 793–803.

Lin, Grace Hui-chin, and Paul Shih-chieh Chien. 2009. "An Investigation into

Effectiveness of Peer Feedback." *Journal of Applied Foreign Languages Fortune Institute of Technology* 3: 79–87.

Ling, Lorraine M., and Noella Mackenzie. 2001. "The Professional Development of Teachers in Australia." *European Journal of Teacher Education* 24: 87–98.

Liu, Meihua, and Yanhui Chai. 2009. "Attitudes towards Peer Review and Reaction to Peer Feedback in Chinese EFL Writing Classrooms." *TESL Reporter* 42: 33–51.

Lomicka, Lara, and Gillian Lord. 2018. "Ten Years after the MLA Report: What Has Changed in Foreign Language Departments?" *ADFL Bulletin* 44: 116–20.

Looney, Dennis, and Natalia Lusin. 2018. "Enrollments in Languages Other Than English in United States Institutions of Higher Education, Summer 2016 and Fall 2016: Preliminary Report." Modern Language Association of America. https://www.mla.org/content/download/83540/2197676/2016-Enrollments-Short-Report.pdf.

Lord, Gillian. 2015. "'I Don't Know How to Use Words in Spanish': Rosetta Stone and Learner Proficiency Outcomes." *Modern Language Journal* 99: 401–5.

Lortie, Dan C. 1975. *Schoolteacher: A Sociological Study*. Chicago: University of Chicago Press.

Ludemann, Pamela M., and Deborah McMakin. 2014. "Perceived Helpfulness of Peer Editing Activities: First-Year Students' Views and Writing Performance Outcomes." *Psychology Learning and Teaching* 13: 129–36.

Lyster, Roy. 2007. *Learning and Teaching Languages through Content: A Counterbalanced Approach*. Philadelphia: John Benjamins.

Lyster, Roy, and Leila Ranta. 1997. "Corrective Feedback and Learner Uptake: Negotiation of Form in Communicative Classrooms." *Studies in Second Language Acquisition* 20: 37–66.

MacIntyre, Peter D., Susan Baker, Robert Clément, and Leslie A. Donovan. 2003. "Talking in Order to Learn: Willingness to Communicate and Intensive Language Programs." *Canadian Modern Language Review* 59: 589–607.

Magnan, Sally. 1985. "Teaching and Testing Proficiency in Writing: Skills to Transcend the Second-Language Classroom." In *Proficiency, Curriculum, Articulation: The Ties That Bind*, edited by Alice Omaggio, 109–36. Middlebury, VT: Northeast Conference on the Teaching of Foreign Languages.

Magnan, Sally, Diana Murphy, and Narke Sahakyan, eds. 2014. *Goals of Collegiate Learners and the "Standards for Foreign Language Learning."* Modern Language Journal Monograph Series.

Magnin, Michèle Claude. 1997. "The Building: An Adaptation of Francis Debyser's Writing Project—A Global Simulation to Teach Language and Culture." *China-U.S. Conference on Education: Collected Papers*, 55–62.

Malinowki, David. 2015. "Opening Spaces of Learning in the Linguistic Landscape." *Linguistic Landscape* 1: 95–113.

Manchón, Rosa M. 2009. *Writing in Foreign Language Contexts: Learning, Teaching, and Research*. Bristol: Multilingual Matters.

Martin, J. R. 1984. "Language, Register, and Genre." In *Children Writing: Reader*, edited by Frances Christie, 21–29. Geelong, Australia: Deakin University Press.

———. 2009. "Genre and Language Learning. A Social Semiotic Perspective." *Linguistics and Education* 20: 10–21.

Martin, J. R., Frances Christie, and Joan Rothery. 1987. "Social Processes in Education: A Reply to Sawyer and Watson (and Others)." In *The Place of Genre in Learning: Current Debates*, edited by Ian Reid, 35–45. Geelong, Australia: Deakin University Press.

Maxim, Hiram. 2005. "Articulating FL Writing Development at the Collegiate Level: A Curriculum-Based Approach." In *Language Program Articulation: Developing a Theoretical Foundation*, edited by Cathy Barrette and Kate Paesani, 78–93. Boston: Cengage.

———. 2006. "Integrating Textual Thinking into the Introductory College-Level Foreign Language Classroom." *Modern Language Journal* 90: 19–32.

———. 2008. "Developing Formal Language Abilities along a Genre-Based Curriculum." In *Conceptions of L2 Grammar: Theoretical Approaches and Their Application in the L2 Classroom*, edited by Stacey L. Katz and Johanna Watzinger-Tharp, 172–88. Boston: Cengage.

———. 2009. "'It's Made to Match': Linking L2 Reading and Writing through Textual Borrowing." In *Crossing Languages and Research Methods*, edited by Cindy Brantmeier, 97–122. Charlotte, NC: Information Age.

———. 2015. "Raising Methodological Awareness among Study Abroad Participants: Reflections from a Student-Driven Linguistic Landscape Research Project." Presentation at the 7th International Linguistic Landscape Workshop, Berkeley, CA, May 7–9.

McCarthy, Michael, and Ronald Carter. 1995. "Spoken Grammar: What Is It and How Can We Teach It?" *ELT Journal* 49: 207–18.

Medgyes, Peter. 1996. "Native or Nonnative: Who's Worth More?" In *Power, Pedagogy and Practice*, edited by Tricia Hedge and Norman Whitney, 31–42. Oxford: Oxford University Press.

Michaelis, Laura. 2012. "Making the Case for Construction Grammar." In *Sign-Based Construction Grammar*, Center for the Study of Language and Information, edited by Hans C. Boas and Ivan A. Sag. Chapter available at https://www.colorado.edu/faculty/michaelis/sites/default/files/attached-files/making_the_case-2.pdf.

Millner, Michael. 2018. "Why I Stopped Writing on my Students' Papers." *Chronicle of Higher Education*, February 12. https://www.chronicle.com/article/Why-I-Stopped-Writing-on-My/242477.

Mills, Nicole. 2011. "Situated Learning through Social Networking Communities: The Development of Joint Enterprise, Mutual Engagement, and a Shared Repertoire." *CALICO Journal* 28: 345–68.

———. 2012. "Encouraging Student Collaboration, Negotiation, and Engagement in Meaningful and Relevant Environments." Presentation at the National Middle East Language Resource Center, George Washington University, Washington DC.

———. 2013. "Action Research: Bridging Theory and Practice." *Academic Exchange Quarterly: Second Language Acquisition and Pedagogy* 17: 95–100.

———. 2014. "Language as a Tool for Creative and Critical Thinking in the Beginning French Classroom." Presentation at the Teaching of Language Division panel "Raising the Bar: Academic Rigor in the Language Classroom," Modern Language Association Conference, Chicago.

———. 2016. "The Charlie Archive: A Pedagogical Resource for Foreign Language Teachers." Presentation at the American Council of Teachers of Foreign Languages Conference, Boston.

Mills, Nicole, and Heather Allen. 2007. "Teacher Self-Efficacy in Native and Non-native Teaching Assistants of French." In *From Thought to Action: Exploring Beliefs and Outcomes in the Foreign Language Program*, edited by Jay Siskin, 213–34. Boston: Heinle.

Mills, Nicole, and R. Kirk Belnap. 2017. "Beliefs, Motivation, and Engagement: What Every Teacher of Arabic Should Know about Self-Efficacy." In *Handbook for Arabic Language Teaching Professionals in the 21st Century*, vol. 2, edited by Kassem M. Wahba, Zeinab A. Taha, and Liz England, 62–75. 2nd ed. Mahwah, NJ: Lawrence Erlbaum.

Mills, Nicole, Chris Dede, and Arnaud Dressen. 2019. "Cultural Immersion in Virtual Reality Narratives." Presentation at the Mobile Language Learning Experience International Conference, New York.

Mills, Nicole, and Rus Gant. 2018. "Virtual Reality and Authentic Cultural Immersion." Presentation at the HUBweek Conference, Boston.

Mills, Nicole, and Samuel Moulton. 2017. "Students' and Instructors' Perceived Value of Curricular Content." *Foreign Language Annals* 50: 717–33.

MLA (Modern Language Association). 2007. "Foreign Languages and Higher Education: New Structures for a Changed World." Report of the MLA Ad Hoc Committee on Foreign Languages. www.mla.org/flreport.

Muir, Christine, and Zoltán Dörnyei. 2013. "Directed Motivational Currents: Using

Vision to Create Effective Motivational Pathways." *Studies in Second Language Learning and Teaching* 3: 357–75.

Nassaji, Hossein, and Sandra Fotos. 2011. *Teaching Grammar in Second Language Classrooms.* New York: Routledge.

Nation, I. S. P. (Paul). 2000. "Learning Vocabulary in Lexical Sets: Dangers and Guidelines." *TESOL Quarterly* 9: 6–10.

———. 2001. *Learning Vocabulary in Another Language.* Cambridge: Cambridge University Press.

———. 2015. "Principles Guiding Vocabulary Learning through Extensive Reading." *Reading in a Foreign Language* 27: 136–45.

Nattinger, James R., and Jeanette S. DeCarrico. 1992. *Lexical Phrases in Language Teaching.* Oxford: Oxford University Press.

NEA Research. 2007. "The Benefits of Second Language Study." Connecticut State Department of Education. http://portal.ct.gov/-/media/SDE/World-Languages/BenefitsofSecondLanguage.pdf.

New London Group. 1996. "A Pedagogy of Multiliteracies: Designing Social Futures." *Harvard Educational Review* 66: 60–92.

Nicodemo, Allie. 2017. "Robot-Proof: President Aoun Outlines Plan for Reinventing Higher Ed in the AI Age." News @ Northeastern, September 13. https://news.northeastern.edu/2017/09/13/robot-proof-president-aoun-outlines-plan-for-reinventing-higher-ed-in-the-ai-age/.

Norris, John, and Nicole Mills. 2014. *Innovation and Accountability in Language Program Evaluation.* Boston: Cengage.

Norton, Bonny, and Kelleen Toohey. 2004. *Critical Pedagogies and Language Learning.* Cambridge: Cambridge University Press.

Nunan, David. 1999. *Second Language Teaching and Learning.* Boston: Heinle.

Oberg, Andrew. 2011. "Comparison of the Effectiveness of a CALL-Based Approach and a Card-Based Approach to Vocabulary Acquisition and Retention." *CALICO Journal* 29: 118–44.

Olds, Kris. 2012. "Global Citizenship—What Are We Talking About and Why Does It Matter?" *Inside Higher Ed*, March 11. https://www.insidehighered.com/blogs/globalhighered/global-citizenship---what-are-we-talking-about-and-why-does-it-matter.

Omaggio, Alice C. 1986. *Teaching Language in Context.* Boston: Heinle and Heinle.

O'Neal, Chris, Deborah Meizlish, and Matthew Kaplan. 2007. "Writing a Statement of Teaching Philosophy for the Academic Job Search." *CRLT Occasional Papers* 23. Center for Research on Learning and Teaching, University of Michigan, Ann Arbor.

Paesani, Kate. 2005. "Literary Texts and Grammar Instruction: Revisiting the Inductive Presentation." *Foreign Language Annals* 38: 15–24.

———. 2006. "*Exercices de style*: Developing Multiple Competencies through a Writing Portfolio." *Foreign Language Annals* 39: 618–39.

———. 2009. "Exploring the Stylistic Content of *Exercices de style*." *French Review* 82: 1268–80.

Paesani, Kate, Heather Willis Allen, and Béatrice Dupuy. 2016. *A Multiliteracies Framework for Collegiate Foreign Language Teaching*. Boston: Pearson.

Paivio, Allan. 1971. *Imagery and Verbal Processes*. New York: Holt, Rinehart and Winston.

Pajares, Frank. 2002. "Gender and Perceived Self-Efficacy in Self-Regulated Learning." *Theory into Practice* 41: 116–25.

Parra, Maria Luisa, and Elvira Di Fabio. 2015. "Languages in Partnership with the Visual Arts: Implications for Curriculum Design and Training." In *Integrating the Arts: Creative Thinking about FL Curricula and Language Program Direction*, edited by Lisa Parkes and Colleen Ryan, 11–36. Boston: Cengage.

Pavlenko, Anita, and Bonnie Norton. 2007. "Imagined Communities, Identity, and English Language Learning." In *International Handbook of English Language Teaching*, edited by Jim Cummins and Chris Davison, 669–80. Dordrecht, Netherlands: Springer.

Péron, Mélanie. 2010. "Writing History in the Voice of an Other: Debyser's *Immeuble* at the Advanced Level." *Foreign Language Annals* 43: 190–215.

Peyton, Joy Kreeft. 2000. "Dialogue Journals: Interactive Writing to Develop Language and Literacy." Washington DC: ERIC.

Phillips, June K., ed. 1997. *Collaborations: Meeting New Goals, New Realities*. Northeast Conference Reports. Lincolnwood, IL: NTC.

Pica, Teresa. 2002. "Subject-Matter Content: How Does It Assist the Interactional and Linguistic Needs of Classroom Language Learners?" *Modern Language Journal* 86: 1–19.

Queneau, Raymond. 1947. *Exercices de style*. Paris: Gallimard.

———. 2009. *Exercises in Style*. Translated by Barbara Wright. New York: New Directions.

Rabiner, Susan, and Alfred Fortunato. 2002. *Thinking like Your Editor: How to Write Great Serious Nonfiction and Get It Published*. New York: Norton.

Ramanathan, Vai, and Dwight Atkinson. 1999. "Individualism, Academic Writing, and ESL Writers." *Journal of Second Language Writing* 8: 45–75.

Ramos, Fernando Prieto. 2001. "'Why Do They Hit the Headlines?': Critical Media Literacy in the Foreign Language Class." *Journal of Intercultural Studies* 22: 33–41.

Rankin, Jamie. "der|die|das." German language learning website. Princeton University. https://dddgerman.org.

Rasdal, James. 2009. "Some Truths (and Not) of Norman Rockwell in Cedar Rapids." *Gazette* (Cedar Rapids), December 1. http://www.thegazette.com/2009/12/01/some-truths-and-not-of-norman-rockwell-in-cedar-rapids.

Rassaie, Ehsan. 2014. "Scaffolded Feedback, Recasts, and L2 Development: A Sociocultural Perspective." *Modern Language Journal* 98: 417–31.

Read, John. 2004. "Research in Teaching Vocabulary." *Annual Review of Applied Linguistics* 24: 146–61.

Redden, Elizabeth. 2017. "Call to Action on Languages, 10 Years Later." *Inside Higher Ed*, January 6. https://www.insidehighered.com/news/2017/01/06/survey-looks-foreign-language-programs-response-decade-old-call-transform-teaching.

Reichelt, Melinda, Natalie Lefkowitz, Carol Rinnert, and Jean Marie Schultz. 2012. "Key Issues in Foreign Language Writing." *Foreign Language Annals* 45: 22–41.

Richards, Jack C. 2018. "Difference between an Approach and a Method?" https://www.professorjackrichards.com/difference-between-an-approach-and-a-method/.

Richards, Jack C., and Richard Schmidt. 2010. *Longman Dictionary of Language Teaching and Applied Linguistics*. 4th ed. Harlowe, UK: Longman.

Ricoeur, Paul. (1970) 2008. *Freud and the Philosophy of Interpretation*. Translated by Denis Savage. New Haven: Yale University Press.

Rinnert, Carol, and Hiroe Kobayashi. 2009. "Situated Writing Practice in Foreign Language Settings: The Role of Previous Experience and Instruction." In *Writing in Foreign Language Contexts: Learning, Teaching, and Research*, edited by Rosa M. Manchón, 23–48. Bristol: Multilingual Matters.

Rios-Font, Wadda C. 2017. "Proficiency or Exposure? Rethinking Foreign Language Requirements within College Curriculum Reviews." *Hispania* 100: 16–29.

Robin, Richard. 2002. "Should We Teach Grammar? Part II." National Capital Language Resource Center Newsletter 6, October 8.

Rodgers, Daryl. 2006. "Developing Content and Form: Encouraging Evidence from Italian Content-Based Instruction." *Modern Language Journal* 90: 373–86.

———. 2015. "Incidental Language Learning in Foreign Language Content Courses." *Modern Language Journal* 99: 113–36.

Rott, Susanne. 1999. "The Effect of Exposure Frequency on Intermediate Language Learners' Incidental Vocabulary Acquisition and Retention through Reading." *Studies in Second Language Acquisition* 21: 589–619.

———. 2007. "The Effect of Frequency of Input-Enhancements on Word Learning and Text Comprehension." *Language Learning* 57: 165–99.

Rubio, Fernando, and Joshua Thoms. 2012. *Hybrid Language Teaching and Learning: Exploring Theoretical, Pedagogical and Curricular Issues*. Boston: Cengage.

Rumelhart, David E. 1980. "Schemata: The Building Blocks of Cognition." In *Theoretical Issues in Reading Comprehension*, edited by Rand J. Spiro, Bertram C. Bruce, and William F. Brewer, 33–58. London: Routledge.

Ryan, Stephen, and Zoltán Dörnyei. 2013. "The Long-Term Evolution of Language Motivation and the L2 Self." In *Fremdsprachen in der Perspektive lebenslangen Lernens*, edited by Annette Berndt, 89–100. Frankfurt: Peter Lang.

Ryan, Stephen, and Kay Irie. 2014. "Imagined and Possible Selves: Stories We Tell Ourselves about Ourselves." In *Multiple Perspectives of the Self in SLA*, edited by Sarah Mercer and Marion Williams, 109–26. Bristol: Multilingual Matters.

Salaberry, Rafael. 2010a. "Lesson 1: Definitions of Grammar—A Contextualized Definition." Foreign Language Teaching Methods, Center for Open Educational Resources and Language Learning, University of Texas at Austin. https://coerll.utexas.edu/methods/modules/grammar/01/contextualized.php.

———. 2010b. "Lesson 4: Implementing a Guided Induction Approach." Foreign Language Teaching Methods, Center for Open Educational Resources and Language Learning, University of Texas at Austin. https://coerll.utexas.edu/methods/modules/grammar/04/.

Sanders, Ashley. 2014. "Going Alt-Ac: How to Begin." *Inside Higher Ed*, January 26. https://www.insidehighered.com/blogs/gradhacker/going-alt-ac-how-begin.

Savignon, Sandra. 1976. "Teaching for Communication." *Language Association Bulletin* 27: 17–8.

Scanlan, Timothy M. 1997. "Another Foreign Language Skill: Analyzing Photographs." In *Pathways to Culture*, edited by Paula Rae Heusinkveld, 351–62. Yarmouth, ME: Intercultural Press.

Schmitt, Norbert. 2008. "Review Article: Instructed Second Language Learning." *Language Teaching Research* 12: 329–63.

Schunk, Dale, Judith Meece, and Paul Pintrich. 2014. *Motivation in Education*. Boston: Pearson.

Scott, Virginia. 1996. *Rethinking Foreign Language Writing*. Boston: Heinle.

———. 2010. *Doubletalk*. Upper Saddle River, NJ: Pearson.

Shapiro, Johanna, Lois L. Nixon, Stephen E. Wear, and David J. Doukas. 2015. "Medical Professionalism: What the Study of Literature Can Contribute to the Conversation." *Philosophy, Ethics, and Humanities in Medicine*, June 27. https://www.ncbi.nlm.nih.gov/pmc/articles/PMC4484639/.

Shulman, Lee S. 2000. "Teacher Development Journal of Applied Developmental

Psychology: Roles of Domain Expertise and Pedagogical Knowledge." *Journal of Applied Developmental Psychology* 21: 129–35.

Silvia, Paul J. 2007. *How to Write a Lot: A Practical Guide to Productive Academic Writing*. Washington DC: American Psychological Association.

Slade, Diana. 1997. "Stories and Gossip in English: The Macro-structure of Casual Talk." *Prospect* 12: 72–86.

Snow, Marguerite Ann, Myriam Met, and Fred H. Genesee. 1989. "A Conceptual Framework for the Integration of Language and Content in Second/Foreign Language Programs." *TESOL Quarterly* 23: 201–17.

Snyder, Delys Waite, Rex P. Nielson, and Kendon Kurzer. 2016. "Foreign Language Writing Fellows Programs: A Model for Improving Advanced Writing Skills." *Foreign Language Annals* 49: 750–71.

Spinelli, Emily, and Jay Siskin. 1992. "Selecting, Presenting and Practicing Vocabulary in a Culturally-Authentic Context." *Foreign Language Annals* 25: 305–15.

Spiro, Rand J., Bertram C. Bruce, and William F. Brewer, eds. 1980. *Theoretical Issues in Reading Comprehension*. London: Routledge.

Staton, Ann Q. 2008. "Teacher Socialization." In *The International Encyclopedia of Communication*, edited by Wolfgang Donsbach. https://onlinelibrary.wiley.com/doi/10.1002/9781405186407.wbiect016.

Swaffar, Janet, and Katherine Arens. 2005. *Remapping the Foreign Language Curriculum: An Approach through Multiple Literacies*. New York: MLA.

Swaffar, Janet, Katherine Arens, and Heidi Byrnes. 1991. *Reading for Meaning: An Integrated Approach to Language Learning*. Englewood Cliffs, NJ: Prentice Hall.

Swaffar, Janet, and Andrea Vlatten. 1997. "A Sequential Model for Video Viewing in the Foreign Language Curriculum." *Modern Language Journal* 81: 175–88.

Swain, Merrill. 1985. "Communicative Competence: Some Roles of Comprehensible Input and Comprehensible Output in Its Development." In *Input in Second Language Acquisition*, edited by Susan Gass and Carolyn Madden, 235–53. Rowley, MA: Newbury House.

Swender, Elvira. 2003. "Oral Proficiency Testing in the Real World: Answers to Frequently Asked Questions." *Foreign Language Annals* 36: 520–26.

Sykes, Julie M., and Jonathon Reinhardt. 2013. *Language at Play: Digital Games in Second and Foreign Language Teaching and Learning*. Boston: Pearson.

Taylor, Florentina. 2013. *Self and Identity in Adolescent Foreign Language Learning*. Bristol, UK: Multilingual Matters.

Thornbury, Scott. 2002. *How to Teach Vocabulary*. Harlow, UK: Pearson.

Thorne, Steven, and John Hellerman. 2017. "Mobile Augmented Reality: Hyper Contextualization and Situated Language Usage Events." In *CALL in Context: Pro-*

ceedings, 2017, edited by by Jozef Colpaert, Ann Aerts, Rick Kern, and Mark Kaiser, 721–30. Antwerp: University of Antwerp. Available at http://call2017.language.berkeley.edu/wp-content/uploads/2017/07/CALL2017_proceedings.pdf.

Tierney, John. 2013. "Why Teachers Secretly Hate Grading Papers." *The Atlantic*, January 9. https://www.theatlantic.com/national/archive/2013/01/why-teachers-secretly-hate-grading-papers/266931/.

Todhunter, Susan. 2007. "Instructional Conversations in a High School Spanish Class." *Foreign Language Annals* 40: 604–21.

Truscott, John. 1996. "The Case against Grammar Correction in L2 Writing Classes." *Language Learning* 46: 327–69.

———. 1999. "The Case for 'The Case against Grammar Correction in L2 Writing Classes': A Response to Ferris." *Journal of Second Language Writing* 8: 111–22.

———. 2007. "The Effect of Error Correction on Learners' Ability to Write Accurately." *Journal of Second Language Writing* 16: 255–72.

Tyron, Francis J. 2016. "Learning to Mean in Spanish Writing: A Case Study of a Genre-Based Pedagogy for Standards-Based Writing Instruction." *Foreign Language Annals* 49: 317–35.

Ushioda, Ema. 1996. *Learner Autonomy 5: The Role of Motivation*. Dublin: Authentik.

———. 2009. "A Person-in-Context Relational View of Emergent Motivation, Self, and Identity." In *Motivation, Language, Identity, and the L2 Self*, edited by Zoltán Dörnyei and Ushioda, 215–28. Bristol: Multilingual Matters.

Vandergrift, Laurens. 1998. "Successful and Less Successful Listeners in French: What Are the Strategy Differences?" *French Review* 71: 370–94.

Van Deusen-Scholl, Nelleke. 2003. "Toward a Definition of Heritage Language: Socio-political and Pedagogical Considerations." *Journal of Language, Identity, and Education* 2: 211–30.

Van Deusen-Scholl, Nelleke, and Stéphane Charitos. 2016. "Shared Course Initiative: Toward Curricular Collaboration across Institutional Boundaries." In *The Interconnected Language Curriculum: Critical Transitions and Interfaces in Articulated K–12 Contexts*, edited by Per Urlaub and Johanna Watzinger-Tharp, 32–50. Boston: Cengage.

Van Houten, Jacque Bott, Ruta Couet, and Gregory Fulkerson. 2014. "From Fact to Function: How Interculturality Is Changing Our View of Culture." *Language Educator*, January, 42–45.

VanPatten, Bill. 2015. "Where Are the Experts?" *Hispania* 98: 2–13.

———. 2017. *While We're on the Topic: BVP on Language, Acquisition, and Language Practice*. Alexandria, VA: American Council on the Teaching of Foreign Languages.

VanPatten, Bill, and Jason Rothman. 2014. "Against 'Rules.'" In *The Grammar Dimension* in *Instructed Second Language Learning*, edited by Alessandro G. Benati, Cécile Laval, and Maria J. Arche, 15–35. London: Bloomsbury.

VanPatten, Bill, and Jessica Williams. 2007. *Theories in Second Language Acquisition: An Introduction*. Mahwah, NJ: Laurence Erlbaum.

Vélez-Rendón, Gloria. 2010. "From Social Identity to Professional Identity: Issues of Language and Gender." *Foreign Language Annals* 43: 635–49.

Vogel, Séverine, Carol Herron, Steven P. Cole, and Holly York. 2011. "Effectiveness of a Guided Inductive versus a Deductive Approach on the Learning of Grammar in the Intermediate-Level College French Classroom." *Foreign Language Annals* 44: 353–80.

Vygotsky, Lev. 1978. *Mind in Society: The Development of Higher Psychological Processes*. Cambridge, MA: Harvard University Press.

Wandel, Reinhold. 2003. "Teaching India in the EFL Classroom: A Cultural or Intercultural Approach." In *Context and Culture in Language Teaching and Learning*, edited by Michael Byram and Peter Grundy, 72–80. Clevedon, UK: Multilingual Matters.

Wesely, Pamela. 2012. "Cross-cultural Understanding in Immersion Students: A Mixed Methods Study." *L2 Journal* 4: 189–213.

Widdowson, Henry G. 2004. *Text, Context, Pretext: Critical Issues in Discourse Analysis*. Malden, MA: Blackwell.

Wiggins, Grant, and Jay McTighe. 2005. *Understanding by Design*. Alexandria, VA: Association for Supervision and Curriculum Development.

Wilkins, D. A. 1972. *Linguistics in Language Teaching*. London: Edward Arnold.

Willis, Dave. 1990. *The Lexical Syllabus: A New Approach to Language Teaching*. London: Collins ELT.

Wong, Wynne, and Bill VanPatten. 2003. "The Evidence Is IN: Drills Are OUT." *Foreign Language Annals* 36: 403–23.

Wylie, Laurence, and Jean-François Brière. 2001. *Les Français*. 3rd ed. Upper Saddle River, NJ: Pearson.

Zamel, Vivian. 1985. "Responding to Student Writing." *TESOL Quarterly* 19: 79–101.

Zhang, Lihua. 2011. "Teaching Chinese Cultural Perspectives through Film." *L2 Journal* 3: 201–31.

Zhao, Huahui. 2010. "Investigating Learners' Use and Understanding of Peer and Teacher Feedback on Writing: A Comparative Study in a Chinese English Writing Classroom." *Assessing Writing* 15: 3–17.

Zietlow, Alex. 2017. "Foreign Language 'Emergency' Hinders U.S. Economy and Foreign Policy, Report Warns." *Washington Times*, June 15. https://www.washingtontimes.com/news/2017/jun/15/foreign-language-learning-disparity-an-american-em/.

Index

acquisition-learning hypothesis, 16
ACT exams, 130
ACTFL. *See* American Council for the Teaching of Foreign Languages
action research, 47
advertisements, 117–18, 138–39, 151–55. *See also* commercials
affective filter hypothesis, 16
Allen, Heather Willis, 32, 45, 146
ALM. *See* audiolingual method
American Council for the Teaching of Foreign Languages (ACTFL) proficiency guidelines, 18. *See also* World-Readiness Standards for Language Learning
Aoun, Joseph, 23
application, 224
AR. *See* augmented reality
Asher, James, 15
aspect, 112–14
assessment, 193–97, 228–30, 242–43
Assessment and Evaluation Language Resource Center, Georgetown University, 67
Atlas complex, 99
Atwood, Margaret, 179
audiolingual method (ALM): Atlas complex in, 99; criticisms of, 14, 100; and grammar instruction, 94, 95; overview of, 13–15; reactions to, 17–18; vocabulary instruction in, 123, 134
audio texts, 160
augmented reality (AR), 87–88. *See also* virtual reality

authentic assessment, 228, 242–43
authentic discourse, 63–68, 120
autocratic instructional style, 73–74
Available Designs, 149
avoidance, 122–23

Backward Design, 191, 224–44
Barnes-Karol, Gwendolyn, 31, 156, 217–18
Bartlett, Frederic, 148
Bass, Randy, 33
Baudelaire, Charles, 178–79
Beck, Isabel L., 130
behaviorism, 13
beliefs: of students, 47–51; of teachers, 42–47
Belnap, R. Kirk, 71
Berg, William J., 146
Berlitz programs, 12
Bernhardt, Elizabeth, 38
Bhatia, Vijay K., 146
binary options, 101–2
binding, 123
Block, David, 61
Bloom's taxonomy, 217
Blyth, Carl S., 37, 90, 98, 111, 112, 137
Bourhis, Richard Y., 117
Bourns, Stacey Katz, 116, 136. *See also* Katz, Stacey L.
Bown, Jennifer, 82
Brennan, Karen, "Requiem," 113–14, 139–42, 265–67
bridge courses, 24, 250
Bridges, Ruby, 157

Broner, Maggie, 156, 217–18
Brooks, Frank B., 171
Brown, Alan, 49
Brown, N. Anthony, 82
bundles. *See* chunks
Busse, Vera, 49–50
Byram, Michael, 209, 217, 218
Byrnes, Heidi, 146–47

Calvino, Italo, 79
Campbell's soup advertisement, 151–55
Canale, Michael, 18, 90, 121
Carter, Ronald, 111
CBI. *See* Content-Based Instruction
Celce-Murcia, Marianne, 18, 36, 63, 109
Center for Advanced Research on Language Acquisition, University of Minnesota, 29, 208
Center for Applied Second Language Studies, University of Oregon, 67
Charitos, Stéphane, 33, 87
Charlie Archive, Harvard University, 225, 229, 236
Charlie Hebdo (magazine), 224–25, 228, 230–31, 234–36
chunks, 14, 127
CLT. *See* communicative language teaching
cognition: as basis of language learning, 61; in process-based writing, 183–86
Colette, 178, 203
Comer, William, 97–98
commentaire composé, 205–6
commercials, 161–63. *See also* advertisements
communication, features of, 62–63
communicative competence, 18, 22, 26, 62–64
communicative language teaching (CLT): criticisms of, 19, 35; and grammar, 92, 98–99; natural approach compared to, 17; overview of, 17–19; precursor to, 15; task-based activities in, 75; technology and, 21; vocabulary instruction in, 123–24
complexity language pedagogy, 34

comprehensible and meaningful input, 69
consciousness raising (CR), 111–14, 193
Construction Grammar, 126–27
Content-Based Instruction (CBI): balanced approach in, 28–29; overview of, 27–30; shortcomings of, 27–28; vocabulary instruction in, 124
content-compatible language, 29
content knowledge, pedagogical, 42
content-language spiraling, 27–35, 107, 223–44, 250
content-obligatory language, 29
content words, 128–29
conversation. *See* authentic discourse; discussion forums, online; instructional conversations
Cook, Guy, 74
Cook, Vivian, 51
corpora, 119
correction of errors. *See* error correction
corrective feedback, 70–73
Couet, Ruta, 20
Council of Europe, 216
cover letters, 253
CR. *See* consciousness raising
critical media literacy, 84–86
critical thinking, 4
Cultura, 209–10
cultural agility, 23
culture, 207–22; "big-C" vs. "little-C," 207; comparisons of, 209–10; defined, 212; films as means of teaching, 219–21; grammar instruction linked to, 106–8; heterogeneity of, 211; images as means of teaching, 216–19; in language classroom, 207–11; language in relation to, 212; modernist conception of, 211, 213; narrative approaches to, 213–15; pedagogical approaches to, 213–22; postmodernist conception of, 212–13; products, practices, and perspectives in, 207–8; vocabulary instruction and, 134–37. *See also* target cultures
Cummins, Jim, 29

curriculum: ACTFL Standards and, 24; contemporary context for, 20; goals, activities, and assessment in, 191–94, 224–44; institutional identity as influence on, 39; lower- vs. upper-level (two-tiered), 24–26, 39, 144–45, 204–6, 246–51; models merging language and content, 27–35, 107, 223–44, 250; writing's role in, 177–78

debate, 82–83
deBenedette, Lynne, 97–98
democratic instructional style, 73–74
Demy, Jacques, *Umbrellas of Cherbourg*, 167
de Nooy, Juliana, 83–86
departments, socialization provided by, 46
DeWaard, Lisa, 21, 134–35
dictoglosses, 137–38
Di Fabio, Elvira, 217
directed motivational current, 57–58
direct method (DM): natural approach compared to, 15; overview of, 12–13; vocabulary instruction in, 123
discourse competence, 18, 109
discourse grammar, 109–14
discussion forums, online, 84–86
DM. *See* direct method
Donato, Richard, 72, 171
Dörnyei, Zoltán, 48, 52, 53, 57, 58, 73, 74
Doughty, Catherine, 100
drills, grammar, 95–98
Dubreil, Sébastien, 33–34, 221
Dupuy, Béatrice, 32, 146

ecological language pedagogy, 34
Edmundson, Mark, 259
Ellis, Rod, 111
Elmendorf, Heidi, 33
emotions: associated with language, 4; in natural approach, 16
empathy, 224
English, as foreign language, 118
error correction, 11, 14, 15, 16, 18, 25, 28, 72, 92. *See also* corrective feedback

expectancy value theory, 50
experiential learning, 33, 54
explanation, 224
explicit instruction, 108–9
extensive reading, 129–30

facets of understanding, 224
Fecteau, Monique L., 172
feedback: interactional competence fostered by, 70–73; from peers, 198–99; on teaching, 252; on writing, 193–94, 198–99
Felski, Rita, 259
films: in cultural instruction, 219–21; grammar instruction utilizing, 116–17; as texts, 163–71
Firth, Allen, 61
Five Cs (ACTFL). *See* World-Readiness Standards for Language Learning
Flaubert, Gustave, 179
Folse, Keith S., 129, 130, 132
Foreign Languages across the Curriculum (FLAC), 31, 124
Fortune, Tara Williams, 29
Freeman, Donald, 42
Fryer, Bronwyn, 258
Fulkerson, Gregory, 20
function words, 128–29
Fund for the Improvement of Postsecondary Education, 31
Furstenburg, Gilberte, 209

gaming, 87–88
Garrett, Nina, 98
Gee, James Paul, 146
genre-based models: pedagogy grounded in, 32, 39; principles of, 187; in text-based pedagogy, 146–48; textual borrowing central to, 188–90; in writing pedagogy, 187–90
Ghanem, Carla, 44
Gibbons, Pauline, 28
Glisan, Eileen, 72
global citizenship, 20, 24

globalization, 212
global simulation, 54–55, 56–57
goal setting, for curriculum, 191–94, 224–25, 227–28, 242
Golde, Chris M., 46
graduate students: professional life of, 246–47, 252–53, 256, 259, 262; reflective thinking of, 46–47; socialization of, 46
Graff, Gerald, 214
graffiti, 118
grammar, 90–120; CLT and, 92, 98–99; contextual factors in, 115–20; defining, 90–93; discourse grammar, 109–14; drills in, 95–98; evolution of, 91; explicit instruction in, 108–9; input processing and, 100–106; traditional instruction in, 93–98; value of, 92; vocabulary pedagogy and, 125–28
grammar translation (GT): and grammar instruction, 94, 95; overview of, 11–12; reactions to, 12, 13; vocabulary instruction in, 123
grammatical competence, 18, 90, 116
GT. *See* grammar translation
guiding principles, 4–5, 240, 242, 244, 261–62
Guilloteau, Nancy, 121, 124

Hacking, Jane, 125
Hall, Joan Kelly, 63–64, 66
Halliday, Michael Alexander Kirkwood, 145, 146
Hanna, Barbara E., 83–86
Harley, Birgit, 110
Harvard University, 225, 236
Henry, Alistair, 53, 58
heritage language learners, 48–49
Heron, John, 70
Horwitz, Elaine, 50–51
Hu, Guangwei, 45
humanics, 23
humanities, 257–60
humor, 114–15

Hyland, Ken, 186, 187
Hymes, Dell, 18

identity: course/curriculum based on, 59, 147; institutional, 38–39; language learning's effect on, 3, 51–52; multilingual, 34–35; student, 51–52, 135–36; teacher, 46, 245–46, 262
images: in cultural instruction, 216–19; as texts, 156–60
Images of Others: An Autobiography of Intercultural Encounters through Visual Media (AIEVM), 216–18
immersion programs, 27–28, 110
induction, 108, 111
input, 69
input flood, 103–4
input hypothesis, 16, 69
input processing, 100–105
instruction. *See* pedagogy
instructional conversations, 65–67
instructional styles: autocratic, 73–74; democratic, 73–74; laissez-faire, 73–74
intake, 100
intensive reading, 129–30
interaction, language learning through, 61–64
interactional competence, 90–120; authentic discourse and, 65–68; concept of, 18, 63–64; debate as means of developing, 82–83; development of, 65–75; elements of, 218; feedback and, 70–73; input and, 69; instructional styles and, 73–74; language play and, 74–75; online media as means of developing, 83–88; tasks as means of developing, 75–78; texts as means of developing, 79–82
Intercultural, Pragmatic, and Interactional Competence (IPIC) Measure, 67–68
intercultural competence, 209–10, 212. *See also* transcultural competence
interdisciplinarity, 249
interference, in vocabulary knowledge, 132

interpretation, 224
interpretation devices, 23
intertextuality, 188
IRE model, 63–64, 65
Irie, Kay, 54

Johnson, Karen E., 42
Jones, Robert E., 65
journal writing, 203

Kahlo, Frida, 106–7
Kaiser, Mark, 221
Katz, Stacey L., 90, 98, 137. *See also* Bourns, Stacey Katz
Kearney, Erin, 214, 215
Kern, Richard, 31–32, 36, 83, 143, 145
Klee, Carol, 31
Knutson, Elizabeth, 214–15
Kramsch, Claire, 2, 3, 20, 26, 51, 145, 209, 211–12
Krashen, Stephen D., 16, 69
Kristeva, Julia, 188
Krueger, Cheryl, 184
Kubanyiova, Magdalena, 53
Kucan, Linda, 130
Kurzer, Kendon, 199, 204

laissez-faire instructional style, 73–74
Landry, Rodrigue, 117
language: content spiraled with, 27–35, 107, 223–44, 250; culture in relation to, 212
language learning: identity shaped by, 3, 51–52; motivations for, 20; outcomes of, 3, 38; psychology of, 49–51; value of, 3–4, 257–60; visions of, 53–55. *See also* second language acquisition (SLA)
language play, 74–75
Languages for Specific Purposes (LSP), 30, 124
Lan zhihe (*Blue Paper Crane*) (film), 219–21
Leaver, Betty Lou, 97
Lee, James, 75–76, 97, 99–106, 108, 128
Lee, Jin Sook, 48
Levet, Sabine, 209

Levine, Glenn S., 34–35, 54
Lewis, Michael, 126, 127
Lexical Approach, 126–28
Li, Defeng, 45
Ling, Lorraine M., 47
linguistic landscape, 117–18
literacy, 31–32, 145–46
literacy-based learning, 148
Lomicka, Lara, 26, 247
Lord, Gillian, 22, 26, 135, 247
Lortie, Dan C., 42
L2 motivational system, 52–53

Mackenzie, Noella, 47
Malinowski, David, 118
Mandela, Nelson, 4
Manhattan (film), 169–70
Martin-Berg, Laurey K., 146
Maxim, Hiram, 146–47, 248
McCarthy, Michael, 111
McDonald's, 138–39
McKeown, Margaret G., 130
McTighe, Jay, 223–25, 228
media literacy, 84–86
Meece, Judith, 50
memorization, 128, 129
Mentira (AR game), 87–88
metalinguistic awareness, 11, 28, 45, 94, 97, 109, 114, 120, 137–38
methods: approaches vs., 9; defined, 9; history of, 11–19
Mills, Nicole, 45, 50, 54
Modern Language Association (MLA) report (2007, "Foreign Languages and Higher Education"), 25–26, 33, 94, 114–15, 119, 212, 246–48, 250
monitor hypothesis, 16
monitor model, 16, 91
motivations: goal formation as influence on, 52; intrinsic vs. extrinsic, 49–50; of students, 20, 47–53
Moulton, Samuel, 50
Muir, Christine, 53, 57, 58
multilingual identities, 34–35

multiliteracies, 32, 79, 124, 146, 148
Murphey, Tim, 74

narrative, 65, 213–15
Nation, I. S. P., 129, 130, 132–34
National Endowment for the Humanities, 31
natural approach: CLT compared to, 17; direct method compared to, 15; overview of, 15–17
natural order hypothesis, 16
New London Group, 32, 146
Nielson, Rex P., 199, 204
Norton, Bonnie, 51

Obama, Barack, 157
Olshtain, Elite, 36, 109
online media, interactional competence developed through, 83–88
Oral Proficiency Interview (OPI), 18
ordering and ranking activities, 104–5

PACE model, 149
Paesani, Kate, 32, 146
Pajares, Frank, 71–72
Paris terrorist attacks (2015), 224–41
Parra, Maria Luisa, 217
Pavlenko, Anita, 51
pedagogical content knowledge, 42
pedagogy: Atlas complex in, 99; autocratic style of, 73–74; in contemporary context, 20–27, 124–25; democratic style of, 73–74; explicit instruction, 108–9; laissez-faire style of, 73–74; motivation-based, 55, 57–60; principles of, 4–5, 240, 242, 244, 261–62; stage-based models of, 148–55, 158–63, 166–71, 173–76, 189–90; teaching statements and, 253–57; traditional grammar, 93–98. See also teachers
peer reading/editing, 198–200
perceived value, 50–51
Performance Descriptors (ACTFL Standards), 24

Péron, Mélanie, 215
perspective, 224
Phipps, Alison, 34
Pica, Teresa, 28
Pintrich, Paul, 50
portfolios, teacher, 252–53
post-methods era, 9
pragmatic competence, 67
profession, 245–62; changes in, 260–61; developing one's profile within, 251–57, 262; diverse roles within, 246; economic and ideological challenges for, 257–61; identities within, 246, 262; journals for, 271; organizations within, 270; politics in, 257; role of humanities in, 257–60; teacher education, 262; two-tiered system in, 246–51
proficiency guidelines (ACTFL), 18–19
project-based learning, 58–60

Queneau, Raymond, *Exercices de style*, 188–90, 268–69

Ramos, Fernando Prieto, 84
Rankin, Jamie, 125
Rassias, John, 14
Rassias method, 14
reading: in two-tiered curriculum, 144–45; vocabulary learning in relation to, 129–31
reflective thinking: of graduate students, 46–47; of teachers, 42–43, 46–47
Reichelt, Melinda, 180
Reinhardt, Jonathon, 88
Richards, Jack C., 9, 112, 129
Ricoeur, Paul, 259
Rifkin, Benjamin, 97
Rios-Font, Wadda C., 94
Rivera, Diego, 106–7
Robin, Richard, 92–93
Rockwell, Norman, *America at the Polls*, 157–60
Rodgers, Daryl, 25
Rosetta Stone, 21–22, 134–35

Rothman, Jason, 108
Rott, Susanne, 121
rubrics, 194–97
Rumelhart, David E., 148
Ryan, Stephen, 48, 54

Salaberry, Rafael, 111, 115
Salvo television commercial, 161–63
SAT exams, 130
scaffolding, 70
Scanlan, Timothy M., 156–57, 216
schema theory, 148
Schmidt, Richard, 112
Schmitt, Norbert, 127, 128, 129
Schunk, Dale, 50
second language acquisition (SLA): acquisition vs. learning models, 16; cognitive basis of, 61; research on, 9–10, 35–36, 47; social basis of, 61; technology and, 21–22
Seinfeld (television show), 114–15
self-determination theory, 49
self-editing, 198
self-efficacy, 59
semantic maps, 132–34
semantic sets, 132
Shapiro, Johanna, 258
Shekhtman, Boris, 97
Shibahara, Chika, 221
Shulman, Lee S., 44
Siskin, Jay, 134, 137–38
SLA. *See* second language acquisition
Slade, Diana, 65
Snyder, Delys Waite, 199, 204
socialization, of teachers, 46
social networking, 86–87
social pedagogies, 33–35, 124
social turn in second language acquisition, 61
speech acts, 115
Spinelli, Emily, 134, 137–38
strategic competence, 18, 121, 123
structured input, 101–5, 233
structured output, 105–6

students: beliefs of, 47–51; expectations held by, 49, 50–51; motivations of, 20, 47–53. *See also* graduate students
study abroad, 34–35, 117, 129
Summers, Lawrence, 3
Swain, Merrill, 18, 27, 90, 110, 121
Sykes, Julie M., 88
symbolic competence, 34, 145, 212

target cultures, 5
tasks: defined, 4; example of, 76–78; features of, 76; for interactional competence, 75–78; tips for lessons based on, 76
teacher education, 262
teachers: beliefs and backgrounds of, 42–47; and change, 260–61; diversity of, 6; education of, 262; expectations held by, 49, 50–51; knowledge required of effective, 44; nonnative, 45; observation of/by, 252; portfolios of, 252–53; professional profile of, 251–57; reflective thinking of, 42–43, 46–47, 50, 99; self-perceptions of, 45; socialization of, 46; teaching statements of, 253–57. *See also* pedagogy
teaching. *See* pedagogy
teaching statements, 253–57
Tec de Pachuca, Mexico, 210
technology: CLT and, 21; criticisms of, 21–22; language acquisition and, 21–22; translation/interpretation software/devices, 23
Tedick, Diane J., 29
tense, 112–14
terrorist attacks (Paris, 2015), 224–41
texts, 143–76; audio, 160; defined, 4, 143; examples of interaction based on, 79–82; films as, 163–71; for interactional competence, 79–82; literacy concerning, 145–46; in lower-level courses, 148–71; pedagogical role of, 36; selection of, 146–48; sequenced interaction with, 148–63; in two-tiered curriculum,

texts (continued) 144–45; in upper-level courses, 171–76; video, 161–63; visual, 156–60; written, 151–56
textual borrowing, 188–90
themes, 4, 227, 242
Thornbury, Scott, 127–28
Thorne, Steven L., 33–34
3 Is of grammar instruction, 111
3 Ps of grammar instruction, 94–95
Todhunter, Susan, 65
Total Physical Response (TPR), 15
TPR. *See* Total Physical Response
transcultural competence, 25–26, 94, 114, 212–13. *See also* intercultural competence
translation, 115
translation software, 23
translingual competence, 25–26, 94, 114–20, 212–13
Tschirner, Erwin, 125
Twitter, 86–87, 180

understanding, 224
unit plans, 241–44
Ushioda, Ema, 49

Van Deusen-School, Nelleke, 33, 48, 87
Van Houten, Jacque Bott, 20
VanPatten, Bill, 35–36, 62, 69, 97–106, 108, 128
video texts, 161–63
virtual reality (VR), 53–54. *See also* augmented reality
vision, 53–55
visual texts, 156–60
vocabulary, 121–42; closely related words, 132–34, 138; contextualized, 137–40; culture in relation to, 134–37; gaps in, 122–23; grammar pedagogy and, 125–28; importance of, 121; instruction within previous approaches, 123–25; intentional learning of, 129–42; pedagogy concerning, 123–42; proficiency in, 125; reading-based, 129–31
VR. *See* virtual reality
Vygotsky, Lev, 70

Wagner, Johannes, 61
Wakim, Nabil, 230
Waryn, Shoggy, 209
Wei, Vanessa, 124
Whiteside, Anne, 212
Wiggins, Grant, 223–25, 228
Williams, Jessica, 100
willingness to communicate, 74
Wong, Wynne, 97
workshops, writing, 201–3
World-Readiness Standards for Language Learning (ACTFL), 24, 30, 34, 39, 207–9, 263–64
writing, 177–206; attitudes toward, 178–80; in contemporary context, 180–81; in curriculum, 177–78; designing assignments for, 194, 198–203; genre-based approaches to, 187–90; goals and assessment in teaching of, 191–94; in-class workshops for, 201–3; journal activities, 203; models/examples for, 205–6; pedagogical approaches to, 181–90; process-based approach to, 183–86; product-based approach to, 182–83; in second language contexts, 181–90; textual borrowing as approach to, 188–90; in upper-level courses, 204–6

Zhang, Lihua, 219–21
Zietlow, Alex, 258
zone of proximal development, 70, 72